# TELLING IT TO THE JUDGE

McGill-Queen's Native and Northern Series
(In memory of Bruce G. Trigger)
SARAH CARTER and ARTHUR J. RAY, Editors

# TELLING IT
# TO THE JUDGE

Taking Native History to Court

ARTHUR J. RAY

FOREWORD BY JEAN TEILLET

INTRODUCTION BY PETER W. HUTCHINS

McGILL-QUEEN'S UNIVERSITY PRESS

Montreal & Kingston · London · Ithaca

© McGill-Queen's University Press 2011

ISBN 978-0-7735-3952-5

Legal deposit fourth quarter 2011
Bibliothèque nationale du Québec

Printed in Canada on acid-free paper that is 100% ancient forest free
(100% post-consumer recycled), processed chlorine free

McGill-Queen's University Press acknowledges the support of the Canada
Council for the Arts for our publishing program. We also acknowledge the
financial support of the Government of Canada through the Canada Book
Fund for our publishing activities.

Library and Archives Canada Cataloguing in Publication

Ray, Arthur J., 1941–
Telling it to the judge : taking native history
to court / Arthur J. Ray; foreword by Jean Teillet ;
introduction by Peter W. Hutchins.

(McGill-Queen's native and northern series ; 65)
Includes bibliographical references and index.
ISBN 978-0-7735-3952-5 (bound)

1. Native peoples–Legal status, laws, etc.–Canada.  2. Native
peoples–Canada–Claims.  3. Native peoples–Canada–History.
4. Ray, Arthur J., 1941–. 5. Evidence, Expert–Canada. I. Title.
II. Series: McGill-Queen's native and northern series ; 65.

KE7709.R39 2011          342.7108'72          C2011-904804-3
KF8205.R39 2011

Designed and typeset by studio oneonone in Sabon 10.2/13.5

In memory of my courageous sister Nancy (1940–2010)

# CONTENTS

# LIST OF TABLES

# LIST OF FIGURES

## ABBREVIATIONS

AO Archives of Ontario, Toronto, Ontario.
DIA Department of Indian Affairs
GAA Glenbow Alberta Archives, Calgary, Alberta
LAC Library and Archives Canada, Ottawa, Ontario
PAMHBCA Provincial Archives Manitoba, Hudson Bay Company Archives, Winnipeg, Manitoba
ROM Royal Ontario Museum, Toronto
SAB Saskatchewan Archives Board

# ACKNOWLEDGMENTS

When I immigrated to Canada to take up an appointment in the Geography Department at York University in 1970, I was unaware of the battles over history that were underway in the courts as Canadian Native People pressed for legal recognition of their rights. My awareness began only a few months before the publication of my *Indians in the Fur Trade* (1974) with the Supreme Court of Canada's decision in the Nisga'a land title suit in 1973. It would be another ten years before I was drawn into the fray. By that time I had moved (1981) to the West Coast, which was the centre of the action, to join the History Department at the University of British Columbia. Soon after my arrival, one of my new colleagues, Keith Ralston, encouraged me to get involved with rights litigation in British Columbia. I also am indebted to Professor Frank Tough, Native Studies Department, University of Alberta for encouraging me to take an interest in Métis rights litigation.

Over the past twenty-five years I have had the great pleasure of working closely with a number of dedicated Aboriginal rights lawyers who introduced me to the many dimensions of the legal system and helped me find my away around the courtroom. They are, roughly in the order that I worked with them: Ken Staroszik, QC; Stuart Rush, QC; Murray Adams; Louise Mandel, QC; Peter Grant; Mary Bird, Francis Thatcher, Peter Hutchins, QC, Jim O'Reilly, Clem Chartier, QC and president of the Métis National Council, Jean Teillet, Michelle Leclair-Harding, and Jason Madden. When I began, the courtroom seemed like a very strange and unfriendly place to me, a place where opposing sides appeared to wear white hats or black hats. Along the way I came to appreciate the professionalism of both parties and the roles each had to play. This appreciation enabled me to learn a great deal from opposing council also.

My deepening involvement in aboriginal and treaty rights litigation as an expert witness in Canada peaked my curiosity about the history of Aboriginal and treaty rights litigation in former British colonies. In support of this ongoing, comparative, research, I received a Canada Council National Killam Research Fellowship (2000–02), a Canada Council Bora Laskin Fellowship (2005–06), and a Woodrow Wilson International Fellowship (2005–06). After presenting my research at the Woodrow Wilson International Center for Scholars in Washington, D.C. in 2006, Fellow Lawrence Rosen, William Nelson Cromwell Professor of Anthropology at Princeton University, suggested that I write at least one monograph about claims litigation from the perspective of a participant-observer. Subsequently others have encouraged me to do so; chief among them are Professor Dianne Newell, director of the Peter Wall Institute of Advanced Studies at the University of British Columbia, Philip Cercone, director, McGill-Queen's University Press, and Walter Hildebrandt, director, Athabasca University Press.

As an expert witness, I have been called to testify mostly about the research in historical economic geography that I have undertaken for the past forty-five years in the extraordinarily rich Hudson's Bay Company Archives. I owe an enormous debt of gratitude to Ms Shirlee Anne Smith, former Keeper of the Records, Hudson's Bay Company Archives, Provincial Archives of Manitoba, her successors, and their staff for facilitating this work. I am also grateful for the help that many former student research assistants provided over the years, particularly Dr Kenichi Matsui, Tsukuba University, my collaborator on an ongoing project in Métis history, and Dr Susan Roy. I would also like to thank David Harrison and Jane McWhinney for their editorial advice.

I am especially grateful to my spouse, Dianne Newell. Her encouragement and support for this project have been an extension of the generous mentoring she has provided for so many years.

# FOREWORD

## JEAN TEILLET

*Telling It to the Judge* is Professor Arthur Ray's account of his experiences of telling "it" – that is, the history of Aboriginal peoples – to the judge in court. Dr Ray's engaging story makes clear that he has brought his considerable skills to the courtroom at the request of several lawyers, including me. Historical work in court is a task unsought and largely unrewarded, and not of the historian's own design. After all, it is not historians who initiate court cases to resolve Aboriginal lands and resources claims. They generally research, write, publish, and teach. I can think of no historian who has taken up history and academia as a profession with the goal of having his work judged in court.

However, litigating history is precisely what Canadian courts are now engaged in. More than forty aboriginal rights cases have gone to the Supreme Court of Canada since 1982, and each has engaged at least one historian – usually more. This is because the courts work on an adversarial system, the basis of which is the testing of evidence through intense and extensive cross-examination. From Aboriginal people judges hear stories previously unknown, and the stories are always longer than the history of Canada as a nation-state. Canada and the provinces are the newcomers on the block. The other side in aboriginal rights cases is the Crown, represented by the federal or provincial government, or both. Lawyers for the Crown are assigned the task of proving that the claimant aboriginal group in court has always had less, known less, claimed less, used less, and perhaps never existed at all. There are real consequences to these contests.

Litigating history is fraught with problems. The first is that judges, like most educated people in this country, believe they already know the history of Canada. It is a challenge to add water to a cup that is already full and bring forth a whole new story that may contradict the history the judge thinks she or he fully comprehends. The second problem is that the history judges have learned is coloured by the assumptions and prejudices of European perspectives. The earliest Europeans to come to America saw Aboriginal peoples through their own lens. They sought leaders who aligned with their own concept of leadership; finding none, they created all-powerful chiefs. They sought concepts of ownership when many North American Aboriginal peoples did not even have words of possession in their languages. They looked for bounded geographic territories with clear separations between peoples. They found peoples who were very mobile users of the land and resources, with different concepts of ownership and shared territories. They assumed that Aboriginal peoples had no commercial economies. They assumed that the Aboriginal peoples of North America were primitive and could be civilized and assimilated into greater and better Euro-Canadian cultures. The task of the historical expert representing Aboriginal claimants is to present facts and theories that will challenge and perhaps displace these ideas. This is a difficult task because judges are as tenacious of their learned convictions as anyone else, and the tendency of most judges is to wedge new facts into old assumptions and beliefs.

Another problem is that older published histories are either silent with respect to the role Aboriginal peoples played or influenced by the assumptions mentioned above. Previous generations of historians were also seduced by stories of violence and power struggles. Even today our news is replete with winners and losers, with the language of attack and ascendancy. This is one reason why Canadians know the story of the Riel rebellions; it is a story they can relate to. But the countless other stories of how Aboriginal peoples lived, their economies – and even the basic fact that they are still here – these stories are mostly absent from our school texts. Many people live next to places called "Indian Point" or "Indian Springs" but don't relate those names to the Aboriginal people who still live just down the road. I have had more than one judge tell me he has lived all his life in (insert name of any small town in Canada) and "there are no Aboriginal people there today."

The historian expert in court is required to do more than simply recount unknown history. The expert's job is to do the primary research, put all the documents together, and form an opinion on what the record means and what story it tells. While it may seem that academics are by nature opinionated, I have not found it easy to locate historians who are able to deliver an analysis and opinion to the court in an engaging and informative manner and sustain them under cross-examination. Many are very skilled at examining records and gathering information but seem incapable of analysis and in the end do not actually form an opinion. Instead, they simply reiterate the substance of the documents or regurgitate other historical opinions. This is highly problematic because when a historian is retained he or she is not told to form a particular opinion. My practice is to provide a series of broad questions about the Aboriginal people. Were they there? What was their economy? How did they use the lands and resources? The brilliance of Dr Ray as an expert was clear from the start. He was a careful researcher and had no problem putting voluminous documents into a cohesive story. His opinion, once formed, was articulate, and he was fully capable of defending it – usually with humour and with an eye to sustaining his big-picture story. It takes a special ability to do that.

For those of us who are engaged in litigating history, *Telling It to the Judge* is an important resource. More people need to know about the kind of historical work that underlies the monumental Aboriginal rights court decisions that are so fundamentally changing our development of Canadian lands and resources. Litigated history, the dialogue between the academy and the courts, is a new strand in the historical record in Canada. Dr Ray is one of the important and valuable voices in this dialogue.

# HOLDING THE MIRROR UP TO NATURE

## Law, Social Science, and Professor Arthur Ray

### PETER W. HUTCHINS

> *That is why it is so important to have one's own,*
> *distinct identity, a sense of its strength,*
> *value and maturity. Only then can a man boldly confront*
> *another culture. Otherwise he will lurk in his hiding place,*
> *fearfully, isolating himself from others. All the more since*
> *the Other is a looking glass in which I see myself, and in which*
> *I am observed – it is a mirror that unmasks and exposes me,*
> *something we would prefer to avoid.*
> – Ryszard Kapuściński[1]

> *To actually have him play a song for us, this is – this*
> *is a courtroom, this is – this is a court of law, we're here*
> *to deal with legal issues, it's not a concert.*
> – Crown Objection to Mr Boulette, a renowned Métis fiddler, playing his
> fiddle in Court to demonstrate Métis culture[2]

> *Critical legal theory requires above all – realisation that*
> *law is made by those on the riverbank and not*
> *those who are drowning.*
> – David Ritter and Frances Flannegan[3]

To advance the law of Indigenous-State relations we need principled and knowledgeable social science scholars and courageous judges – without the combination, the law stalls or retreats. Experienced counsel on the Indigenous side appreciate the absolute necessity of engaging the former, but can only pray for the latter. It is no accident that

Professor Arthur Ray has played such a dominant role in this rapidly evolving area of law. Win, lose, or draw, counsel and clients know that with Professor Ray's excellent scholarship in play and with his willingness to leap into the den of lions that Aboriginal litigation sometimes imitates, the Holy Grail of reconciliation between Indigenous peoples and the State becomes just that much more possible.

I was honoured to be asked by Arthur Ray ("Skip" to his friends) to write an introduction to this book, *Telling It to the Judge*. I have spent close to forty years in Aboriginal law practice "telling it to the judge" in written and oral argument. In November 1972 I made my first appearance before the court as part of the legal team for the Cree of James Bay, in what was to be the epic injunction proceedings against the original James Bay hydro-electric project taking place before Justice Albert Malouf.[4] This was in the time before the courts had provided any clear recognition of the existence of Aboriginal title. At the outset opposing counsel smugly pronounced one of the law's grandest conceits, "the King can do no wrong." But after hearing the testimony of 167 witnesses, Justice Malouf decidedly disagreed, granting the Cree's request for an injunction against the project and opening the door for the negotiation of Canada's first modern-era treaty, the *James Bay and Northern Quebec Agreement*.[5]

I came quickly to appreciate that the purpose of the law in our area is to seek and ensure justice (in the Natural law sense) out of the chaos, cruelty, dispossession, and mendacity of the past and that Indigenous peoples are locked in a struggle with the most sinister of humankind's creations, which is not the doctrine of *terra nullius*, not the Seventh Cavalry, and not the residential school system, as these are but derivatives of our most sinister creation: the State. The odds are formidable and the obstacles great: the public treasury, a "frontier" to be tamed, the development imperative and, sad to say, sometimes the law itself – made by those on the riverbank, rather than those whose rights and concerns are engaged.

Over time, the law has embraced various doctrines and tests, often vestiges of the original colonial powers, which function to further dispossess and marginalize Indigenous peoples. This includes the law of *terra nullius*, decreeing that Indigenous peoples possessed no souls and therefore could not be said to be proprietors of their ancient homelands; the law of "organized society," requiring Indigenous peoples to establish that their ancestors lived "in a rational and recognized society" (rather than in ... what? Packs?); and the law of extinguishment, devised to conveniently "clear the land" of competing claims – through European "assertions" of sovereignty, installing pitiable administrative regimes, or simply occupying, developing, or flooding indigenous territories.

The Eurocentric viewpoint will suggest, thanks to the use of these devices, that Indigenous culture cannot justify legal protection or has been lost and, correspondingly, that Indigenous claims to territory cannot be valid. This is a strategic misunderstanding, for make no mistake that the prize is land and resources. For example, in the James Bay injunction proceedings, the Crown argued that many of the James Bay Cree's hunting territories had not been used for several years, with the suggestion that the conclusion to be drawn was that the Cree had "abandoned" their attachment to their homeland, Eeyou Istchee. In fact, as the Cree hunters simply explained to the court, they were exercising Indigenous conservation strategies, letting their hunting territories rest and the living resources recuperate, as their ancestors had done for eons. The Cree culture and economy was alive and well. At the end of the day, Justice Malouf agreed.[6]

My good friend and respected colleague Louise Mandell has remarked that, in Aboriginal-State relations, we should be dealing with "rights not relics." One of the cruellest contemporary paradoxes in Indigenous-State relations is the courts' insistence on Indigenous claimants' proving the continuity of a cultural practice in order to establish an Aboriginal right under the prevailing legal tests, while modern society and governments require Indigenous peoples to swear off many of the traditional ways in order to "deserve" economic support and be eligible to conclude "modern treaties."[7] Social science, with history at the forefront, is capable of shattering this paradox. Historians are not only tasked with explaining the facts of history; they are capable of encouraging judges and non-Indigenous society to recognize that Indigenous culture is at once fluid and tenacious – the umbilical cord linking and feeding the past, present, and future – and that present-day Indigenous peoples *are* their Indigenous ancestors and have the right to remain so in the process of reconciliation and contemporary relations with the State. Skip Ray's work with the Métis provides a vivid example.

Lawyers and jurists have numerous flaws – among them are professional arrogance, an obsession with departmentalizing, and an instinctual conservatism parading as *stare decisis* or precedent. Each of those attributes represents the antithesis of useful scholarship and can lead to distortions of historical understanding. As Professor Ray writes:

> In my opinion, there are three reasons why judges tend to value historical experts roughly equally. The first is the common underlying notion that anyone can be an historian. The second is the lingering notion that documents are mostly "plain on their face." The third is the belief that historians are essentially clerks, whose primary role is to bring to the court's attention those documents that historians deem to be relevant.[8]

And again:

> Succeeding generations of academics have deployed different theoretical and methodological frameworks, thereby continually altering our understandings of Native history. In this way, scholarship has helped to keep the Aboriginal past alive in the academy and connected to its present interests.
>
> Courts, on the other hand, use history to bury the past rather than to continually revisit it.[9]

Arthur Ray has our number!

Despite these flaws present in our profession, Skip graciously acknowledges my own efforts in preparing and leading experts through their evidence. An expert's methodology and approach to the discipline seems to me to be essential information for a judge – it is an opportunity, not always seized, for the court to determine whether it is dealing with an "expert witness-educator"[10] or a charlatan. Professor Ray provides his view of why some judge-students presiding over trials in which he testified were not interested in "debates about the nature of history."[11] Succinctly put, it is because judges search for "facts" that address the current relevant case law. The pursuit of facts is aimed at weighing Aboriginal histories against legal tests, not at questioning those tests.[12]

Ironically, Supreme Court Justice Ian Binnie's name arises in this context. It is true that Justice Binnie, in addressing criticism over the courts' "cut and paste" treatment of history, rather testily pronounced in *R. v. Marshall*:

> While the tone of some of this criticism strikes the non-professional historian as intemperate, the basic objection, as I understand it, is that the judicial selection of facts and quotations is not always up to the standard demanded of the professional historian, which is said to be more nuanced. Experts, it is argued, are trained to read the various historical records together with the benefit of a protracted study of the period, and an appreciation of the frailties of the various sources. The law sees a finality of interpretation of historical events where finality, according to the professional historian, is not possible. The reality, of course, is that the courts are handed disputes that require for their resolution the finding of certain historical facts. The litigating parties cannot await the possibility of a stable academic consensus. The judicial process must do as best it can.[13]

It is also true that this perception of incompatibility may be on the wane. Justice Binnie has provided leadership in moving the jurisprudence forward in a search for what the historical Aboriginal perspective might have been, at least with respect to treaty-making, notwithstanding documentation ostensibly "clear on its face."[14] In this progress, Justice Binnie begins to push back from Professor Ray's "three reasons." But it is because of Justice Binnie's keen interest in the opinions of social scientists like Professor Ray that this pushback has begun.[15]

Other judges have demonstrated how history and law can work together quite nicely. Justice Lamer in *R. v. Sioui* provides proof with his contextual reading of what was found by the Court to be a 1760 treaty of peace between the Huron Nation and the British.[16] The origin of the document was a brief encounter between General James Murray and Huron sachems during Murray's final advance on Montreal in the fall of 1760. The document itself was signed only by Murray and was devoid of usual treaty language, yet the unanimous Supreme Court, speaking through Justice Lamer, found that military and diplomatic events of the French and Indian War justified finding that a treaty of peace had been concluded. Justice Lambert of the

Court of Appeal of British Columbia, in his Reasons in the *Delga-muukw* appeal, characteristically hits the nail on the head:

> Historians and anthropologists and other social scientists do not always agree with each other. Circumstances change and new raw material is discovered and interpreted. The tide of historical and anthropological scholarship could, in a few years, leave a trial judge's findings of fact stranded as forever wrong.[17]

All this appears to me to demonstrate the judicial process "doing the best it can." Professor Ray and his kindred spirits should take heart in this judicial sea change. In my view, they played and continue to play a role, and an important one, in this process.[18]

One aspect not always appreciated by the non-lawyer is the considerable importance to be given to the findings of fact of the trial judge.[19] It is the trial judge who sees and hears the witness, for our purposes the expert witness, and who has the opportunity to assess the credibility of the expert and the testimony.[20] For this reason, the trial judge's findings of fact and credibility will be treated deferentially on appeal, and overturned only in cases where a clear error was made. However, if the trial judge fails to appreciate the social science evidence, an appellate court may still rescue the day if the evidentiary base has been well laid. As the appeal judges will be working only with the transcripts, it is important that an expert's methodology and approach to the discipline is well fleshed out at the trial level. This is why the work of expert witnesses such as Professor Ray is so important.

We have seen instances in the field of Aboriginal law where the Supreme Court has returned to the trial evidence, including the expert testimony, making new and different findings of fact.[21] In *Marshall*, Justice Binnie focused in on expert evidence provided by historian Dr Patterson at trial and concluded:

> I think the view taken by the Courts below rather underestimates Dr. Patterson. No reason is given for doubting that Dr. Patterson meant what he said about the common understanding of the parties that he considered at least implicit in this particular treaty arrangement.[22]

Justice Binnie was ready to accept expert historical evidence based upon Dr Patterson's assumptions regarding what was "implicit" in the treaty.[23] This is an interesting example of a case where we have the highest court looking back to the historical evidence provided at trial, which explained the historical context of the Mi'kmaq 1760 Treaty. The Supreme Court was not prepared to hold that the treaty was "clear on its face." In overturning the courts below, Justice Binnie wrote:

> The trial judge erred, I think, because he thought he was boxed in by the March 10, 1760 document.
>
> In my view, the Nova Scotia judgments erred in concluding that the only enforceable treaty obligations were those set out in the written document of March 10, 1760, whether construed flexibly (as did the trial judge) or narrowly (as did the Nova Scotia Court of Appeal). The findings of fact made by the trial judge taken as a whole demonstrate that the concept of a disappearing treaty right does justice neither to the honour of the Crown nor to the reasonable expectations of the Mi'kmaq people. It is their common intention in 1760 – not just the terms of the March 10, 1760 document – to which effect must be given.[24]

Aboriginal law concerns itself with big issues about which it is important not to be stranded as "forever wrong." Elsewhere, I have written of Aboriginal litigation:

> In the tug-of-war between power and principle, look at what has been and continues to be at issue: universal human rights versus special rights and privileges; individual versus collective rights; acquired rights versus expropriated rights; Western liberal democracy versus clans, kinship, and heredity; natural resource extraction versus the seasonal round of harvesting; the crown as protector of indigenous cultures and economies versus the crown as facilitator of settlement and development; Aboriginal peoples with treaties versus those without them; universal principles of human rights versus the exercise of self-determination; domestic laws and politics versus international

laws on human rights and constraints on state power; and, perhaps most importantly, as raised in this volume, claims to "tradition" versus claims to "modernity." These are all principles and positions devoutly held and bitterly contested. The jurisprudence is replete with these struggles.[25]

There is no doubt in my mind that judges and lawyers in Aboriginal litigation need the assistance of social science. The courts must have in hand a sophisticated diagnosis of the present malady through an understanding of the past – not a snapshot but a full-length feature with plot, characters, context, a quest, and good and evil at play – an understanding that also includes movement, evolution, adaptation, deterioration, and renewal. All of this is necessary to diagnose the illness, recognize and acknowledge the causes, and bring the remedial, transformational, and curative properties of the law to bear. It is therefore not surprising that Professor Ray and his fellow experts, as he tells it, "faced formidable challenges as educators." They "had to lead trial judges from secondary school levels of historical knowledge about Canada and about First Nations and Métis defendants and plaintiffs to advanced university graduate understandings in an unreasonably short period of time."[26] They are not to be faulted for not always succeeding.

Skip Ray's work demonstrates remarkably how historical events, even silences in the record, can be fused to form a revealing narrative, how accepting the elusiveness of history and revisiting the past can, in fact, lead us closer to the "Other's" reality[27] – and how not proceeding in this way can "leave a trial judge's findings of fact stranded as forever wrong."[28] The chapters of this book reveal his struggles in the courtroom to persuade counsel and the judiciary that *not* everyone can be an historian, that documents *are mostly not plain on their face* and that the primary role of historian is *not* "clerical" sorting of documents for the judge.

In each of the recounted trials, Skip Ray's insightful contextual reading of the historical record brought us all closer to the truth. In *Horseman* (a prosecution for killing a grizzly bear and selling the pelt), he provided the revelation, through fur trade and government records, that the First Nations people of the Treaty 8 region earned a substantial part of their livelihood through commercial hunting and that local native hunters had traded grizzly bear skins on a regular basis. In *Del-*

*gamuukw* (Aboriginal title and governance), he was responsible for educating the court on chief trader Brown's the "extraordinary reports" made after Brown's arrival in Gitxsan and Wet'suwet'en territory in 1821. This material demonstrated Brown's sense of "discovery and difference" from his experience on the eastern side of the Rockies, which in turn confirmed the unique systems of hierarchical social structure with hereditary leaders and the House/territorial organization of the Gitxsan and Wet'suwet'en – all central issues in the claim. In the cases of *Regina v. Spade* and *Regina v. Wassaykessic* (fishing prosecutions), Hudson's Bay Company records were juxtaposed against the academic consensus, showing the importance of subsistence and commercial fishing for hunters and gatherers in the Treaty 3 and Treaty 9 areas.

I have personal knowledge of Skip Ray's long and intense study of the Hudson's Bay Company's fur trading reports for the *Victor Buffalo* case, which concerned the true meaning of Treaty 6, as we were both involved in the Treaty and historical phase of the trial. Based upon the Cree's long trading experience with the company, including the protocols, periodic renewal of arrangements, and what he referred to as the "social safety net" offered by the company, he provided insight into the Cree's understanding of what occurred during treaty time with the Crown. Again in the landmark Métis rights case *Powley* (a distinctive Sault Ste Marie Métis community and section 35 hunting rights), Professor Ray's expertise in examining trading records was instrumental in establishing that Métis had a well-developed self-consciousness and notions about their rights – efforts for which he earned the headline in the local newspaper: "UBC Professor declares the Métis a People!" Recently, he has continued to define Métis communities and customs, in the cases of *Regina v. Belhumeur* (fishing prosecution) and *Regina v. Goodon* and *Regina v. Jones and Hirsekorn* (Métis fisheries and harvesting rights).

Skip Ray's retort to the "plain on its face" approach to historical documents is always, "not so fast!"

For my work on the preparation of the James Bay injunction proceedings, I spent much time in the Cree and non-Cree communities of Northern Quebec. In 1973 one would see posted in hotels and bars the admonition "No Indians." Was this the "historical fact," the snapshot that explained Quebec society in the 1970s? Was it evidence of a permanent racial antipathy? Not if one fast-forwarded only five years to the year that the *James Bay and Northern Quebec Agreement*, Canada's first "modern-era" treaty, was concluded. From then on hotels, bars, and skidoo/truck dealerships, not to mention local mayors, courted the "Indians." Later came progressive modifications to the Treaty, many of which have vindicated and protected Cree traditional values. Our common understanding of the past continued to be radically transformed in the following decades through developing mutual respect. The "no Indian moment" had now to be explained in the context of Canada's first modern-era treaty, the recognition of the strength and cohesiveness of Cree traditional society and culture, and the economic clout that treaty relations brought to the racial mix.

What Professor Ray argues for is a more dynamic approach to history in court, one that accommodates a changing academic consensus or the evolution of one expert's views. As a witness, he was challenged during his testimony in *Victor Buffalo* on an apparent disparity between his early writings and his expert report prepared for the case. His explanation was that his research had continued following the publication of his *Indians in the Fur Trade* in 1974, when the First Nations' "voice on treaty history had been largely silent,"[29] and that since that time considerable work had been done on oral history research. His research and opinions now included First Nations' history on their Treaties. It is never too late to learn. The law must devise, with the critical assistance of social science, a more malleable method of resolving disputes, one that allows for adjustment or evolution in outcomes, as we continue to converse with each other, learn from each other. Perhaps most important, we must not fear peering steadfastly into Ryszard Kapuściński's looking glass or Shakespeare's mirror.

Skip Ray is a no-nonsense scientist. He advocates for his discipline and its insights and testifies to his studies. This is what has advanced the law in my area of practice. He is a consummate, even passionate, professional – not a fellow traveller. It is this professionalism that will save the day for Aboriginal peoples because the resulting historical integrity has and will continue to vindicate the Indigenous peoples' cause.

The point is that there is a dawning realization on the part of the judiciary that justice for Indigenous peoples will not be achieved by requiring Indigenous people to meet metaphysical judicial tests but rather by accepting that the law must extend its formidable protection to the "Other" by honouring their past struggles – first, for survival in the face of self-serving doctrine justifying overwhelming force and, subsequently, for full social and economic partnerships based upon an evolving understanding of our shared past.³⁰ This will not happen if we perpetuate Eurocentric versions of the past or the present. It will happen if we exercise a humility regarding the law's limitations and an openness to the teachings of trained, professional, and principled social scientists in whose front rank Professor Arthur Ray is securely ensconced.³¹

NOTES

1 Ryszard Kapuściński, *The Other* (London: Verso, 2008), 88.

2 Transcript of *Regina v. Belhumeur*, 2007 SKPC 114, (2007) 301 Sask R 292, as quoted by Arthur Ray in this volume, 116 [*Telling It to the Judge*].

3 David Ritter and Frances Flannegan, "Lawyers and Rats: Critical Legal Theory and Native Title," in Sandy Toussaint, ed., *Crossing Boundaries: Cultural, Legal, Historical and Practice Issues in Native Title* (Carlton: Melbourne University Press, 2004), 131.

4 *Kanatewat v. James Bay Development Corp.*, [1974] R.P. 38, reversed [1975] (C.A.) 166, leave to appeal dismissed [1975] 1 S.C.R. 48 [*Kanatewat*].

5 Ibid. at para. 1.

6 Ibid., at paras. 139–40.

7 See Peter W. Hutchins, "What Makes Them Who They Are: Bribery and Coercion in Cultural Compromise" (paper presented at Insight's 9th Annual Aboriginal Law Conference, Toronto, 4–5 October 2010) [available from the author].

8 Ray, *Telling It to the Judge*, 158.

9 Ibid., 152.

10 Ibid., chapter 8.

11 Ibid., 153.

12 Ibid., 154. This approach is reflected in the Supreme Court's reasons in *R. v. Van der Peet*, [1996] 2 S.C.R. 507, 137 DLR (4th) 289 [*Van der Peet*] and *Mitchell v. M.N.R.*, 2001 SCC 33, [2001] 1 S.C.R. 911.

13 *R. v. Marshall*, [1999] 3 S.C.R. 456, at para. 37 [*Marshall*].

14 *Mikisew Cree First Nation v. Canada (Minister of Canadian Heritage)*, 2005 SCC 69, [2005] 3 S.C.R. 388; *Marshall*.

15 In fact, in *Marshall*, Justice Binnie cites Arthur Ray's article "Creating the Image of the Savage in Defense of the Crown: The Ethnohistorian in Court," *Native Studies Review*, 1993 6 (2): 13–28.

16 *R. v. Sioui*, [1990] 1 S.C.R. 1025.

17 *Delgamuukw v. British Columbia*, 104 DLR (4th) 470 (BCCA) at para. 886.

18 Not long before his Reasons in *Marshall*, Justice Binnie attended a very interesting conference at Osgoode Hall entitled "History Goes to Court," and I could not help but remark that a number of the historical works he cited in *Marshall* had been on display and discussed at the conference. *Marshall*, at para. 36.

19 Typically, appellate courts are deferential to the trial judge's finding of fact, unless there was a clear error in the finding of fact. The general rule applied by the courts, that a court of appeal should not interfere with a trial judge's reasons unless there is a palpable and overriding error, was restated by the Supreme Court in *Housen v. Nikolaisen*, [2002] 2 S.C.R. 235.

20 *Van der Peet*, at paras. 81–2.

21 In *Delgamuukw v. British Columbia*, [1997] 3 S.C.R. 1010, Chief Justice Lamer indicated that there are specific situations in which an appeal court could interfere with a finding of fact made at trial. Specifically, "In cases involving the determination of aboriginal rights, appellate intervention is also warranted by the failure of a trial court to appreciate the evidentiary difficulties inherent in adjudicating aboriginal claims when, first, applying the rules of evidence and, second, interpreting the evidence before it" (para. 80). In *Delgamuukw*, the Chief Justice found that there had been serious errors in the way the trial judge had dealt with the oral history evidence adduced at trial (para. 107). As a result, he concluded that the factual findings of the trial judge (which were the basis for the lower court's decision that the Gitxsan and Wet'suwet'en did not have Aboriginal title) could not stand and ordered a new trial (para. 108).

22 *Marshall*, at para. 38.

23 This opinion was generally agreed to by the defence experts.

24 *Marshall*, at paras. 39–40.

25 Peter W. Hutchins, "Power and Principle: State-Indigenous Relations across Time and Space," in Louis A. Knafla and Haijo Westra, eds., *Aboriginal Title and Indigenous Peoples: Canada, Australia, and New Zealand* (Vancouver: University of British Columbia Press, 2010), 221.

26 Ray, *Telling It to the Judge*, 147.

27 As Ryszard Kapuściński writes in his work, *The Other*, 22. The terms 'Other' or 'Others' can be understood in all sorts of ways and used in various meanings and contexts, to distinguish gender, for example, or generation, or nationality, or religion, and so on. In my case I use these terms mainly to distinguish Europeans, people from the West, whites, from those whom I call 'Others' – that is, non-Europeans, or non-whites, while fully aware that for the latter, the former are just as much 'Others.'

28 Citing J.A. Lambert in *Delgamuukw v. British Columbia*, 104 DLR (4th) 470 (BCCA) at para. 886.

29 Ray, *Telling It to the Judge*, 83.

30 During the trial of the *Victor Buffalo* case, Dr Winona Wheeler, an expert

in indigenous histories, spent some time explaining to the Court the notion of other ways of knowing the past and recent changes in academic scholarship among historians regarding interpreting "Other" histories: "there is a growing respect in [the] scholarly community for recognizing other ways of knowing, but not just recognizing other ways of knowing ... recognizing it is vital to understand people within people's own sense of themselves in order to understand them in general." *Buffalo v. Canada* (30 November 2005), Ottawa T-2022-89, (F.C.), (Transcript, 1 November 2001).

31  "With appreciation to Nancy Bono and Robin Campbell, associates with Hutchins Legal Inc, for their research and editorial work."

# PROLOGUE

The Seven Years' War (1756–63) had brought the English and French battle for empire in North America to an end, but in the immediate aftermath the conquerors faced a number of critical problems. Key among them was the need to secure Aboriginal people's loyalty to the Crown and prevent them from clashing with newcomers over land. This was an especially difficult and urgent challenge, as many Native groups had earlier sided with the defeated French. For many years, moreover, all Native groups had benefited economically and politically from having both the English and the French court their favour. Now Aboriginal people were very anxious about the potential adverse effects that British domination would bring. Indeed, in the Great Lakes region, Aboriginal discord about this turn of events boiled over in May 1763 in Pontiac's Uprising (1763–64).

To quell unrest and gain the favour of Native people, King George III issued the Royal Proclamation of 1763 declaring that lands "of our dominions and territories" that had not been "ceded to us" were reserved for Indians "as their hunting grounds." The Proclamation further professed that it was "our Royal Will and Pleasure" that the territories beyond the existing colonies and the region granted to the Hudson's Bay Company be reserved for the present "under our Sovereignty, Protection and Dominion, for the use of the said Indians." Finally, the decree specified that only the Crown had the right to purchase Indian land at public assemblies of Indians convened specifically for that purpose. Although the purpose of these pronouncements was to win Native loyalty, they subsequently served as foundational principles in Canadian Native rights law.

The Proclamation had this impact partly as the consequence of a late nineteenth-century federal-provincial legal battle that most Canadians have never heard about. This feud, which is remembered in law as *St. Catherine's Milling and Lumber Company v. Regina* (1888), arose when the federal government granted a small timber company a licence to harvest trees from off-reserve Crown lands in the Treaty 3 (1873) area of Northwestern Ontario. The Ontario government objected, saying that the lands in question belonged to the province. In doing so, the province raised questions about the nature of Aboriginal rights in land that the Ojibwa had surrendered to Canada in 1873. The Judicial Committee of the Privy Council in England, which was the final arbiter of Canadian legal disputes until 1949, ultimately decided the issue based on its interpretation of the Royal Proclamation. The Judicial Committee concluded that the Ojibwa had only held personal rights to use lands in unceded territories "at the pleasure of the Crown." In other words, the Ojibwa had not surrendered outright ownership of the Treaty 3 area to Canada. Accordingly, the British justices ruled in favour of Ontario.

In this way, although Aboriginal people had not even been party to *St. Catherine's Milling*, the case had the effect of narrowly defining their land rights in Canadian law until late in the twentieth century, when Canadian courts revisited the issue in response to legal petitions by First Nations. Needless to say, when First Nations eventually learned about the implications of *St. Catherine's Milling*, they were affronted by the notion that their land rights derived from the Crown and continued only at its pleasure. Understandably, they believed that their rights originated from their use and occupancy of traditional territories before Europeans arrived on the scene and should continue in force until they were to surrender them voluntarily through negotiations.

First Nations had begun pressing these perspectives even before *St. Catherine's Milling*. In 1881 the Nisga'a sent a delegation from their Northwest Coast homeland to Victoria to demand that their land rights be respected. Subsequently, other First Nations from British Columbia joined in the struggle, sending petitions to Victoria, Ottawa, and London. Soon the Nisga'a decided to seek legal redress also. Accordingly, in 1910 they hired a lawyer to prepare a petition to the Judicial Committee of the Privy Council. Politicians and government officials feared the potential outcome of a Nisga'a petition. Accordingly, the federal government took steps to block the Nisga'a and others from petitioning the Judicial Committee or taking other legal action. One of the most egregious moves involved amending the Indian Act in 1927 to bar Indians from soliciting funds to hire lawyers to fight claims cases. This ban remained in effect until 1951. By that time, the Supreme Court of Canada had become the final arbiter of the country's legal disputes. Politicians were confident that the court would rule in their favour.

After the ban against hiring lawyers was lifted, the Nisga'a resumed the quest to have their Aboriginal title recognized in Canadian law. In 1969 they finally had their day in court in the now-famous case of *Calder v. British Columbia*. Through their lawyer, Thomas Berger (subsequently B.C. Supreme Court Justice Berger), the Nisga'a argued in the Supreme Court of British Columbia that their Aboriginal title had never been extinguished in accordance with the procedures specified by the Royal Proclamation. Indeed, this had not happened elsewhere in British Columbia either, except for small scattered tracts of land on Vancouver Island that were covered by the Douglas Treaties of 1850–54 and the Treaty 8 (1899) area of the northeastern portion of the province. The provincial government replied in its defence that the British government had never intended that the Royal Proclamation be applied in British Columbia, and even if it had, colonial land legislation had implicitly extinguished any Native titles.

The Nisga'a claim eventually reached the Supreme Court of Canada where, in 1973, six of the seven justices (one abstained) concluded that Aboriginal title had existed in the province prior to colonization; three of them held that colonial and provincial legislation had not extinguished that title, while three rejected this idea. Although this split decision disappointed the Nisga'a, *Calder* raised the probability that Aboriginal title existed in all areas of Canada that had not been surrendered by treaties publicly negotiated for that express purpose. The decision did not define what the scope of any existing Aboriginal titles might be, however. The Liberal government of Prime Minister Pierre Elliott Trudeau reacted to the worrying issues *Calder* raised by creating a complex claims procedure. For the first time, substantial funding became available for historical research concerning Aboriginal title claims (referred to as comprehensive claims) and those pertaining to disputes arising from the interpretation and implementation of historic treaties (known as specific claims).

While *Calder* progressed through the courts, other developments were taking place that also would have a profound impact on Aboriginal rights litigation in Canada. The late 1960s and 1970s was a time of growing political activism by First Nations and the Métis. By the time Trudeau pushed for constitutional reform in the late 1970s and early 1980s, Aboriginal political leaders had become very effective on the national stage in advancing their agendas. They demanded inclusion in federal-provincial discussions about repatriating the Constitution. Their activism bore fruit in Section 35 of the Constitution Act (1982). This clause afforded protection to existing Aboriginal and treaty rights. Also, it broadly defined Aboriginal people to include First Nations, the Inuit, and the Métis. Section 35, however, failed to specify the extent and nature of existing Aboriginal and treaty rights. The politicians left it to the courts to settle these contentious issues.

In these crucial ways, *Calder* and Section 35 set the stage for the modern claims litigation era in Canada. Together they raised several fundamental questions: What Aboriginal and treaty rights had survived in various parts of Canada? What was the scope of Aboriginal title? Who are the Métis and where do they live? What is the nature of their culture and their rights? All these questions had major historical components.

As Canada moved toward *Calder* and the Constitution Act, a development took place in the United States that would affect the nature of some of the historical evidence that other experts an I would eventually present in Canadian court battles from the mid-1980s on. In 1946 Congress passed the Indian Claims Commission Act, which created the United States Indian Claims Commission (USICC) to address the grievances that American Indian tribes held against the federal government. The commission operated for thirty years. Very quickly it focused on title and land cession issues. The federal government (the defendant) and tribal groups (the plaintiffs) from across the country hired experts to present and challenge historical evidence regarding the use and occupancy of traditional tribal territories by hundreds of tribal claimants.

The operation of the USICC had a lasting impact on North American Native history for several reasons. Substantial funding for research in the field of American Indian history became available for the first time. This new research focused on economic life, especially land use and tenure, topics that had not previously been of primary scholarly concern. Claims work also acted as a catalyst for an interdisciplinary approach to Indian history because initially most of the experts who appeared before the commission were anthropologists and archaeologists. They applied anthropological and archaeological theories and perspectives in their interpretations of diverse documentary evidence. Their approach came to be known as ethnohistory. During the latter half of the 1950s and 1960s, these ethnohistorical experts published aspects of their research in leading scholarly journals and monographs.

When I was a graduate student in historical geography at the University of Wisconsin–Madison in the late 1960s, I was drawn to the emerging ethnohistorical scholarly literature because it was especially relevant to my developing interests. As an historical geographer, I was fascinated by the effects that Western Canadian Native peoples' participation in the European fur trade had had on their inter-tribal relations, migrations, economic life, and ecological circumstances. At the time, I was unaware that much of this scholarship had originated with Claims Commission cases. Perhaps ironically, I did not learn of this connection until I began appearing as an expert witness in Canada over thirty years later. Acting in that capacity, I became interested in studying the claims resolution processes in which I had become involved. Many years earlier during my graduate student days, however, *Calder* was just beginning to wind its way through the Canadian courts, a journey that did not end until two years after I completed my doctorate in 1971. The Constitution Act was still eleven years away. Thus, when I immigrated to Canada in 1971, I had no idea that one day I would head down the path described in the following chapters and be drawn into some of the country's most important landmark legal cases.

# TELLING IT TO THE JUDGE

# CHAPTER 1

# TAKING FUR TRADE
# HISTORY TO COURT

In 1985 Calgary lawyer Ken Staroszik phoned me at the University of British Columbia and asked me if I would be willing to appear as an historical expert in a treaty rights case in Alberta (*Regina v. Horseman* 1986).[1] Knowing nothing about appearing in court as an expert, I asked him what he expected me to do. He replied, "You will be there to educate the court about Native and fur trade history." Because that seemed like a reasonable and straightforward task – somewhat like the obligation of a citizen – I agreed. I was completely unaware that my acceptance in 1985 was drawing me into the intensifying struggles of Aboriginal people to use history to define and defend their Aboriginal and treaty rights in Canadian courts. Until this time, I had thought my work on the historical geography of Aboriginal people in Canada had little applied significance. I had been drawn to this topic out of curiosity as a consequence of having grown up in Wisconsin, where histories of the state emphasized the Indian and fur trade dimensions. My doctoral supervisor at the University of Wisconsin, Andrew H. Clark, who had emigrated from Canada, encouraged me to pursue these topics, but he suggested that I focus on Canada. In particular, he recommended that I study the Métis of Manitoba, a province to which he had strong ties.[2] As part of my plan to follow his suggestion, I began to do background research into the roles First Nations had played in the western Canadian fur trade. This topic became the focus of my doctoral research, which I eventually published a few months after *Calder v. Regina*, the first Aboriginal title case, as *Indians in the Fur Trade*,[3] and it had remained my primary scholarly interest until Mr Staroszik phoned me.

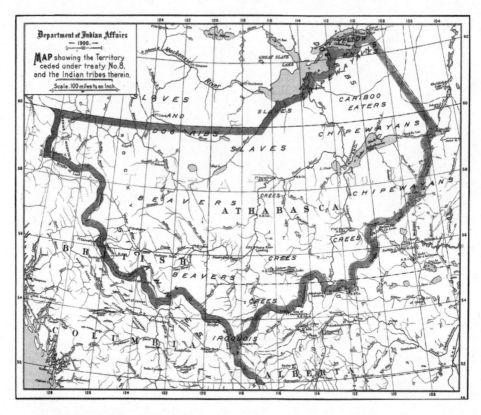

Fig. 1: Map of Treaty 8 Region, 1900.

Mr Staroszik's client, Bert Horseman, a Cree living in northern Alberta, had been charged under the Alberta Wildlife Act[4] for selling a grizzly bear skin. The act banned commercial hunting of this endangered species. The agreed facts of the case were that Mr Horseman had killed the bear in self-defence when the animal attacked him while he was out fur-trapping. He skinned the bear and took the bearskin home. About a year later he sold the skin to alleviate his dire financial circumstances. Mr Horseman asserted that he had a right to do so because Treaty 8, which his ancestors had signed in 1899, promised Indians they would be able to pursue their long-established livelihood pursuits. Indeed, the treaty explicitly states:

> And Her Majesty the Queen HEREBY AGREES with the said
> Indians that they shall have right to pursue their usual vocations
> of hunting, trapping and fishing throughout the tract surren-

dered as heretofore described, subject to such regulations as may from time to time be made by the Government of the country, acting under the authority of Her Majesty, and saving and excepting such tracts as may be required or taken up from time to time for settlement, mining, lumbering, trading or other purposes.[5]

Through his lawyer, Mr Horseman contended that commercial fishing, hunting, and trapping had become customary vocations in the Treaty 8 region (fig. 1) long before the end of the nineteenth century. He thought, therefore, that selling a bearskin should be considered one of the "usual vocations" protected by the treaty.

Mr Horseman's claim made sense to me on the basis of what I had learned in the previous twenty years. The European fur trade probably had penetrated northern Alberta almost two centuries before his ancestors signed the treaty in 1899.[6] Furthermore, the trade is still operating in the region. I told Mr Staroszik that I thought these historical and present-day facts were common knowledge. He agreed that they were, but added that the Crown prosecutors were arguing otherwise. They claimed that commercial hunting, fishing, and trapping had not been the usual practice of the northern Alberta Cree when they signed Treaty 8. Thus, Mr Staroszik needed an expert "to educate" the court about the history of the fur trade of northern Alberta. This expert had to be someone whom the trial judge would recognize as being a bona fide authority on the subject.

GATHERING HISTORICAL EVIDENCE: THE HUDSON'S BAY
COMPANY ARCHIVES

Fortunately for me as a novice expert witness, the relevant historical evidence was quite straightforward. Mr Staroszik required proof that when the local native people signed the treaty they had been making their livelihoods off the land at least in part by commercial hunting, trapping, and fishing. Although I knew enough about the history of the European/Aboriginal fur trade in the region to affirm this was the case, I decided to visit the Hudson's Bay Company (HBC) Archives in Winnipeg, Manitoba, to see if any documents survived that had a specific bearing on the case.

I had been using the company's archives since the summer of 1968, when I began research for my doctoral dissertation in Ottawa.[7] The HBC records had become readily available to scholars for the first time only in the late 1960s, and I was fortunate to be among the small vanguard of researchers to consult them.[8] Significantly, the late 1960s and early 1970s also happened to be the time when the modern Aboriginal claims era in Canada was just beginning. The Nisga'a Aboriginal title case (*Calder*), which finally reached the Supreme Court in 1973, heralded that beginning.[9] The pace with which such cases were heard quickened after the the Canadian Constitution Act was adopted in 1982, because Section 35 of the act protected existing Aboriginal and treaty rights. As noted, since the politicians did not define these rights, the implications of Section 35 were unknown. Slowly – in piecemeal fashion – the meaning and impact of the act are becoming clear, mostly through Aboriginal and treaty rights litigation in which ethnohistorical evidence plays a central role.[10] *Horseman* was one of the trials that began to define existing Aboriginal and treaty rights.

By the time of the *Regina v. Horseman* trial in 1985, HBC records had facilitated the rise of Native History in Canada, especially in the West.[11] Since *Horseman*, this archive also has provided crucial evidence in Aboriginal and treaty rights cases, especially those in Ontario and western Canada. The reason for this is that the company's archive contains a wealth of detailed historical information about all aspects of the lives of Aboriginal Peoples from across Canada. This is one of the legacies of the Hudson's Bay Company's having slowly built a vast network of posts outward from its original Hudson Bay–James Bay base after it was chartered in 1670. By the early nineteenth century, its sprawling trading empire included most of present-day Canada.[12] HBC posts effectively served as observation stations where traders collected an eclectic array of information about Canada's Aboriginal people. Of particular relevance to Aboriginal rights litigation are post records in the form of account books, daily journals, correspondence books, and a wide variety of other company documents. They are rich sources of information about local environments and the livelihoods Aboriginal peoples derived from them.

Thanks to this rich material, I thought HBC records would be pertinent to Mr Horseman's case. He had killed the grizzly bear near the site of the abandoned HBC post of Fort Vermilion, which had been located on the lower Peace River. For this reason, I checked to see if a

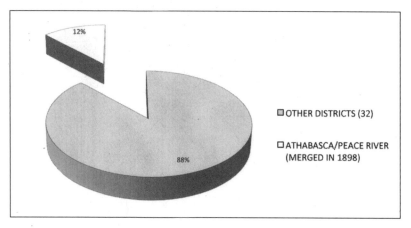

12%

☐ OTHER DISTRICTS (32)

☐ ATHABASCA/PEACE RIVER
(MERGED IN 1898)

88%

Fig. 2: Athabasca & Peace River District as share of total value of Hudson's Bay Company returns, 1892–1900.

set of records from this trading post and nearby ones (especially those of Fort Dunvegan and Lesser Slave Lake) had made their way into the archives. Fortunately, they had. Sets of account books and districts reports were among the surviving documents.[13] As is typical, the trading post accounts provided information about the annual "returns" at the fort, which were the furs and hides that Native people brought to exchange for trading goods and the bartering of "country produce."[14] Fur traders applied the latter term to a wide range of commodities that they bought from their native clientele to support local trading operations. Country produce included a variety of food, clothing and clothes-making materials, boat- and canoe-building and repairing supplies (such as birch bark, cedar ribs, spruce root, pine tar), firewood, timber, and packing resources (leather and leather cording), to name only a few. The local HBC account books and headquarters records were explicit enough for me to construct for the court a detailed picture of the fur trade of the region in the 1890s (fig. 2).

Other HBC documents supplemented the trading post records and strengthened Mr Horseman's case. These had been created at district and department headquarters and in London. By the early nineteenth century, company directors and managers had organized the sprawling fur trading business into districts and departments. Company managers drew upon records generated at individual trading posts to compile annual reports for districts, departments, and London headquarters.

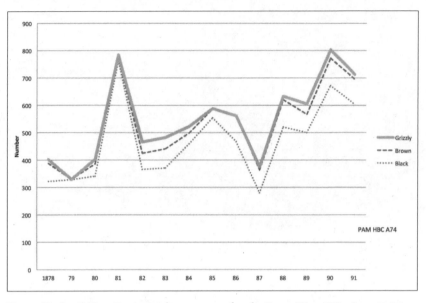

Fig. 3: Hudson's Bay Company bear returns for the Peace River District, 1878–91. The *Horseman* litigation raised the question of whether First Nations had traded grizzly bear skins in the vicinity of Fort Vermilion on the Peace River before 1899.

Fig. 4: Treaty 8 negotiations at Fort Vermilion on the Peace River, August 1899. Native People received assurances from government officials that the treaty would not adversely affect their economic way of life.

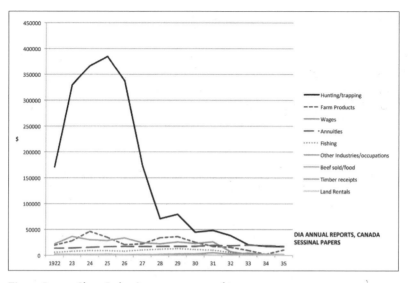

Fig. 5: Lesser Slave Lake Agency sources of income, 1922–35.

Of particular relevance to the *Horseman* case was the fact that the latter records, especially the Fur Trade Department annual reports, showed that local native hunters had traded grizzly bear skins on a regular basis (fig. 3). Other London records enabled me to show that the eastern portion of the Treaty 8 area, which encompassed most of the Atha-basca District of the Hudson's Bay Company (where Fort Vermilion was located), had been one of the company's most important trading districts at the end of the nineteenth century (fig. 4). It remained so dur-ing the early twentieth century.

Published federal government records also enabled me to corrob-orate the picture I had generated from the HBC archives.[15] Officers of the North West Mounted Police (NWMP),[16] for example, were among the first government officials to arrive in the area, and they were fil-ing patrol reports as early as the 1890s.[17] Their reports mentioned not only the commercial hunting and trapping activities of the Cree and Dene inhabitants, but also the sales of fish to non-Natives living in the region.[18] Department of Indian Affairs (DIA) records would tell a similar story for a later time. Agents of this department arrived in the region just over twenty years after the negotiation of the treaty and, as required, they filed annual agency reports, which included appendices of economic statistics. Their reports made it abundantly clear that the

Native people of the Treaty 8 region continued to earn a substantial portion of their livelihood from the land by commercial hunting, trapping, and fishing, even though the DIA had made concerted efforts to promote agriculture (fig. 5). This kind of evidence from the early post–Treaty 8 era is important because it demonstrates that the treaty had not significantly altered Native economic life, and suggests in turn that Indians and government officials likely intended that the treaty clause concerning "usual vocations" guarantee Indians the right to continue to earn an income from fishing, hunting, and trapping.

### CAN TRADE AND SUBSISTENCE ACTIVITY BE SEPARATED?

To guide me in drafting my research report for the Provincial Court of Alberta,[19] Mr Staroszik gave me a list of questions to address. They concerned the general aspects of the economic history of the western Canadian fur trade before and after 1899, and specific details about the Treaty 8 area.[20] In preparing my response, I took the opportunity to make the general point that it was very difficult to differentiate subsistence activities from commercial ones in the post-European contact era. I cited the trade of beaver pelts as probably the best example of the problem. This commodity had been the staple of the fur trade in Canada from its inception in the late sixteenth century until the mid-nineteenth century.[21] Long before European contact, however, beaver had been a mainstay in the economies of Native Peoples throughout most of what is now Canada, especially among those who lived in the sprawling evergreen woodlands of the Canadian Subarctic. The women of First Nations from this vast region fashioned warm winter coats from pelts turned inward. These people also ate beaver meat, especially when populations of moose or woodland caribou were at the low points of their cycles. At these times, beaver could be a crucial component of the diet.[22] The meat of three or four of these animals was roughly equal to that obtained from one woodland caribou. In other words, beaver trapping[23] was crucial for making clothes and obtaining food. After contact, the economies of the Native peoples and newcomers became increasingly interdependent. Native trappers bartered their beaver pelts (and those of other animals) to obtain ammunition, guns, knives, metal hatchets, traps, twine, fish nets and net lines, and a variety of other imported items that had become essential components of their toolkits. In this way, commercial and subsistence activities became inseparably linked.

In making this point to the court, I was revisiting an issue that the Hudson's Bay Company had faced during the 1830s when it introduced to what is now western Canada the first European-conceived beaver conservation program. Faced with faltering returns caused by over-trapping during the previous thirty years, the company devised a scheme that featured district trapping quotas and closed seasons. These measures anticipated the kinds of management practices that would be central to federal and provincial conservation programs of the late nineteenth and early twentieth centuries. The problem the company faced, however, was that the depletion of moose and woodland caribou throughout the subarctic woodlands, which also was a consequence of ruinous fur trading competition during the pre-1821 era, had forced Native people to be more reliant on beaver for food. Consequently, they trapped the animals even when local HBC traders, as a matter of conservation policy, refused to accept their beaver pelts. Indeed, Native trappers sometimes hid their beaver pelts to avoid incurring the anger of local company men.[24]

Significantly, the inextricable intertwining of the subsistence and growing commercial sectors of native economies that were enmeshed in the fur trade, as well as the economic interdependence of Aboriginal people and Euro-Canadians that developed soon after contact, were issues that I would return to in subsequent cases, most notably in *Regina v. Powley* (2002), which concerned the hunting rights of Métis living in the area of Sault Ste Marie, Ontario.

THE EXPERT WITNESS IN COURT: ACCEPTING A REPUTATION

My appearance in court in *Horseman* was a very brief affair compared to most of my subsequent trial experiences. The whole event lasted barely a morning. There were two primary reasons for this brevity. First, the Crown apparently had changed its strategy and decided not to focus on contextual issues concerning the treaty. Second, the *Horseman* trial took place very early in the era following the *Calder* case and the passage of the Canadian Constitution. Since *Horseman*, court proceedings have become increasingly adversarial and often feature protracted battles of phalanxes of opposing historical experts bearing myriad documents and espousing conflicting historical interpretations and theories about the nature of pre- and post-contact Aboriginal cultures.

My appearance in court as an expert witness began pleasantly with Mr Staroszik asking me questions about my *curriculum vitae* so that I could highlight the aspects of my academic career that would demonstrate to the court that I was qualified to give testimony about Native and fur trade history. Opposing counsel raised no questions or objections to cast doubt on my qualifications. Mr Staroszik then proceeded to the evidence-in-chief[25] phase of the trial by posing a series of questions about my written report, or "evidence." This brief had not been submitted to opposing counsel in advance because the trial was a criminal rather than a civil proceeding.[26] As is the general practice when leading evidence-in-chief, Mr Staroszik asked questions that afforded me the opportunity to highlight my major conclusions. After he had finished, it was Crown counsel's turn to cross-examine me. However, by that time, the Crown had dropped their argument that the Cree and other native groups had not fished, hunted, or trapped for commercial purposes before 1899. Instead, Crown counsel had determined to focus on issues relating to the textual interpretation of the treaty and those arising from federal and provincial legislation that had been enacted after Treaty 8 had been concluded. Because I had not been asked to address these topics, I was spared the ordeal of a rigorous cross-examination.

In 1986 Alberta Provincial Court Justice Wong acquitted Mr Horseman.[27] In her written reasons for judgment, she accepted my portrayal of the pre-1899 Native economy and the notion that subsisting by hunting and fishing necessarily entailed some production for exchange. This led her to conclude that Treaty 8 had included the right to barter produce obtained from Native hunting and fishing. She held, therefore, that Mr Horseman had not exceeded his treaty right. The Crown promptly filed an appeal to the Court of Queen's Bench. There, Justice J. Stratton overturned Mr Horseman's acquittal. Mr Horseman then appealed all the way to the Supreme Court of Canada.

Significantly, Justice Stratton and the appeal courts that followed him shifted their attention from the evidence of historical context that I had presented at trial to the question of the extent to which the rights protected by Treaty 8 had subsequently been curtailed by the federal Crown, acting unilaterally through the Natural Resources Transfer Agreement (NRTA) of 1930.[28] The NRTA had transferred ownership of

Crown lands from federal to provincial ownership in Alberta, Manitoba, and Saskatchewan.[29] The act was an amendment to the British North America Act 1930, which had been renamed the Constitution Act 1930.

## THE IMPORTANCE OF HISTORICAL CONTEXT

In addressing this question, the appeal courts focused on the intended meaning of Paragraph 12 of the NRTA concerning Indian hunting and fishing rights. This brief section of the much more extensive act states:

> In order to secure to the Indians of the Province the continuance of the supply of game and fish for their support and subsistence, Canada agrees that the laws respecting game in force in the Province from time to time shall apply to the Indians within the boundaries thereof, provided, however, that the said Indians shall have the right, which the Province hereby assures to them, of hunting, trapping and fishing for food at all seasons of the year on all unoccupied Crown lands and on any other lands to which the said Indians may have a right of access.[30]

From my perspective as an ethnohistorical expert, the problem with having the appeal courts focus their attention on this section of the NRTA was that neither party had brought forward evidence at trial to provide the historical context that these higher courts should have considered when they tried to ascertain what the drafters of the act had intended.

Justice Stratton of the Court of Queen's Bench essentially took the view that Paragraph 12 was "plain on its face." He was convinced that the drafters of the NRTA had meant to restrict Treaty 8 rights because the act specifically stated that Indians would continue to have the right to hunt and fish "for food." For Stratton, these two words signalled that the drafters of the agreement had envisioned that Indian hunting rights were to be limited only to activities directly related to subsistence after 1930. Accordingly, he flatly rejected the suggestion that this section of the NRTA made any allowance for a multi-stage process such as that suggested by HBC records, whereby some of the proceeds of the hunt could be used to buy the articles Indians needed for subsistence. Seeking further support for his conclusion about the intended meaning of the act, Stratton turned to the clause in Paragraph 12 that states that Indians were to have the right to hunt for food "on all unoccupied Crown lands and on any other lands to which the said Indians may have a right of access." This clause made it clear that the treaty rights of individual Indians no longer would be limited to the boundaries of their respective treaties (treaties 6, 7, and 8).[31] Rather, Alberta Indians could exercise them anywhere in the province that was legally accessible to them. Justice Stratton surmised that this spatial expansion of the right was intended by the drafters of the NRTA to be a *quid pro quo* for restricting the nature of that right.

In taking this textual rather than contextual approach to the interpretation of Paragraph 12, Justice Stratton was following a precedent that had been established in a body of case law concerning the application of the NRTA in the Prairie provinces that can be traced back to 1935.[32] This case law approach is problematic, however. One of the most notable difficulties is that it offers divergent paths of interpretation that lead to opposing conclusions about whether the paragraph was intended to curtail Treaty 8 rights or shield them from provincial encroachment. Stratton opted for the former perspective, which theorizes that the drafters of the NRTA consciously merged and consolidated all the treaty and statutory rights that Indians held and reduced the scope of those rights solely to subsistence-oriented practices.[33] Subsequently, the Alberta Court of Appeal and a majority of the Supreme Court of Canada upheld his approach and conclusion.

However, Justice Bertha Wilson, when writing for the dissenting Supreme Court justices (C.J. Dickson and J.J. L'Heureux-Dubé), emphasized aspects of case law that construed Paragraph 12 as having been intended to protect existing treaty rights.[34] This led her to emphasize the need to consider carefully what the paramount concerns of the Indians were when they signed Treaty 8. After reviewing the historical evidence that had been presented in *Horseman* and consulting published scholarship on Treaty 8, she emphasized that the overriding concern of Indians in 1899 had been to protect their existing way of life.[35] Justice Wilson noted that Indians had signed the agreement only after government negotiators had solemnly and repeatedly assured them that their way of life would continue as before ("as long as the land shall last"). Accordingly, Justice Wilson thought that if Indians were restricted to hunting only for food it would be a fundamental violation the spirit and intent of Treaty 8.

## THE HAZARDS OF INFERRING (OR INVENTING) INTENT

When viewed from the perspective of an ethnohistorian/historical expert, the decisions of the majorities in appeal courts in *Horseman* serve to highlight an inherent problem of Aboriginal and treaty rights litigation. Once a case begins to wind its way through the legal process, it takes on a life of its own. Historical questions that lawyers and experts representing opposing parties had not anticipated at the outset frequently arise and sometimes take centre-stage. When such questions come up at the trial phase, they can possibly be addressed, but rarely in a satisfactory manner. Good historical research cannot be done on the fly. Worse, if new questions arise after this initial phase, as happened in *Horseman* concerning the NRTA, new historical evidence cannot be introduced. So, in this instance, the appeal court justices resorted to existing case law and textual analysis to infer (invent) legislative intent. While this is an accepted practice in law, it is egregious historical practice. Historical geographer Frank Tough's detailed research on the history of the drafting of the NRTA, which he undertook after the *Horseman* case, provides a stunning example of why this is so. Tough's work conclusively demonstrates that the court's textual analysis of the act was flawed and the justices' conclusions about legislative intent were wrong.

On the issue of commercial rights, for example, Tough observes that the appeal courts' readings of Paragraph 12 failed to take into consideration the fact that this part of the act mentioned "trapping" as one of the livelihood rights. Given the close association of trapping with the commercial fur trade, that fact should have raised alarm bells for the justices who argued that this paragraph was meant to bar commercial activities. In his analysis of the drafting of the 1930 agreements, which began in Alberta in 1926, Tough shows that "trapping" was inserted late in the process to address concerns raised by the Hudson's Bay Company. The company, of course, had a longstanding vested interest in protecting Indians' commercial harvesting rights. Tough also demonstrates that the "for food" reference was inserted to address the concerns of DIA officials, who wanted to make sure that Indians were not barred from obtaining food during any seasons that were closed to hunting by provincial legislation. They had a vested interest in preventing this from happening, because the DIA faced the risk of spiralling relief costs if Native people were barred from hunting.[36] In other words, the phrase "for food" was intended to protect, not restrict, extant rights. Finally, Tough shows that federal-provincial officials never expressed any desire to merge and consolidate Indians' treaty and statutory rights during negotiations leading to the NRTA, which took place sporadically over a four-year period.

Tough's research clearly demonstrates the need to introduce at trial all relevant historical evidence in order to minimize historical invention by the courts. Concern about this issue in the post-*Horseman* Aboriginal and treaty rights claims era has created another daunting problem for plaintiffs, defendants, and the courts, however. Since *Horseman,* legal counsel have been increasingly disposed to enter into the court record any historical evidence that they believe might be even remotely relevant to the legal issues at hand. As a consequence, it is increasingly common for trial judges to be snowed under by masses of highly diverse ethnohistorical and historical evidence, and they are forced to listen to ever more lengthy sessions of evidence-in-chief and cross-examination. Worse, judges are sometimes presented with massive records without the benefit of any context. Jammed court calendars and soaring litigation costs are the result. *Delgamuukw v. Regina* (1997), the 1980s land title claim of the Gitxsan-Wet'suet'en of British Columbia, heralded the beginning of this trend. I now turn to my involvement in that case, in which teams of experts attempted to educate the court by presenting masses of evidence and diverse historical perspectives in an extremely adversarial setting.

# CHAPTER 2

# ROLES AND REVERSALS OF THE HISTORICAL RESEARCHER

From colonial times to the present, British Columbia has been a hot-bed of the Aboriginal rights struggle in Canada. Successive colonial and provincial B.C. governments have steadfastly refused to acknowledge that Aboriginal people held title to the lands their ancestors had occupied from time immemorial. Undaunted, the various First Nations pressed their rights, using all the means available to them. They were particularly active in political and legal arenas.[1] A key consequence is that a disproportionate number of landmark legal decisions have resulted from cases originating in British Columbia. Indeed, as I have mentioned, the land title claim of the northwest coast Nisga'a (*Calder v. British Columbia*) marked the beginning of the modern claims era in the country.

Soon after taking up an appointment in the History Department at the University of British Columbia in 1981, I was drawn into the legal battles of the province's First Nations. My participation began in 1984, not as an expert witness but as an historical researcher. Keith Ralston, one of my colleagues at the University of British Columbia, encouraged me to attend a meeting at the Vancouver law offices of Stuart Rush to discuss a research program that the Gitxsan-Wet'suet'en – at the time incorporated as the Gitksan[2]-Carrier Tribal Council[3] – were planning as part of their opposition to the Aluminum Company of Canada's[4] proposal to develop the hydroelectric generation potential of the Bulkley River.[5]

## A FIRST NATION DEFENDS ITS LANDS

The Gitxsan-Wet'suet'en, who are the inland neighbours of the Nisga'a and Coast Tshimsian, were afraid that the projected and contentious hydroelectric development, known as Kemano 11,[6] would adversely affect the salmon fisheries in their traditional territories. The tribal council intended to gather historical evidence about the use and occupation of their territories from "time immemorial" to the present to demonstrate that the Gitxsan-Wet'suet'en had a vested interest in the lands that would be affected by Kemano 11.[7] At the Vancouver office meeting with Mr Rush, tribal council president Neil Steritt stated that the far-reaching historical research program being planned would also serve other purposes. Most notably, he indicated that some of the historical evidence gathered would eventually be used to prepare and pursue a comprehensive land title claim. This was because the Gitxsan-Wet'suet'en, similar in this respect to most First Nations in British Columbia, had never agreed to share or surrender their lands through treaties with the Crown. In the absence of treaties, they were unwilling to allow any further development that affected their traditional lands (fig. 6).

Prior to the Vancouver meeting, I had not undertaken any research that focused on First Nations who lived west of the Rocky Mountains. Furthermore, at the time I was heavily engaged in a project concerning the history of the Canadian fur trade of the late nineteenth and twentieth centuries.[8] Nonetheless, I agreed to prepare a report on the fur trade in Gitxsan-Wet'suet'en territory from its inception in the late eighteenth century to the end of the pre-Confederation era in British Columbia (pre-1871). My research agenda at the time was already leading me to spend considerable time in the HBC archives in Winnipeg and in the national archives in Ottawa. Accordingly I proposed to the Gitxsan-Wet'suet'en that they reimburse me for any additional costs that I incurred gathering data for their project. They agreed, and my subsequent work for them proved to be exciting and eye-opening.

As I would do very shortly thereafter for *Horseman*, I began my Gitxsan-Wet'suet'en project in the HBC archives in Winnipeg. The plaintiffs' traditional territory sprawls over the vast drainage area of the middle and upper Skeena River basin. Prior to 1821, the Hudson's Bay Company had been unable to penetrate this area via the Peace River corridor because of the staunch opposition of its archrival, the

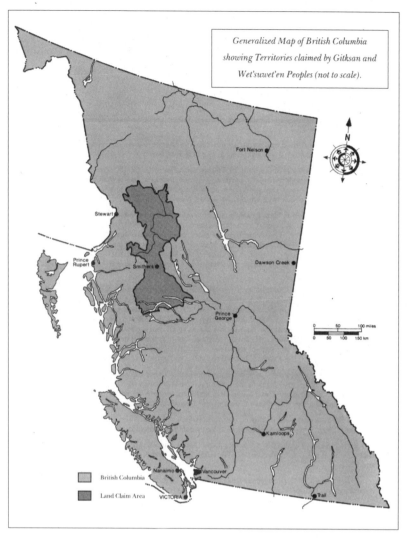

Fig. 6: Map of claimant's territory from *Delgamuukw v. A.G.: Reasons for Judgment.*

North West Company, which from the first decade of the nineteenth century had operated in the region bordering Gitxsan-Wet'suet'en territory to the east[9] and southeast.[10] The company's Scottish traders referred to these and other lands lying west of the Rocky Mountains in north central British Columbia as New Caledonia, in memory of their homeland. When the two companies merged in 1821, the former trading rivals operated under a renewed HBC charter and an expanded trading licence.[11] After the amalgamation, the reorganized Hudson's

Bay Company extended its operations in New Caledonia to the margins of the Gitxsan-Wet'suet'en lands by establishing a post on Babine Lake, which is remembered today as Old Fort Babine.[12] I started my research for the Gitxsan-Wet'suet'en with the records from this post, which, as it happened, yielded some of the most important historical documents that were used in the Gitxsan-Wet'suet'en litigation.

William Brown, chief trader for the Hudson's Bay Company, established Old Fort Babine in 1821, naming it Fort Kilmaurs after the place where he had grown up in Scotland. Up until 1821, Brown had been stationed in various HBC districts east of the Rocky Mountains. These included the York Factory area on western Hudson Bay (his first posting), the Brandon District of Western Manitoba, and the Athabasca District. Although the First Nations of these districts varied considerably, they did have characteristics in common. Most notably, all were what anthropologists classify as fishing, hunting, and gathering band societies. For much of the year they lived in small groups of closely related families. During the summer, these related groups and their neighbours usually gathered together for short periods of time at productive fishing places. Although some groups had hereditary leaders, people predominately followed the adult male who was best suited to lead the group in the task at hand (hunting, trading, warfare, and so on). Leaders also were those who were able to gain a consensus among their followers.

CULTURE THROUGH THE EYES OF A FUR TRADER

When Brown crossed the mountains and entered Gitxsan-Wet'suet'en country, he moved into a very different cultural world. His growing awareness of this is clear from the records he kept. This is why I found Brown's narratives so fascinating. Beginning my foray into Gitxsan-Wet'suet'en history through his accounts allowed me to be initiated to the region through the eyes of a newcomer who already had gained a great deal of fur trading experience elsewhere. Of particular relevance to me and my later testimony on behalf of the Gitxsan-Wet'suet'en was the fact that prior to 1981 all my research had focused on the areas where Brown had cut his teeth as a fur trader. As a result I was especially atuned to his sense of discovery and difference. Questions about the dissimilarities between the fur trading experiences of the Gitxsan-

Wet'suet'en and those of the First Nations who lived east of the Rocky Mountains would loom large in the Crown's cross-examination of me as an expert witness.

Undoubtedly the most striking difference between the native societies of the Subarctic and Plains regions, which trader Brown knew well, and those of the western Pacific slope, which he was now encountering for the first time, was that the latter were anchored on well-developed salmon fisheries and had hierarchical social structures that featured hereditary leaders. Furthermore, the extended family, or lineage, was the basic social unit, and family members lived most of the year in large cedar-plank houses. In other words, the "house" was a social and residential unit. Members of a house collectively owned a distinct tract of land that their hereditary leader managed. A number of houses clustered together during the long winter season, forming settlements near good salmon fishing sites. However, these settlements lacked any type of extra-kin governing organization. In addition to their salmon-fishing settlements, lineages also seasonally occupied berry-collecting and hunting sites, as well as others that were associated with an array of resource-harvesting activities. A well-developed network of trails linked these sites together. These trails also facilitated extensive trading connections between Gitxsan-Wet'suet'en settlements and those of neighbouring groups, most notably the downriver Coastal Tshimsian, the Nisga'a, who lived to the north of the latter in the Nass River basin, and the Babine, who lived to the east of the Wet'suet'en on Babine Lake.[13]

The co-residential Gitxsan-Wet'suet'en lineages traced their ancestry to various clans, which formed bonds within and between settlements. All events of major importance to local groups, such as leadership succession, individual acquisition of names and titles, deaths, or conflict resolution, took place at formal public witnessing/gift-giving ceremonies, which we have come to know as "potlatches."[14]

It is clear that when Brown arrived at Babine Lake in 1821, he immediately realized that understanding and working through the house/territory system of the Gitxsan and Wet'suet'en and the latter's close relatives, the Babine,[15] would be essential for trading success in the area. For this reason, he devoted his first two district reports to this topic [Appendix 1]. These extraordinary reports, which are synopses of his first two post journals,[16] demonstrate that he was an astute ethnographic observer who likely had one, or several, knowledgeable

Native informants. Within two years of arriving in Gitxsan-Wet'suet'en territory, he was able to describe, albeit using European terminology, the defining features of these people's house/territory system. Of crucial importance to *Delgamuukw v. Regina* was that the scheme that Brown outlined accorded closely with the one described both by anthropologist Diamond Jenness for the Wet'suet'en in 1943[17] and by the hereditary chiefs in preparation for litigation. Since neither Jenness nor the elders were aware of the Brown records, however, his observations provided independent corroboration.

## OF "NOBLES" AND "MEN OF PROPERTY"

It is clear from his journals and reports that Brown was particularly interested to learn that that the leaders, which he variously referred to as "chiefs" of various rank, "nobles," or "men of property," closely regulated Babine, Gitxsan, and Wet'suet'en economic life. The contexts in which he used these terms when referring to hereditary leaders suggests that he meant the word "chief" to identify the highest ranked "noble" of a settlement or a clan. He referred to the latter social grouping, which usually included people from several settlements, as a "tribe," and indicated that two or more "tribes" were represented in most settlements. He used the expressions "nobles" or "men of property" interchangeably when writing about heads of houses (lineages).[18]

Brown's descriptions of the geography of the area suggest that the settlements were of different economic importance and, perhaps, social rank. Regarding those of the Babine-Wet'suet'en, the chief trader stated that the "village" of "Hot-sett,"[19] located on the Bulkley River near the present-day Wet'suet'en community at Morricetown, British Columbia, was paramount. In his first report (1823), he mentioned that three chiefs and seventeen men of property resided at "Hot-sett" (figs. 7, 8, and 9). He listed them according to rank.[20] Brown also noted their seating order at feasts. What is astonishing about this knowledge is that he had not visited the settlement. He could only have gleaned this information from Wet'suet'en who visited his fort or from local Babine. Regarding the Babine, he noted that they had almost the same number of chiefs and men of property as the Wet'suet'en but lived in three separate settlements on Babine Lake: "Nass-chick," which was the largest, "Nah-tell-cuzz," and "Tachy," the smallest.

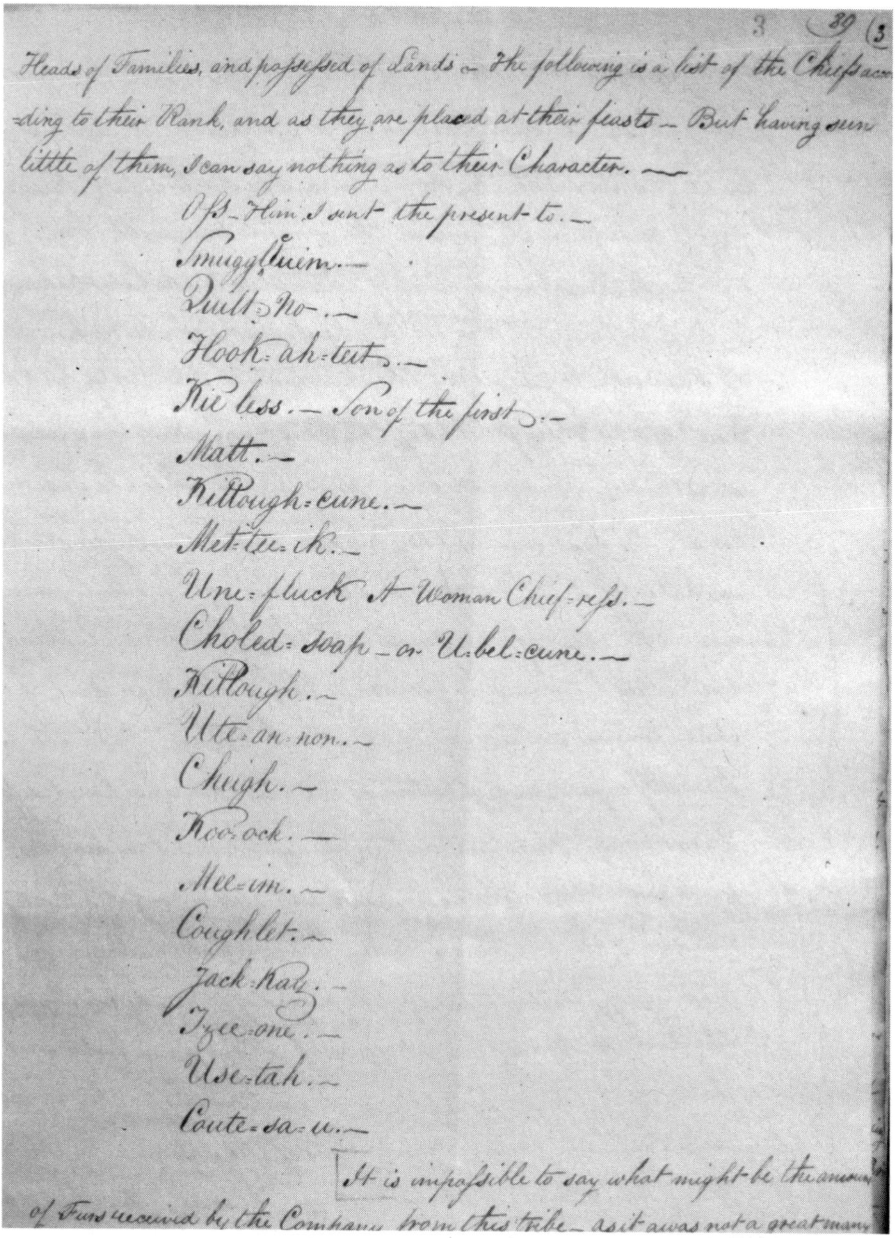

Heads of Families, and possessed of Lands — The following is a list of the Chiefs according to their Rank, and as they are placed at their feasts — But having seen little of them, I can say nothing as to their Character. —

Off — Him I sent the present to. —

Smugglluim. —

Quilt-no. —

Hook-ah-teet. —

Kie less. — Son of the first. —

Matt. —

Killough-cune. —

Met-teu-ik. —

Une-fluck  A Woman Chief-refs. —

Choled-soap — or U-bel-cune. —

Killough. —

Ute-an-non. —

Chigh. —

Koo-ock. —

Mee-im. —

Coughlet. —

Jack-Kay. —

Tzee-one. —

Use-tah. —

Coute-sa-u. —

[It is impossible to say what might be the amount of Furs received by the Company from this tribe — as it was not a great many

Fig. 7: Page from Chief Trader William Brown's District Report of 1823, listing Wet'suet'en chiefs in order of rank. Brown's records were included in Exhibit 964 as a supplement to my brief to the court.

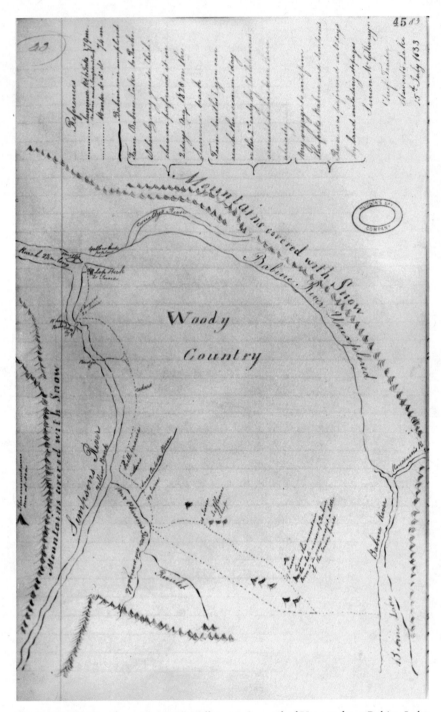

Fig. 8: Sketch Map from Simon McGillivray's Journal of Voyage from Babine Lake to Wet'suet'en Country, spring 1833.

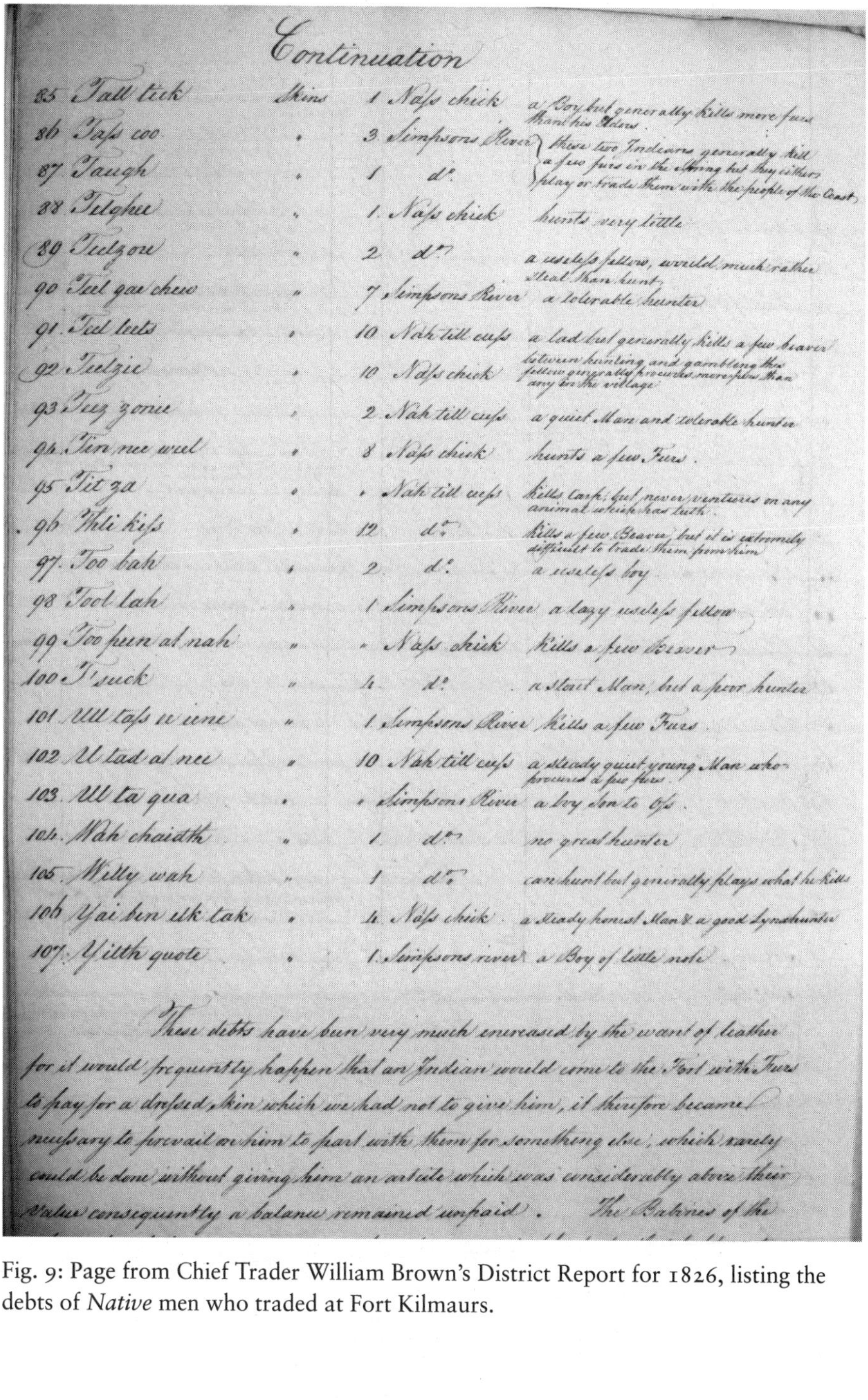

# Continuation

| No. | Name | | No. | Location | Remarks |
|---|---|---|---|---|---|
| 85 | Tall tick | Skins | 1 | Nass chick | a Boy, but generally kills more furs than his Elders |
| 86 | Tass coo | " | 3 | Simpsons River | these two Indians generally kill a few furs in the Spring but they either play or trade them with the people of the Coast |
| 87 | Taugh | " | 1 | do. | |
| 88 | Telghee | " | 1 | Nass chick | hunts very little |
| 89 | Teelzou | " | 2 | do. | a useless fellow, would much rather steal than hunt |
| 90 | Teel gae cheu | " | 7 | Simpsons River | a tolerable hunter |
| 91 | Teel teets | " | 10 | Nah till cuss | a lad but generally kills a few beaver |
| 92 | Teelzie | " | 10 | Nass chick | between hunting and gambling this fellow generally procures more plews than any in the village |
| 93 | Teez zou | " | 2 | Nah till cuss | a quiet Man and tolerable hunter |
| 94 | Ten nee weel | " | 8 | Nass chick | hunts a few Furs |
| 95 | Tit za | " | . | Nah till cuss | kills carp, but never ventures on any animal which has teeth |
| 96 | Thli kiss | " | 12 | do. | kills a few Beaver, but it is extremely difficult to trade them from him |
| 97 | Too bah | " | 2 | do. | a useless boy |
| 98 | Tool lah | " | 1 | Simpsons River | a lazy useless fellow |
| 99 | Too peen at nah | " | . | Nass chick | kills a few Beaver |
| 100 | T suck | " | 4 | do. | a stout Man, but a poor hunter |
| 101 | Ull tass u iene | " | 1 | Simpsons River | kills a few Furs |
| 102 | Ul tad al nee | " | 10 | Nah till cuss | a steady quiet young Man who procured a few Furs |
| 103 | Ull ta qua | " | . | Simpsons River | a boy Son to Ofs |
| 104 | Mah chaidth | " | 1 | do. | no great hunter |
| 105 | Welly wah | " | 1 | do. | can hunt but generally plays what he kills |
| 106 | Yai tin ilk tak | " | 4 | Nass chick | a steady honest Man & a good lynx hunter |
| 107 | Yilth quote | " | 1 | Simpsons river | a Boy of little note |

These debts have been very much increased by the want of leather for it would frequently happen that an Indian would come to the Fort with Furs to pay for a dressed Skin which we had not to give him, it therefore became necessary to prevail on him to part with them for something else; which rarely could be done without giving him an article which was considerably above their value consequently a balance remained unpaid. The Natives of the

Fig. 9: Page from Chief Trader William Brown's District Report for 1826, listing the debts of *Native* men who traded at Fort Kilmaurs.

The chief trader's account of Gitxsan settlements was sketchier than his descriptions of the Babine-Wet'suet'en, even though he visited their territory in 1825 and again in 1826. Referring to the Gitxsan people as the "Atnah," he indicated that they had at least eight settlements, which increased in size in a downstream direction. One of the largest Gitxsan villages, he wrote, was located near the forks of the Skeena and Babine rivers.[21] It is likely that he was referring either to ancestral Kispiooks or to Kiseguecla.

In addition to describing the house/territory organization and locations of Babine-Wet'suet'en and Gitxsan primary settlements, Brown, as would be expected, paid a great deal of attention to their economic activities, especially their trading patterns. He focused on three aspects of the economic geography of the region that were crucial to his struggle to expand the company's fur trade. First, he was struck by the fact that men of property tightly controlled the harvesting and trading of resources in their territory, and expressed particularly concern about the effect of this control on beaver trapping and trading. He reported that no one could trap these animals in a house's territory without the approval of its hereditary head, he reported, and he complained that these nobles barred the majority of young adult males from trapping beaver. His accounts suggest that these leaders limited the yield of beaver pelts from their territories to approximately twenty to thirty animals per year, a restriction that represented a major impediment to his goal of expanding the company's trade.

Second, and equally troublesome for Brown, was his discovery that the fur and other commodities harvested by local natives from the various house territories flowed mostly through the hands of the respective men of property. As was the case with First Nations elsewhere in the Pacific Northwest, trade had been important in Gitxsan-Wet'suet'en-Babine country long before Brown arrived on the scene, and most nobles already had well-established trading connections. Making matters worse for him, by the time he arrived on the scene, the coast Tshimsian were deeply involved in the maritime fur trade. This contact led them to strengthen their traditional trading links with their Gitxsan-Wet'suet'en neighbours and reach out to the Babine. To his annoyance, Brown learned that the Tshimsian traders had access to cheaper European goods on the coast than the company could supply from York Factory, which was located more than half a continent away on Hudson Bay. In dealing with Brown, the Tshimsian used their economic advantage, their traditional ties to interior settlements, and threats to use force against their traditional partners if the latter changed their trading allegiances.

Brown's 1826 report on Fort Kilmaurs and his accompanying journals thus provide us with a clear glimpse into the struggle he was having with his Tshimsian rivals for the fur trade of the Gitxsan, Wet'suet'en, and Babine. The picture is made more vivid by his list of the men who traded at his post, in which he included thumbnail "character sketches" of each man, as was common practice among company traders at the time. Brown's pithy remarks conveyed his assessment of the degree to which each individual either aided his challenging effort to expand the company's trade or hampered it, and his acerbic descriptions of those who stood in his way often explain why these individuals did not trade with him (Appendix 1).

Having begun my investigation with Brown's exceptional narratives, I extended my research backward in time to the pre-contact era by examining archaeological reports and the accounts of fur traders, mostly NWC men, who operated southeast and east of Babine Lake from 1806 to 1820. I also worked forward in time to the early twentieth century. The fur trade history of the latter period (c. the 1830s to 1915) involved using a variety of documentary (primary) sources, especially those of the Hudson's Bay Company, as well as published ethnographies and histories (secondary sources), to explore how the diversifying regional economy (particularly mining activities and the development of salmon canneries on the lower Skeena River) affected Gitksan-Wet'suet'en economic life. The published literature about the Gitxsan-Wet'suet'en proved to be very limited, especially the ethnographic scholarship; most archaeologists and anthropologists had cast their gaze on the coastal or inland neighbours of the Gitxsan-Wet'suet'en.

On 17 February 1984, I submitted my first report to the Gitksan-Carrier Tribal Council. This twenty-five-page report, which I entitled "HBC Expansion into the Upper Skeena River Region in the 1820s," focused on the Brown records. Mr Rush, who led the litigation team[22] for the Gitksan-Carrier Tribal Council, told me that when the Wet'suet'en received my report, it caused considerable excitement because the names of the chiefs and nobles Brown had listed for Hot'sett had not been found in other documentary records. Mr Rush said that members of the community read the names aloud to determine whether

Brown's English/Scottish renderings approximated the sounds of any of the chiefly titles that were still in use; some did. This is not surprising, given that heads of houses inherited names and titles when they assumed those positions. In this way, names are passed down through the generations.[23]

In January 1985, I filed my final, much lengthier, report.[24] To my surprise, I heard nothing back from the Gitxsan-Wet'suet'en or their lawyers for a couple of years. The reason was that they were intensely engaged in filing their title claim and preparing for the trial. As they planned for the anticipated litigation, the tribal council made the daring decision to have the elders lead off the presentation of evidence. They would be followed by experts from academe and from other disciplines. This plan reversed the normal trial practice in Aboriginal rights cases in Canada, a tactic other First Nations have since followed. The council's idea was that the elders should present the house histories, which were called the *ada'ox* by the Gitxsan and *kungax* by the Wet'suet'en, because they were the custodians of these histories and were the most knowledgeable about them. Accordingly, the Gitksan-Wet'suet'en wanted expert witnesses, mostly scholars, to be called on to provide supporting evidence as was necessary. This precedent-setting litigation decision presented a major challenge to the court. In effect, the Gitxsan-Wet'suet'en were demanding that their oral histories be given at least the same weight as histories written by outsiders. Their challenge eventually reverberated all the way to the Supreme Court. In any event, in 1985 I was uncertain if I would have to present my research in the anticipated trial.


THE COURT'S ATTITUDE TO ORAL HISTORIES


Two years later, in May 1987, the trial of the Gitxsan-Wet'suet'en title claim began before the Supreme Court of British Columbia in Smithers, British Columbia, with Chief Justice Allan McEachern presiding. The small courtroom was packed with people from the two First Nations. In their opening statement, the chiefs asked the court to cast aside evolutionary perspectives that had portrayed their people's culture as being inferior to that of Euro-Canadians. They stressed that to make this change, the court would need to be open-minded about hearing and evaluating new lines of evidence such as oral histories.

Traditionally the Gitxsan-Wet'suet'en presented some of these stories in song, which is an unusual format for court proceedings. The chiefs expressed the evidentiary challenges they were posing for the court in positive terms by stating: "Never before has a Canadian court been given the opportunity to hear Indian witnesses describe *within their own structure* the history and nature of their societies."[25] They also issued a warning: "For the Court, however, to deny the reality of Gitxsan and Wet'suet'en history except where it can be corroborated by expert evidence in the western scientific tradition is to disregard the distinctive Gitxsan and Wet'suet'en system of validating historical facts."[26]

Their opening pleas and warnings had little effect on Chief Justice McEachern. Two years later, it had become clear to the Gitksan-Wet'suet'en's legal team that he was giving little weight to the elders' extensive testimony in the already protracted trial. This led Mr Rush to phone me early in 1989 and tell me that they needed me to testify. During the four-year interval between the filing of my report and his phone call, I had appeared in the comparatively straightforward and low-key *Horseman* trial. So, his request did not seem ominous.

In preparation for my appearance, Mr Rush asked me to shorten my 1985 report and focus on the pre-1850 era,[27] in effect, to submit a brief that was very similar to my 1984 report. He explained that he and his colleagues wanted me to appear because my analysis of chief trader Brown's records and portrayal of the fur trade of the early nineteenth century would independently corroborate the evidence the elders had already presented about their traditional house/territory system.

When I was called to appear, the wisdom of the lawyers' decision to ask their team of experts not to attend court before they were called to testify became clear. It shielded us from the suspicion of having had our testimony "tainted" by listening to those who preceded us in the courtroom. To protect our independence as witnesses, the lawyers had also asked us to work independently, even though some of my fellow experts thought it made better sense, from an academic perspective, for us to work as a research team. Mr Rush decided not to pursue that option, fearing that working together was risky because the failure of any one of us in court could potentially undermine the testimony of us all. These concerns should have been a warning to me that my trial experience in this case would be very different from that of *Horseman*. So, in blissful ignorance, I shortened my report and agreed to appear. I was in for a rude shock! Courtroom 53 of the Vancouver law courts, where the trial had reconvened in January 1988, the 100th anniversary of *St. Catherine's Milling* (see Prologue), proved to be a hostile and suspicious place.

I spent the weekend before my scheduled trial appearance preparing at the Vancouver law offices with Murray Adams, who was going to lead my evidence-in-chief. I had not undertaken such elaborate preparations for *Horseman*. Rather, during the evening before the latter trial, Mr Staroszik and I had spent only a couple of hours at an Edmonton hotel talking generally about the historical issues we would address. When I arrived at the Vancouver law offices and met Mr Adams for the first time, he was very casually dressed in a T-shirt and jeans and was sitting in the board room behind a very long table that was buried under a mound of exhibits (maps, documents, and scholarly publications). In his low-key, deadpan, but earnest way, he made it clear that we had a lot of work to do. He explained that he anticipated that, considering the importance of my testimony, I would be given a rigorous cross-examination. Not having had that experience in *Horseman*, I asked him to give me some idea of what this would entail.

## WHEN CROSS-EXAMINATION BECOMES INQUISITION

When he finished describing the procedure for "testing evidence" in court, I remarked that it sounded somewhat like a doctoral oral examination. Mr Adams smiled and told me this was not the case. He pointed out that in doctoral examinations some or all of the examiners are sympathetic to the candidate, whom they want to succeed. In sharp contrast, he said, cross-examining counsel would seek to discredit me and my testimony. It would be more like an inquisition.[28]

With that sobering thought in mind, we went to work, reviewing my report and focusing on the portions he intended to highlight when he led my evidence. He made his choices in light of the issues that had arisen at trial and in anticipation of the direction my cross-examination would likely take (fig. 8).

On Monday morning (20 March 1989) my ordeal began. It was clear from the outset that I was going to have a rough ride. When Mr Rush proposed calling me as an expert in the field of historical geography, counsel for British Columbia, C.F. Willms, rose to make two basic objections based on his interpretation of my written submission. First, he argued that Chief Justice McEachern did not need me to interpret HBC records for him because "in most cases the documents are plain on their face." His added reasons for making this objection were that he thought the oral opinion I would express about the documents would simply be that they "don't mean what they say" or that, as a cultural historian – "or sorry, not a cultural historian, a historical geographer" – I could somehow "glean the social organization of the plaintiffs at the time of contact from these documents." However, he added, addressing the bench directly: "Those are issues for your lordship, those aren't issues for a historical geographer. The documents say what they mean, they mean what they say, and your lordship can come to your own conclusions."[29]

I had very mixed reactions to Mr Willms's objections. I realized that, apart from his misconstruing the nature of my report, he was introducing me to a world in which ways of thinking and operating differed sharply from those of the academy. For example, a basic premise of historical disciplines (anthropology, archaeology, history, and historical geography being among them) is that evidence (artifacts, documents, and oral history) must be contextualized to be interpreted properly. It is also generally understood that scholarly interpretations are largely shaped in reference to current theoretical frameworks. For these reasons, scholars regard the notion that any line of historical evidence is "plain on its face" as being fundamentally wrong-headed. But, as we have already seen with regard to appeal courts' interpretations of the Natural Resources Transfer Agreement in *Horseman*, this notion, which Mr Willms advanced, was based on precedents of judicial interpretation. As someone who was still a relative novice at being an expert witness and unfamiliar with litigation practices, I thought Mr Willms's proposition was absurd and even potentially counterproductive to the interests of his client. If, for example, Chief Justice McEachern had read Brown's documents as though they were plain on their face, he would have concluded that the Gitxsan-Wet'suet'en had a society like that of England and Scotland. This was because chief trader Brown had described the local Aboriginal social and land ownership system using terms that reflected his European background ("nobles" and "men of property").[30] Given that Mr Willms certainly did not want the court to decide that the Gitxsan-Wet'suet'en traditionally had a private property regime similar to that of Europeans, on reflection I assume he was merely engaged in courtroom strategizing and theatrics.

Mr Willms's second objection to my appearing as an expert had to do with my academic field:

> Historical geography, or history, is not a science at all, it's not a subject at all, it's not a subject of expert opinion, it is not verifiable. The opinions of historians depend completely on their own views of what documents mean. They are arguments about what history is, they don't relate to archaeology or anthropological interpretation, but solely to this is what so and so said on a particular day and in my opinion what he meant was this, and it's my submission that that isn't science.[31]

On its face, this objection seemed especially disingenuous in light of the fact that one of the key experts that Mr Willms intended to call on behalf of the Crown was Dr Sheila Robinson, who was trained as an historical geographer, although he intended to qualify her as a cultural geographer![32] Aside from this issue, I thought that Mr Willms displayed remarkable ignorance about the nature of the academic disciplines at issue. All of them interpret evidence. Moreover, the boundaries between the disciplines he mentioned are not distinct, especially when the scholarly gaze is focused on people of non-literate cultures. In the 1930s Julian Steward recognized this reality when he coined the term "ethnohistory" to describe the interdisciplinary study of Aboriginals in North America. Archaeologists, for example, employ the so-called direct historical approach, which involves using documents of the early contact period to help them interpret artifacts from the late pre-contact era. Ethnographers, historians, and cultural/historical geographers use anthropological concepts and theoretical frameworks to interpret documentary records, which is what I had done in my brief to the court. My own *curriculum vitae*, which had been submitted to the court, made it clear that, among other things, I was trained in anthropology and archaeology,[33] having field experience in the latter discipline, and I had published my research about various aspects of First Nations history in scholarly journals of anthropology, archaeology, ethnohistory, geography, and history.

## THE "TRUTH" OF THE RECORD

Having sparred over my credentials, the lawyers turned to issues raised by the HBC records. Mr Adams wanted to have the documents I cited admitted as evidence and assigned exhibit numbers. Mr Willms demanded to know how extensive the submission would be and what purpose it would serve. He added: "If he [Dr Ray] is not going to rely on them for the truth of them, then there's no underlying factual basis for this witness' opinion. We can argue about what they're worth at the end of the day, my lord, but I think my friend's got to at least say that he's relying on them for the truth of the contents." James A. Macaulay, QC, who represented the Attorney General of Canada, joined the discussion. He stated: "If this witness is relying on a historical document, then it's to be assumed, unless he makes a comment on it and points out why it shouldn't be relied on in that way, it ought to be assumed these documents are being introduced in evidence for the truth of the contents, the accuracy of the contents, given that they're made by Hudson's Bay Company officials; in other words, given the circumstances, but essentially that they're truthful and not untruthful or inaccurate."

At this point Chief Justice McEachern intervened and asked if the HBC records were business records. Mr Macaulay affirmed that they were. With this assurance, the chief justice replied: "I haven't addressed my mind to the question of business records, but I'm not sure that I have to go that far." He continued: "I have heard a lot of assertions by Mr. Willms and other witnesses that certain matters of social or cultural phenomena should be attributed to the fur trade, and I now have before me a witness who has studied the fur trade and its consequences, and it seems to me that he ought to be able to say that my opinion is such and such and I rely upon the Hudson's Bay Company records to a very great extent, but not necessarily upon everything that's in every document." With this consideration, the chief justice admitted the documents for the purpose of identifying them as the basis on which I had formed my opinion, "without committing anyone at this point to be adopting the whole of the document – as the whole of each document as proof of the truth of the fact stated in each document."

After this lengthy discussion about the basis on which the business records of the Hudson's Bay Company should be admitted, Mr Macaulay wryly commented on the copies, which had been printed from microfilm: "I observe, my lord, that this discussion is largely academic, because the vast majority of these pages are illegible." Concluding the conversation, Chief Justice McEachern quipped: "Then there's no harm done," and he admitted the two volumes of HBC documents I had submitted as Exhibit 964.[34]

## LAWYERS' ATTITUDES TO HISTORY AND HISTORIANS

Although Mr Willms's objections were representative of the kinds of courtroom manoeuvres that lawyers make when opposing expert witnesses are brought forward, I think the objections he raised also reflected an attitude about academic disciplines that were commonly held in Canadian legal circles at the time and which persist, to some extent, to the present, as I learned in subsequent trials. Until the 1960s in the United States, and until after *Delgamuukw* in Canada, the assumption was that anthropologists were the scholars best suited to provide the courts with "scientific evidence" about the nature of Aboriginal cultures and the transformations that these cultures underwent after contact with Europeans. In fact, as American anthropologist Nancy Lurie observed in the 1960s, lawyers and courts often treated anthropologists as surrogate Indians.[35] In contrast, as Mr Willms's comments highlighted, many in the legal profession thought that historians lacked the kind of special knowledge that courts could or should recognize in accordance with the accepted rules of evidence. At best, many lawyers regarded (regard) historians as being little more than highly educated clerks, or archivists, who have the special ability to ferret out relevant documents for courts to interpret. This kind of thinking was evident in Mr Macaulay's response to Mr Willms's objection. In his role as counsel for the Attorney General of Canada,[36] he expressed surprise at Mr Willms's suggestion that historians should not be allowed to give expert evidence, noting that expert evidence by historians was commonplace. He then explained that historians can make important contributions to the deliberations of courts because "they have the professional training and discipline that allows them to select relevant documents and to ignore documents that are not really helpful and in some cases are misleading."[37]

After listening to the lengthy sparring over the issue of whether I should be allowed to appear, Chief Justice McEachern ruled that he would hear the evidence "if the historical material gleaned from the records of the Hudson's Bay Company are admissible at all, I suspect they are, that there may be other factors known to the historian but not known to me which will affect the construction to be placed upon the documents."[38] He continued: "For that reason it seems to me that I must hear the evidence and then decide whether I am in as good a position as the historian to reach a conclusion [about] what the documents mean, and if I decide that I am, then some parts of the evidence of the witness may become inadmissible."[39]

This whole episode struck me as being odd, if not comical. It also was very frustrating. I was forced to sit mute in the courtroom while three teams of lawyers and the chief justice discussed the nature of historical research and attempted to define the fields of anthropology, archaeology, and historical geography, subjects about which they knew very little. I was barred from contributing to their deliberations because I had not yet been accepted as an expert by the court. For all practical purposes, I did not yet exist in the eyes of the court. In the end, it was clear that my ability to identify appropriate HBC documents counted most in the chief justice's decision to accept me as an expert. What I did not know at the time was that once I and my discipline had been recognized by a court, whatever the reasoning might have been, I would not face serious challenges in future cases. While this initiation made my subsequent life as an expert easier, it points to problems with the litigation process regarding the accrediting of witnesses and defining the scope of their expertise, issues to which I will return.

After I completed my evidence-in-chief with Mr Adams, the Crown's cross-examination of me began. It was gruelling. Two teams of lawyers took part. Mr Willms led off for British Columbia's team. He took aim at a key point that I had made during my evidence-in-chief about the antiquity of the house/territory system that Brown had described in such detail. I had stated that, in my professional opinion, it seemed most likely that the scheme had been well established long before the Gitxsan-Wet'suet'en had been influenced by the European land-based (beaver-oriented) or maritime (sea otter-oriented) fur trades. I had come to this conclusion because the house/territory institution was so central to these First Nations cultures. For this reason, it seemed most unlikely to me that the Gitxsan-Wet'suet'en would have been able to adopt and so fully integrate it into all aspects of their lives in the relatively short span of time from initial indirect European contacts to the time of Brown's arrival on the scene – a period of twenty to forty years.

Mr Willms sought to undermine my fundamental conclusion. He had two primary reasons for doing so. First, my interpretation contradicted the argument of his leading ethnohistorical expert, Dr Sheila Robinson, who had argued in her written brief to the court, and would do so again later on the witness stand, that the Gitxsan-Wet'suet'en traditionally did not have a house/territory tenure scheme because they had no need for one before they became entangled in the fur trade.[40] Her thesis was that their traditional concepts of ownership, if they had any, would have been limited to places where they fished, hunted, collected berries, built settlements, and blazed trails.[41] Although she was aware of the Brown records, Dr Robinson did not address their relevance to the central thesis of her written report.[42]

The second reason for Mr Willms's vigorous attack on my conclusion was that most of the Gitxsan-Wet'suet'en trial took place at a time when the so-called frozen rights theory of Aboriginal rights still had credibility. According to this theory, the only Aboriginal cultural practices that were eligible for legal protection were those that had not been altered, or invented, in response to interaction with European newcomers.[43] The Supreme Court did not flatly reject this theory until its *Regina v. Sparrow* (1990) decision, which it handed down during the last month of the *Delgamuukw* trial.[44] In *Sparrow*, the court held that traditional practices included those originating in the pre-contact era that survived in modern forms.[45] The problem in *Delgamuukw* was that most of the ethnohistorical evidence had been presented by the time of the *Sparrow* ruling. This meant that one possible way of defeating the Gitxsan-Wet'suet'en title claim during my cross-examination involved demonstrating to the court that the practices Brown described were the products of European contact. Clearly the best way for Mr Willms to advance this proposition was through his cross-examination of me and by leading the testimony of Dr Robinson.

PUBLISH AND BE DAMNED!

Mr Willms deployed a multifaceted cross-examination strategy, a key aspect of which was to cast doubt on my credibility by highlighting the fact that my conclusions about the impact of the fur trade on the house/territory system and land use practices of the Gitxsan-Wet'suet'en were at variance with what I had published about the earlier fur trading experiences of First Nations who lived east of the Rocky Mountains. In particular, he reminded me that my first book, *Indians in the Fur Trade*, emphasized the extensive culture changes that had resulted from the expansion of this industry from the St Lawrence valley and Hudson Bay, and he wanted to know how I could argue otherwise for the Gitxsan-Wet'suet'en. This was a reasonable question and it was a line of questioning I would face in future court appearances. In reply, I repeatedly stressed that the post-contact experiences of First Nations of the Subarctic and Plains regions were not the same as those of Native People who lived in the Pacific watershed. The environments were different, the cultures were different, and the fur trades were different.

The exchange made me very aware that published scholars are more vulnerable as expert witnesses than unpublished experts are. Cross-examining lawyers who do their homework will search back through the publication record of a witness for apparent contradictions that might raise credibility issues. At the time, my record extended back over seventeen years.[46]

Another facet of the Crown's attack was to highlight the fact that Brown's discussion of the house/territory system emphasized the regulation of beaver trapping and trading. Mr Willms noted correctly that trader Brown did not devote much attention to the regulation of other resources in Gitxsan-Wet'suet'en territories. He offered this observation as proof that the scheme had been developed in response to the fur trade. In support of his premise, he noted that published ethnographic studies focusing on the Gitxsan-Wet'suet'en's neighbours, most notably works by Julian Steward and scholars who expanded on his ideas, had argued that the scheme in question was a product of the fur trade.[47] When making this point, Mr Willms clearly was relying on Dr Robinson's brief and was anticipating the testimony she would make several months later.[48]

The problem with relying on published ethnographies in this case was that the Brown narratives were unknown to the scholars cited by Dr Robinson and Mr Willms. Regarding Brown's commentary about the Babine-Wet'suet'en tenure system, I pointed out that it was likely that this fur trader focused on the beaver management aspect because his primary objective was to expand the company's beaver trade in the area. I also emphasized the crucial observation Brown made in his narratives that beaver meat was an important ceremonial food for the Babine-Wet'suet'en. He concluded from this information that their conservation scheme was aimed at securing a steady supply of beaver meat for feasting purposes rather than to husband fur stocks. For me, these crucial observations made it very reasonable to suppose that the expansion of the fur trade into the region after contact gave hereditary leaders an additional incentive to manage the beaver stocks in their territories. In other words, the arrival of the European fur trade in the region had the effect of reinforcing existing resource management practices instead of leading the Gitksan-Wet'suet'en to invent them.

I realized that my conclusion was vulnerable to attack because it challenged interpretations that had been published by ethnographic "authorities." The Crown's advantage in emphasizing this inconsistency was that the court was inherently skeptical of "purposeful" research that had been undertaken or written-up on behalf of the plaintiffs after they had filed their claim. While this suspicion may be understandable – and I experienced it again in later trials – it is nonetheless problematic. The reason is that the litigation process often requires Aboriginal claimants or defendants to commission new research that challenges extant scholarly perspectives. Older outlooks were often based on conceptualizations of Aboriginal people and their cultural history that have served to rationalize their dispossession and economic marginalization. In fact, as I later learned, some theoretical models that the Crown relied on in *Delgamuukw* had been developed out of earlier research undertaken in the United States to oppose Indian tribal claimants who came before the (U.S.) Indian Claims Commission in the 1950s and 1960s.[49] Steward's evolutionary cultural ecology framework, upon which Dr Robinson relied so heavily, was a prime example. In the 1950s Steward had served as an expert for the federal government. Of relevance to *Delgamuukw*, Steward's theoretical speculations, which the Crown introduced through Dr Robinson, were based partly on research he had undertaken for the U.S. Justice Department to counter claims from tribes from the American Southwest (Paiute and Shoshone) and California. Steward's work for the department predisposed him to believe that Athapascan-speaking groups, which included the Babine-Wet'suet'en, had developed their land tenure systems in response to the fur trade.

When Mr Willms finished his cross-examination at noon on my fourth day on the stand, it was Mr Macaulay's turn on behalf of the federal Crown. He took a wholly different tack. His objective was to foster the notion that the Gitxsan-Wet'suet'en lacked the effective system of Aboriginal governance that would have been essential for them to have had a viable land tenure regime.[50] He tried to make his point by suggesting that hereditary leaders were incapable of settling intra- and inter-tribal disputes. Through leading questions, he suggested that widespread bloodshed had been the result. For example, after citing two incidents of murder that had led the relatives of the victims to seek, and in one incident to take revenge, he asked me this pointed question: "I put it to you, Dr Ray, that's really the point of the cross-examination, or one of the points anyhow, that this was a very fragile system and ... it was interrupted by such things as a single killing, and a whole village in this case wouldn't hunt because of the expected revenge, which in fact did come in the middle of the winter? Do you agree that the reciprocal killing system had that effect?"[51]

Mr Macaulay's tactic in advancing this proposition was to introduce fragments of documents, several of which seem to have been couriered to him in court while he was cross-examining me. Most of these snippets featured passages about bloodshed and warfare in Gitxsan-Wet'suet'en territory, which I had not cited because the focus of my report was on the economic geography of the region, rather than dispute resolution practices. Also, most of the exhibits that Mr Macaulay introduced were from accounts that had been written in the late nineteenth and early twentieth centuries. This was a time when epidemics and population losses, alcohol trading, missionary activity, and the increasing encroachments of outsiders had severely disrupted Gitxsan-Wet'suet'en life and society.[52] I reminded Mr Macaulay on more than one occasion that history is not read backward – that events of the late nineteenth century did not influence those that took place at the beginning of the century, which was the period I had focused on in my report.

## INTERPRETING DOCUMENTS WITHOUT CONTEXT

Mr Maculay's cross-examination tactics provided little or no context for most of the documents he introduced or for the episodes they described. I complained to him repeatedly that this made it difficult for me to provide informed commentary about them. In my report and on the witness stand, I emphasized that the Gitxsan-Wet'suet'en had the means to deal with murder and other forms of violence that did not involve resorting to revenge killings. The most important way toward reconciliation was for the family of the perpetrator to pay · compensation to grieving relatives, usually in the context of a feast. On several occasions I reminded him that we would have a warped view of European or Canadian society if we simply judged them in terms of the violence that took place on the meaner streets of our cities or on our countless battlefields. Undeterred, Mr Macaulay kept to his script and paraded more and more documents before the court that detailed violent incidents. Late in the afternoon, after reading to the court yet another description of such an event, which he had extracted from a missionary journal written in 1875, he posed this question: "But I'm putting that to you to ask you whether you agree that there was a certain excitability and ferocity that led to the whole village taking up arms rather than individuals?"[53] Angrily I replied: "I still object to this idea that we're dealing with a bunch of uncivilized savages. Basically the thrust of your argument, as I take it, is that these people had no organized society, that somehow the Indians were more inclined to be violent, to have outbursts ... It's a very stereotypical view of native people and I think it's long out of order. It is after all the twentieth century, not the nineteenth."[54] Not to be deflected from his path, Mr Macaulay dredged up more citations, including one from the twentieth century, to paint a picture of the Gitxsan as being, as he put it, "truculent" by nature.[55]

Toward the end of our exchange, Chief Justice McEachern intervened for clarification: "Macaulay has been suggesting a tendency towards violence and you have been resisting that and you are saying that that just wasn't the state of things, or at least it wasn't the normal diet for the period you are talking about. Yet, there seems to be some pretty strong suggestions that there was warfare on the Skeena, and I take it that you are saying that that was at some later time?"[56] I replied that after the 1830s conflicts did increase for the reasons I had already explained in my testimony. I also reminded him that I had discussed violence in my reports and added: "I'm not denying violence in any of these periods of time. What I object to is this portrayal of native society as violence prone. I would say that that's an ethnocentric point of view."[57]

In the end, the line of questioning Mr Macaulay used when cross-examining me and other witnesses had the effect he intended. In his reasons for judgment (1990), Chief Justice McEachern, quoting seventeenth-century English philosopher Thomas Hobbes, described traditional Gitxsan-Wet'suet'en life as having been "nasty, brutish, and short."[58] These insensitive words created outrage in First Nation communities throughout Canada. The Gitxsan-Wet'suet'en were offended for the additional reason that Chief Justice McEachern had paid little regard to the oral evidence their elders had presented. The scholarly community was also shocked by the dismissal of oral history. Anthropologists were offended for an additional reason: the chief justice had mostly ignored their expert testimony.[59] Anthropologists were not accustomed to being dismissed. In the end, albeit seven years later, joy returned to the Gitxsan-Wet'suet'en and Aboriginal people across Canada when the Supreme Court of Canada ruled that Chief Justice McEachern had not given proper weight to Gitxsan-Wet'suet'en oral evidence and ordered a new trial. In the interim, academic commentators, some as observers and others as experts who had been involved in the case (myself included), assailed the chief justice for his comments about Gitxsan-Wet'suet'en society and his assessments of various lines of ethnohistorical evidence.[60]

My cross-examination in *Delgamuukw* certainly was a painful experience for which I could not have been prepared. Apart from having to endure the line of question already described, when preparing me for the trial Mr Adams had forgotten to mention that, once cross-examination began, I would be barred from talking to anyone about my testimony. Subsequently, I learned that this is standard practice, intended to prevent witnesses from being coached. Not being forewarned, however, I was suddenly left feeling very isolated in a very hostile environment. It is a practice that adds greatly to the stress of serving as an expert witness.

## LIGHT RELIEF AT THE END OF THE ROAD

On reflection, I realize that my cross-examination experience also had its comical moments. Mr Adams had a true poker-face. When he was leading my testimony I could never tell from his expression how well I was doing. This was not the case, however, when Mr Willms was cross-examining me. The recommended practice for trial lawyers is to ask witnesses only questions for which the anticipated answers will advance their case. The problem for Mr Willms was that I often gave him unexpected replies. At these times his brow wrinkled with subtle frowns. On these occasions Mr Rush, who was assisting Mr Adams, often chuckled.

During much of my cross-examination, Don Monet, who is an artist, cartoonist, and actor, was sitting in the back of the courtroom. At the time, he was taking part in the Vancouver Fringe Festival. The day Mr Macaulay was cross-examining me, Monet was dressed in a Dr Seuss–like "cat-in-the-hat" costume that featured a bright chartreuse jacket and stovepipe hat. He looked very out of place in the sombre courtroom, where rows of lawyers sat in the front outfitted in their black and white trial apparel. As Mr Macaulay droned on, I was wondering who this comic character was. Just when my patience with the procedure had stretched to the breaking point, Monet too had had enough. He stood up, shouted, "Shame, shame!" and stalked out of Court Room 53. His outburst is recorded in the trial transcript with the brief entry: "A voice: Shame."[61] The chief justice promptly called for a recess.

After I had finished testifying, Monet phoned me and told me he was creating an installation for a basement gallery in Vancouver that featured my afternoon in court with Mr Macaulay. In the gallery, the artist created a representation of the courtroom, which featured life-size cartoons of the cross-examiner and me. For sound, Monet planned to read aloud and record the court transcript of our exchange. He asked me if I would be willing to "play" my part; he would play Macaulay. I agreed. When visitors to the installation walked into the gallery, they heard, with dramatic and thundering effect, Monet's voice asking me pointed questions about Gitxsan-Wet'suet'en violent acts. In this way he took the theatre of the courtroom to the street. Later, in collaboration with Skanu'u (Ardythe Wilson), he wrote an excellent illustrated (cartoon) history of the trial (fig. 10).[62]

Although my ordeal in *Delgamuukw* was neither as gruelling nor as lengthy as that of many of the other experts who appeared, especially when compared to the taxing trial experiences the Gitxsan-Wet'suet'en elders endured, it has had a lasting impression on me nonetheless. It certainly made me a tougher and more effective witness. The questions raised in cross-examination also made me aware of the need for a comparative economic history of Canada's Aboriginal people that was aimed at a popular readership. With that objective, I expanded the chapter I had written for the *Illustrated History of Canada* into the book *I Have Lived Here Since the World Began*.[63]

Fig. 10: Cartoon of my testimony in *Delgamuukw* by artist Don Monet. Mr Monet regularly attended court and through cartoons he recorded the protracted proceedings in Courtroom 53 of the Law Courts Building in Vancouver, British Columbia.

My time on the witness stand, and the assistance I subsequently provided the lawyers for the Gitxsan-Wet'suet'en as they prepared their cross-examinations of the Crown's witnesses, piqued my curiosity about the ways in which ethnohistorical evidence, both primary sources and published scholarship, has been and is being used for and against Aboriginal claimants and defendants in Canada and other former British colonies, especially the United States, Australia, and New Zealand. To pursue my interest, I shifted the primary focus of my research from native economic history. This work, in which I am still engaged, has made me aware of the extent to which academic scholarship, including my own, has been influenced by Aboriginal and treaty rights claims research that began in the 1950s in the United States.

# CHAPTER 3

# DEFENDING TRADITIONAL

# FISHERIES AND HARVESTING

# RIGHTS

After my gruelling, albeit interesting, experience in *Delgamuukw*, I was immediately drawn back into treaty rights litigation. This new involvement was the direct result of my earlier participation in *Horseman* and my published research, which had begun with *Indians in the Fur Trade*. The litigation concerned First Nations individuals living in the Treaty 9 area of Ontario who had been charged with violating provincial fish and game laws. Like Bert Horseman, they petitioned the courts for exemptions, claiming that Ontario's conservation legislation violated their treaty rights. They based their claim on the fact that Treaty 9 contained a livelihood rights clause that was almost identical to the one included in Treaty 8.[1] In contrast to the Alberta case, however, the Natural Resources Transfer Agreement (NRTA), which had trumped treaty hunting and fishing rights in the prairie provinces, did not apply in Ontario.

My first Ontario case (*Regina v. Spade, Regina v. Wassaykessic*) was held in a small provincial courtroom in Thunder Bay, Ontario, in the autumn of 1992.[2] The defendants, Ivan Spade and Isaiah Wassaykessic, were from the Mishkeegogamang (New Osnaburgh) First Nation. Mr Spade had been charged with unlawfully selling migratory birds, contrary to Section 5 of the Migratory Birds Convention Act, and Mr Wassaykessic with unlawfully selling sturgeon contrary to the provincial Game and Fish Act. Their lawyer, Mary Bird, asked me to appear as an expert on their behalf only two weeks before the trial. Her request came at the eleventh hour because the expert she had retained withdrew unexpectedly at the last moment. Although her late appeal gave me no time to research and write a report for the court, I

Fig. 11: Northern Ontario Treaty Areas.

agreed to testify anyway, because I already was very familiar with the local Native economic history of this region, having included it in my doctoral and later research projects. Also, the primary issue Ms Bird wanted me to address was very familiar and of interest to me. She wanted me to tell the court about the commercial fishing and water-fowl hunting activities of the First Nations in Treaty 9 area of Ontario (fig. 11).

I flew from Vancouver to Thunder Bay the day before the trial began. I remember it well because it happened to be the day (26 October 1992) of the national referendum on the ill-fated Charlottetown Accord to amend the Canadian Constitution. When I arrived late in the afternoon, I suggested to Ms Bird that I prepare a list of questions for her to ask me the following day during my evidence-in-chief. I made this proposal because I had not prepared a brief for the court, she knew little about fur trade history, and she had no prior experience with offering historical evidence in treaty rights cases. Ms Bird liked the idea. So, I headed off to the motel I was staying at to begin work on my list of questions. By this time it was evening, so I decided to walk across the street to a large sports bar/dining room and draft my questions over dinner. As the results of the Charlottetown referendum streamed across the large TV monitors, I wrote the script for my evidence-in-chief, which I handed to Ms Bird the following morning as we headed for court.

## AN "INTERESTING LECTURE," SAYS THE JUDGE

As this was to be my first court appearance since *Delgamuukw*, I expected I would be subjected to a hostile cross-examination. When I saw the Crown prosecutor arrive carrying copies of my published books, my anxiety increased. I assumed he had been using them to prepare his cross-examination of me. This proved not to be the case, however, and my court appearance turned out to be more like what I had experienced in *Horseman*. There were only five of us in the courtroom: the judge, the court clerk, Ms Bird, the crown prosecutor, and me. As has often been my experience, the trial judge had a keen interest in fur trade history. During my evidence-in-chief, he said he had just read journalist Peter C. Newman's *Company of Adventurers*, a popular history of the Hudson's Bay Company.[3] The judge commented that he had been astonished to learn from Newman of the thousands of geese that the Cree had hunted every fall and spring for the company's posts on James Bay and Hudson Bay. His revelation simplified my task. It meant that the judge was not surprised when I told him that it was commonplace for HBC company post managers, and those who worked for rival concerns, to either contract Native hunters and fishers to fill their posts' larders or barter with them to do so. The lawyer for the Crown raised no objections to my testimony and had few questions for me. It turned out that he too was a "fur trade buff." After I had finished testifying, the judge thanked me for my "interesting lecture on fur trade history." To my astonishment, Crown counsel added that he too had enjoyed the hearing and the opportunity to meet me. He then asked me to autograph the copies of my books that that

Fig. 12: Chief Moonias waiting for Treaty 9 signing ceremony, Fort Hope, Ontario, 1905.

he had brought to the courtroom. In this way, *Wassaykessic* proved for me to be a pleasantly different experience from *Delgamuukw*. Since then, I cannot say I have had such a congenial time in court.

Very shortly after my appearance in *Wassaykessic*, Ms Bird's law partner, Francis Thatcher,[4] asked me to prepare a report for a Treaty 9 fishing rights case in which he was involved. It arose in the autumn of 1992 from a charge that the Crown had laid against Eli Moonias, who at the time was chief of the Martin Falls First Nation. One of his ancestors had been involved in Treaty 9 negotiations in 1905 (fig. 12).[5] As sometimes happens, Chief Moonias wanted to be charged so that he could challenge provincial fishing regulations. He operated a fishing company and held a commercial licence to fish for sturgeon on the Albany River. The Crown charged him for exceeding the quota set in his licence. Chief Moonias wanted to confront this charge for two reasons: he believed that his treaty rights exempted him from having a quota imposed and, alternatively, he considered the quota to be arbitrary because the Crown had not provided any biological data about the size or health of the Albany River sturgeon population. In other words, the Crown had not proven the need for the conservation measure it had imposed.

Chief Moonias made his claim in the immediate aftermath of the landmark *Sparrow* (1990) Aboriginal fishing rights case from British

Columbia, a case that resulted from Ronald Sparrow of the Musqueam First Nation being charged with fishing for salmon with a drift net that was longer than the band's Indian food fishing licence permitted.[6] The federal fisheries department had issued the licence with net size restrictions for conservation purposes. Mr Sparrow's defence was that the regulation infringed on his Aboriginal rights according to Section 35 (1) of the Constitution Act of 1982. In response to Mr Sparrow's appeal, the Supreme Court ruled that legislation can curtail Aboriginal rights if there is a valid objective and if the restriction is consistent with the special trust relationship created by history, treaties, and legislation and the responsibility of the government vis-à-vis Aboriginal people. The court concluded that conservation objectives do warrant placing restrictions on Aboriginal rights, provided that they do so with as little infringement as possible in order to accomplish the desired results.[7]

## PREPARING A BRIEF ON NATIVE FISHERIES

With this ruling in mind, Mr Thatcher asked me to prepare a brief on behalf of his client which focused on the Native people's consumption and exchange of fish and wildlife in Northern Ontario before the negotiation of Treaty 9 (also known as the James Bay Treaty) in 1905.[8] He was particularly interested in having me collect information about the size and nature of Native fisheries – especially the sturgeon fishery of the Albany River. This material would be relevant because the Martin Falls First Nation, where his client lived, is located on the Albany River about 200 miles "as the crow flies" from Fort Albany, Ontario. Mr Thatcher anticipated that I would find archival data to establish that commercial fishing was a usual vocation of people from Martin Falls First Nation and their neighbours. He also hoped that I might uncover data that provided an indication of what the long-term sustainability of an Albany River sturgeon fishery might be.

His request appealed to me because it offered me the opportunity to undertake the kind of research for northern Ontario that I had not been able to do in *Wassaykessic*. Also, I suspected that a search of the HBC archives would be as fruitful as Mr Thatcher hoped, as the Albany River had served as a main thoroughfare of the fur trade from the founding of the company in 1670,[9] when it first built Fort Albany, until the early twentieth century. Also, when the Hudson's Bay Company embarked on its inland expansion in the late eighteenth century, it built a number of posts along the river, including one at Martin Fall. As I had anticipated, the company's very long presence in the area had led to the creation and preservation of a voluminous and varied archival record that contained countless observations about Native activities as suppliers of provisions, including fish and fish products. These comments are found in the post journals and accounts covering the period from 1693 until the early twentieth century.[10] In addition, the company's London headquarters records and those of its Southern Department, which was headquartered at Moose Factory after 1821 and encompassed most of present-day northern Ontario,[11] contained data about the isinglass trade.

Isinglass is a gelatine product that Native women made from the swim bladders of sturgeon. Traditionally, they used it for glue and to fix paint. Writing in 1743 at York Factory on Hudson Bay, HBC trader James Isham observed: "The Glue the Natives save out of the Sturgeon is Very Strong and good, they use it in mixing with their paint, which fixes the Colours so they never Rub out."[12] Europeans also used isinglass for glue making, as well as employing it as a clarifying agent for making beer and wine.[13] The local provision trade in sturgeon and isinglass sales[14] together meant that, like beaver trapping, sturgeon fishing provided Native people with use and exchange value for their labour. Sturgeon fishers could sell or use their isinglass and also trade or consume fresh, frozen, dried, and smoked filets and caviar. Also, it was of importance to the Moonias claim that historical geographers had already demonstrated that the number of grams of isinglass that Aboriginal people traded could be used to estimate the minimum number of sturgeon that Native fishers were catching annually, partly for commercial purposes.[15]

To help me conduct the research that Mr Thatcher and his client needed, I hired a team of four senior undergraduate students in the spring of 1993 immediately after classes ended.[16] These students had taken my survey course in Canadian Native history and had demonstrated through class assignments that they would be excellent researchers. I directed them to the HBC post records for the Southern Department, suggesting that they begin with those for the Albany and James Bay districts, and make complete notes[17] of all of the references that they found to Native people bartering "country provisions" or working on seasonal contracts as hunters and/or fishers. Their research in the Fort Albany account books alone yielded 182 single-spaced pages of references to company purchases of provisions during the period from 1693 to 1797. About one-third of the approximately 1,400 entries[18] involved transactions for fish. The journals of the Albany River posts of Fort Albany, Henley House, Martin Fall, and Osnaburgh House, as well as those for Fort Severn, which was located on Hudson Bay, yielded another 143 pages of references to provision harvesting and trading activities.

Frequently the company clerks did not detail the species of fish that they bought from Native suppliers, but when they did, most often they mentioned whitefish and sturgeon. This is not surprising. Traditionally, whitefish, which Native people harvested with fish weirs, seines, and dip nets, was the most important species for Aboriginal People in what.is now the Treaty 9 area in terms of the quantities they caught and ate or fed to their dogs. They prized sturgeon highly as well, but unlike whitefish, sturgeon reproduce very slowly and could not be caught in the same mass quantities. From the HBC records it is impossible to make precise determinations of the size of the various local fisheries, because entries concerning specific transactions often are imprecise about the quantity of fish involved. For example, although clerks often listed the numbers, pounds, or kegs that were involved in specific transactions, journals just as frequently merely said that Indians brought, caught, or traded "some fish" or "a few fish."

## WHEN NATIVE WOMEN PARTAKE IN TRADE

Three of my researchers were young women. They especially enjoyed reading the post journals because they offered interesting glimpses of the roles Native women played in the local Native economies. Their interest in this aspect of the research reflected the period in which they undertood this work. By the early 1990s, undergraduate courses in Canadian history emphasized Native, social, and women's history. By that time, the latter two fields of study had had a considerable impact on fur trade history and Native studies, a trend that had begun in the early 1980s with the publication of Jennifer Brown's *Strangers in Blood* (1980)[19] and Sylvia Van Kirk's *Many Tender Ties* (1980).[20] These two works and the studies that followed from them emphasized the West,

Fig. 13: "Old Betsy" making a fishing net, New Brunswick House, Northern Ontario.

where Native women were tightly enmeshed in social and economic life at trading posts through marriage to traders.

My claims research project gave these female students the opportunity to look at Native women in a different region and consider their involvement in the local economy, not only at trading posts, but beyond them as well. My students were quick to note that the records usually mentioned the men by name, whereas their wives and daughters were often unnamed. I explained to them that this bias in the record reflected the fact that the classic fur trade was based on credit/barter, which involved giving advances to Native families or adult males at the beginning of the trading year. Post managers listed most of the former debts under the names of the male family heads.[21] My students were pleased to note that there were some exceptional cases where women were mentioned specifically. Two of these were "Auld [Old] Betsy" and her daughter from Martin Fall and New Brunswick House. Table 1 lists the journal references to these two women in the early 1870s. It is noteworthy that when the Treaty 9 negotiators visited the region in 1905, they took a picture of Auld Betsy while she was making a fish net at New Brunswick House, which is located about 300 kilometres south-southeast of Martin Fall. The journal entries from the 1870s provide an indication of the range of Auld Betsy's activities and her independent spirit (fig. 13) (Table 1).

Table 1: References to "Auld Betsy" and Her Daughter in Martin Fall Post Journals, 1870–75

| | |
|---|---|
| 1 October, 1870, p. 40 | Mark Ice and Auld Betsy's daughter, one of our fishers came in this noon. Fish are not catching. |
| 26 October, 1870, p. 44 | Auld Betsy and her Son Ned has come in. The N.C. [North Creek][1] fishing is done. They filled 7 kegs and are in the same place as the kegs were last winter. They brought in all the fishing material, nets, etc. |
| 14 January, 1871, p. 15 | Auld Betsy & her daughter came in this afternoon, they have a few white-fish for me. |
| 9 October, 1871, p. 19 | Auld Betsy and her daughter started this morning to Moosewakie for our nets etc. The "Lame Man" and Ned had … at the fishing, as it appears the fellows are not about coming in with them. I don't understand them. |
| 10 October, 1871, p. 20 | Auld Betsy & Her daughter returned in the afternoon and reports [sic] that they saw none at Mooseewakie Lake, therefore has got none of the nets. I hardly believe that they could be at the Lake and back in the time they left here. |
| 15 October, 1871, p. 20 | Auld Betsy & her daughter got up a bark tent and are smoking the white fish we got in yesterday. They would spook [?] if we kept them any longer. So we had (they say) had to be at it on the Sabbath. |
| 22 January, 1872, p. 33 | Auld Betsy & daughter came in with a few fish for us. |

| 12 March, 1872, p. 36 | "Auld Betsy" ... daughter came in yesterday. has 2 martin & 10 white fish which she traded. |
| 10 October, 1873, p. 14 | Auld Betsy & Daughter Sett there [sic] net but getting no fish. |
| 13 October, 1873, p. 14 | no Sign of fishermen Coming down this day Willie & Mother & Betsy & Daughter went to angle at N. Creek they got 9 small Trout among them |
| 21 August, 1874, p. 27 | Auld Betsy & Daughter Came in & Brought a few fish |
| 17 May, 1875, p. 3 | In the afternoon Pat and "Betsys" daughter, "Margret" as her English name turns out to be, set a couple nets at Mouth of Carp Creek |

Another notable instance of a Native woman's involvement in fish trading took place at the small post of Fort Severn. During a three-year period (1874–76) a woman to whom the post journalists refer merely as the "fisher wife" overwhelmingly dominated the small fish trade at the post. The references to this anonymous woman are listed in Table 2. They show that she came only in July and August. It is unclear whether she caught all the fish herself, or if she fished with and traded on behalf of her family. It is most likely that the latter was the case (Table 2).

Their focus on the importance of inland fisheries to the fur trade also gave my researchers and me an opportunity to address another imbalance in fur trade and Native history scholarship. Classical North American anthropology of the early twentieth century had cast the Native societies of the Subarctic culture area, which includes the present- day Treaty 3 and 9 areas of Northern Ontario, as being typical "hunter-gatherer" cultures. This perspective had led scholars to emphasize the economic roles that males played as hunters and trappers. Following this lead, fur trade histories had not emphasized the importance of Native fisheries to the fur trade of the Subarctic. One twentieth century HBC officer, J.W. Anderson, was an exception. In his published memoir, *Fur Trader's Story*, he devoted a whole chapter to this subject. Anderson observed: "It is safe to assert that all down the centuries of the fur trade in Canada fish has been the

Table 2: Trade by the "Fisher Wife" at Fort Severn, 1874–76

| 22 July, 1874, p. 10 | Fisher wife brought 15 Trout and 18 white fish this day. |
| 25 July, 1874, p. 10 | Fisher wife brought 9 Trout and 8 Suckers, Poor fishing. |
| 8 August, 1874, p. 11 | Fisher wife brought 24 fish of all sorts. |
| 24 July, 1875, p. 23 | Fisher wife came up but brought little or nothing. |
| 22 June, 1876, p. 35 | Fisher [wife] brot [sic] 6 fish. |
| 23 June, 1876, p. 35 | Fisher wife brot 11 fish. |
| 24 June, 1876, p. 35 | Fisher wife brought 14 fish. |
| 27 June, 1876, p. 35 | Fisher wife brought 12 fish |
| 29 June, 1876, p. 35 | Fisher wife brot 10 suckers |
| 14 July, 1876, p. 36 | Fisher wife brought about 10 fish |
| 15 July, 1876, p. 36 | Fisher wife brot 40 fish |
| 29 July, 1876, p. 37 | Fisher wife brought 20 fish |
| 31 July, 1876, p. 37 | Fisher wife brot 30 fish |
| 3 August, 1876, p. 37 | Fisher wife brot 20 fish |
| 9 August, 1876, p. 37 | David Anderson and Stonie start for the Goose hunts ... Fisher wife brot 80 fish. |
| 10 August, 1876, p. 37 | Fisher wife brot 130 fish |
| 11 August, 1876, p. 37 | Fisher wife brot 33 fish |

*Source*: PAMHBC Fort Severn Journal, B/198/a/123–1873–77

principal sustaining food for the fur trader and his dog team. And, many a remote inland post was established by one or two white men, a handful of Indians with a few simple tools, and fish nets."[22] At the time we started our research for Mr Thatcher, historical geographers Frank Tough, Victor Lytwyn, and others were just beginning to publish their pioneering scholarship on inland Native fisheries and their importance to Aboriginal people and the fur trade.[23]

Our research in the HBC archives indicated that local fisheries in the Treaty 9 region became increasingly important to fur trading operations in the Hudson's Bay Company's Southern Department from the late eighteenth century onward, as fur and game animal populations declined because of over-hunting and trapping. Aboriginal people participated in various ways. They continued to supply fish as an article of commerce; they continued to fish seasonally on contract, and some of them fished as salaried seasonal or regular company employees. The relative importance of this variety of arrangements to overall fish procurement varied considerably from post to post in the late nineteenth century.

Of particular relevance to Chief Moonias's defence was the discovery that the documentary records indicated that in the late nineteenth century the Martin Fall post relied heavily on whitefish taken by seine fisheries operated mostly by Aboriginal men who were retained on contract.[24] The post managers often referred to them in general terms as "our fishers" or "the fishermen." The fishers named most often from 1869 to 1899, in addition to Auld Betsy and her daughter, included: Lame Man (and his sister), Auld Sturgeon, Moss Sturgeon, Sandy Sturgeon, Osshkapay (and his brother), and Patrick and Jack Wich ee capay (and his sister).[25] The post supplied these and other Native contract fishers with salt, kegs, nets, and sometimes canoes and tents. For example, on 19 July 1870, the Martin Fall journal entry reported: "The Lame Man came in this morning. Had 9 sturgeons but not large ones ... They came in so well [timely] for us. He started in the afternoon. I let him have a larger canoe than his own and a couple of kegs & salt to get fish for us. He himself proposed it. Therefore he ought to make a good job of it."[26] Fishers on contract usually received small advances and were paid for their catches once they delivered them to the post. Sometimes the post manager hired Native people to pack the fish in kegs for the fishers and haul them to the post.[27] Of the various seasonal fisheries, the autumn whitefish fishery was the most crucial for Martin Fall, as it was for most posts.

Whereas the majority of the fish that Native fishers caught on contract were salted, those that other Native fishers brought in to trade had mostly been "hung," that is, dried, although some was fresh (fig. 14).[28] Whitefish and suckers dominated the trade, judging from the journals, but sturgeon also was important (fig. 15).[29] The Martin Fall journals reveal that some of the Native men who fished on contract also sold fish in the off-season. As noted, women also took part in the trade.

The records from other HBC posts on the Albany River are much less extensive than those for Martin Fall, but suggest similar patterns nonetheless. Fort Hope was the closest establishment upriver. For the years after 1870, only five reports have survived covering the years 1890–93.[30] These brief records indicate that the post manager con-

Fig. 14: Putting bark on a smoking lodge, Long Lac, Ontario. Native women played an important role in all aspects of the fisheries that sustained the northern fur trade.

Fig. 15: Philip Mathew, Fort Severn, removing whitefish from gillnet.

Fig. 16: Native women drying isinglass, Northern Ontario.

tracted Aboriginal people to operate fish camps for him, and he hired at least one individual – Sugar Head – as a fisherman at the post.[31] In addition, a number of other Aboriginal people arrived from time to time to sell their fish. Sturgeon was included among the varieties of fish that they exchanged.[32]

Another 200 kilometres upriver (as the crow flies) from Fort Hope lay Osnaburgh House. The only surviving journals for the post-1870 era for this post encompass the years from 1871 to 1877. They indicate that the largest supply of fish came from three or four fisheries operated by full-time company servants and their Native wives, and by Native men and their wives, whom the company retained on seasonal contracts. One husband and wife team, "Fanny and his wife" operated two of the fisheries. Whitefish overwhelmingly dominated the catch at Osnaburgh. In sharp contrast to Martin Falls, there is only a single reference to sturgeon in this set of journals.[33] Once we had finished gathering information from the HBC post records we turned to the company's Southern Department and London headquarters records for Isinglass returns and sales for the period 1822–1900 (fig. 16).[34] As I have mentioned, the department encompassed most of the lands covered by the Robinson Treaties (1850) and all of the area that was encompassed by Treaty 3 (1874) and Treaty 9. We extracted information from the company's London "fur sales" and auction catalogues, and I presented it in my report to Mr Thatcher in a series of graphs, two of which I have reproduced here (figs. 17 and 18). Figure 17 shows the quantities of isinglass from the Southern Department that the company sold each year in London. What is striking is that sales volumes rose sharply from the early 1820s until 1855 and declined abruptly thereafter. Using the measure developed by Holzkamm, McCarthy, and Lytwyn, which assumes it took about twenty-five sturgeon of average size to produce one kilo of isinglass,[35] we estimated what the minimum catch sizes would have been based on these annual sales data (fig. 18). Other data obtained from the archives showed that the prices buyers paid in London for isinglass from the Southern Department trended downward after 1855.

At first glance it might be tempting to conclude that it was over-fishing that had caused the precipitous drop in commercial harvesting and sales after 1855. This would be an erroneous conclusion, however. The data reflect the fact that the company reorganized the Southern Department in 1857. When doing so, it removed the old Lake Huron district and some of the posts along Lake Superior (all of which now lay within the boundaries of the 1850 Robinson Treaties). An analysis of Southern Department returns reveals that the Lake Huron and Albany River districts accounted for most of the isinglass production before 1857. It became clear that the elimination of the Lake Huron district was what caused the sharp drop in the overall production of the Southern Department after 1857. We also obseved that after 1857 the Albany River district accounted for a larger share the department's isinglass trade (probably one-fifth to one-sixth of the total, judging from figure 18).

Of great relevance to the concerns of Mr Thatcher and his client was that the returns for the Albany District (fig. 18) do not imply that there was any major decline in the estimated sturgeon harvest over time. On the contrary, after 1857 output increased slowly. Although information about isinglass returns for the Albany River district apparently are unavailable for the years after 1870, London data suggest that production was fairly steady, considering that the total value of sales did not decline significantly even though London prices for this commodity were falling.

Unfortunately, the HBC records do not give us a breakdown of the trade in isinglass on a post-by-post basis, so it was not possible to get data specifically for Martin Fall. Scattered references in the post journals do suggest, however, that most of the Albany River District production came from the area between Martin Fall and Osnaburgh House.

Another limitation of the HBC records about this trade is that the company clerks made very few observations about the character of this commerce, apparently because it was not their prime concern. None-

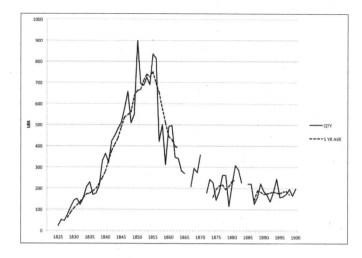

Fig. 17: London sales of Hudson's Bay Company's Southern Department isinglass, 1822–1900.

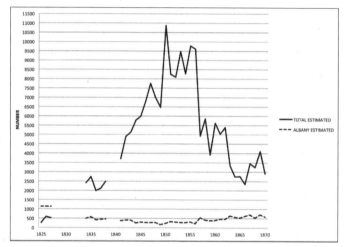

Fig. 18: Estimated minimum sturgeon harvests for Hudson's Bay Company's Southern Department based on isinglass trade.

theless, my researchers did glean a few clues from the record that were specifically relevant to Chief Moonias's claim. For instance, the 5 August 1869 entry in the Martin Fall post journals states that "Moonee ass, his Brother & a few others [came in], they had nothing but rats [muskrat] & Isinglass."[36] The post journals give some indication of the families who were involved in sturgeon harvesting and isinglass production. The dominant family at Martin Falls and Osnaburgh was the Sturgeon family (clan). The Osnaburgh House Indian debt book for 1853–54, for example, indicates that they were heavily involved in the isinglass trade. This particular record also provides us with a rare insight into the general nature of this commerce. The entries in the debt book relating to company purchases of isinglass (also of sturgeon for food) reveal that most individual transactions (25 of a total of 39) involved sales of one-half pound to one pound (the modal transaction). It would have taken at least five and one-half to eleven sturgeon to yield these amounts. The debt books also suggest that most sales probably represented a family's (wife's) annual production, since the named individuals appear only once. Quite striking is the fact that a few families produced substantially greater amounts than the norm. For instance, the top four producers accounted for nearly one-third of the total. Their combined contribution would have required a catch of at least 225 sturgeons.

After my research team completed its work, I summarized the results in a 271-page report entitled "Aboriginal Fishing for Commercial Purposes in Northern Ontario before Treaty 9: A Report for the Martin Fall First Nation." I submitted it to Mr Thatcher in June 1993. In light of the massive body of evidence that we had gathered, I decided to provide a very short contextual analysis (eighteen pages) and let the material mostly "speak for itself." Accordingly, I appended to my brief essay seven graphs, four tables of the data I had used to generate them, and nine lengthy appendices of extracts from post records concerning transactions that involved company purchases of country produce.

In addition to the information we had obtained from the HBC archives, in the course of our research we noted that the federal government's Treaty 9 negotiating team kept a log of its expenses when it visited northern Ontario in 1905. On several occasions, they bought fish from Native people. Because this was clear evidence that the Crown's treaty negotiators were aware that selling fish was a customary practice, I included a table of the treaty party's purchases of fish and other provisions.

After I submitted my report to Mr Thatcher, he sent a copy to the Crown. I waited to hear from him about when I would be expected to appear in court. I was actually looking forward to having a chance to present the evidence we had gathered, being convinced that it overwhelmingly supported Mr Moonias's defence. This was not to be. The province withdrew the charges against Chief Moonias ten days before the scheduled four-week trial. The reason given was that provincial attorneys had concluded there was insufficient scientific evidence to prove or to justify the element of conservation beyond a reasonable doubt.[37] For a time it appeared as if I might have the opportunity to present the evidence we had gathered in another case that arose in 1993 when the province laid a charge against a Native fisherman from

New Osnaburgh First Nation. The charge was very similar to the one Ontario had filed against Chief Moonias. I agreed to Mr Thatcher's request to appear as an expert in this additional case on the understanding that the report I had prepared for Chief Moonias's claim would be re-submitted. Once again the litigation did not proceed; the trial had been scheduled for June 1994, but the defendant died in the interim.

Shortly after the termination of this research related to Treaty 9, I became involved in yet another abortive fishing rights case. This one concerned a member of the Waterhen First Nation of the Treaty 2 area of Manitoba. As with the Treaty 9 territory, fishing for subsistence and exchange purposes had been very important to Native people in the northern two-thirds of the Treaty 2 region for at least a century and a half before the negotiation of the latter agreement in 1871 (fig. 19).[38] Indeed, some of the best inland Aboriginal fisheries in Canada were located in this portion of central Manitoba, as Tough's scholarship had already shown.[39] So, when the Public Interest Law Centre in Winnipeg asked me to prepare a report, I assumed I would have no trouble uncovering a body of evidence that would be as massive as the one my researchers had collected for Mr Thatcher. I was mistaken. Although the HBC records pertaining to the woodland section of Treaty 2 were sufficient for me to demonstrate the importance of the commercial and subsistence fisheries generally, few records survived for the Waterhen River outpost.[40] Furthermore, the few documentary scraps that do exist in the HBC archives are mostly from the late 1890s and early twentieth century – a time well after Treaty 2 had been concluded.

I was able to track down one journal that covered the brief period from 6 September 1849 to 5 June 1850, however. This document is located in the Washington State University–Pullman archives.[41] Four men constituted the small labour force at the outpost. They were James Monkman (senior and junior), Joseph Monkman, and James Whiteway. Of relevance to the claims case is that the Monkman family appears in the annuity lists of Treaty 2 in the 1870s. It is unclear which of these four men kept the journal, but the entries reveal that competition for the local Aboriginal trappers' furs was very strong. As was often the case after 1821, Métis traders were the key HBC rivals. The most notable among them was a man named Paullet (also spelled Pollet) "Shatrand." This phonetic spelling undoubtedly is a reference to the Indian/Métis Chartrand family.[42] The Chartrands also appear on Treaty 2 annuity lists for Waterhen. Paullet and his sons did some trapping of their own and traded with the local "Indians." The anonymous

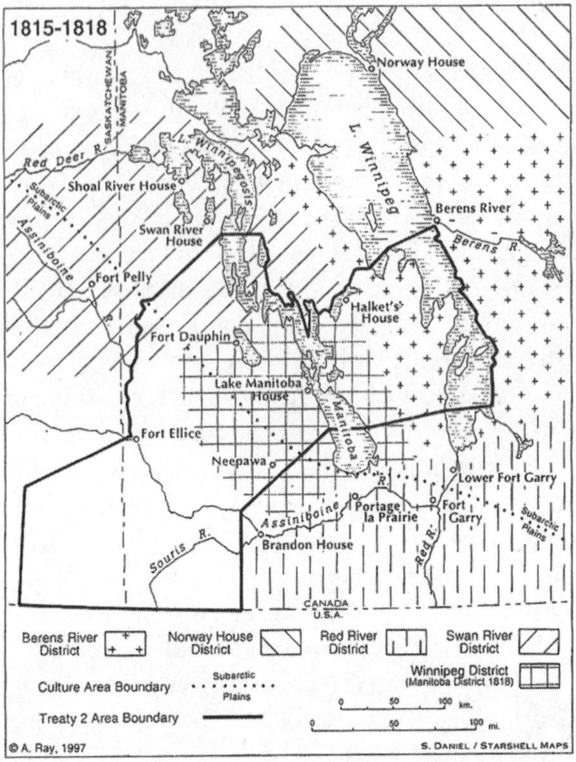

Fig. 19: (*Right and opposite page*) Historical geography of the Treaty 2 Area.

HBC journal noted that Chartrand's kinship ties with the company's Native clients made members of this family formidable opponents:

> On the 25th [March] when the Shatrands arrived they began a drinking and was heard to say that all these Indians would be his the next winter a day or two before we was told by an Indian that all the Indians in this quarter had Combined and promised to give all there [sic] furs to the Shatrands the next winter and it appears much like it for we have some trouble to get a skin from them and no wonder for they are all relations together.[43]

An observation of importance to the legal issues at hand was that the journal made it clear that the economic strategy of the "Indians" at this time involved concentrating their commercial activities on trapping rather than fishing. They clearly made this change because the fierce competition for their furs, especially beaver, had driven up local fur prices, making trapping more lucrative than fishing. Thus, many

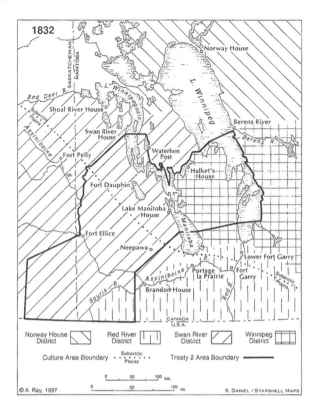

local Natives turned away from the productive local fisheries, such as the one located nearby at Partridge Crop River. This specialization had two consequences. When food was scarce, as it was in parts of the hinterland of Waterhen Post during the winter of 1849–50, Native people bought fish at the post. In other words, they relied on Waterhen Post fishery, which was operated by the "men" who included members of the Monkman family.[44] Yet, at other times during the same winter, Aboriginal people sold surplus meat they had obtained from hunting /trapping.[45] This kind of economic behaviour often seemed imprudent and paradoxical to European traders, who thought Aboriginal people should stockpile their food as a hedge against lean times. From the Native perspective, on the other hand, it made good sense to let the trading posts stockpile the surplus, provided they had access to it when necessary.

In these ways, the abbreviated Waterhen journal for 1849–50 showed the opportunistic nature of Native economic behaviour and demonstrated how it could create complex local socioeconomic relations. In this instance, it meant that Native trappers bought, rather than sold, fish at the post so they could take advantage of the upswing in fur prices that were in part the consequence of the activities of local Métis competitor, Mr Chartrand. And yet, the fish the "Indian" trappers bought at Waterhen Post had been supplied by company servants, some of whom were "Indian" (Monkman).

## THE RISKS OF DOCUMENTARY EVIDENCE

Whereas the research for the Treaty 9 cases had yielded overwhelming evidence in support of Aboriginal and treaty commercial and subsistence fishing rights claims, the information I collected for the Waterhen area of Manitoba was ambiguous. Clarity could not be obtained because only a single, incomplete, pre-treaty post journal had survived for the Waterhen outpost. This discovery made me very aware of the risks that Aboriginal people face if they are forced to rely heavily, if not exclusively, on documentary records when advancing claims. For First Nations who are fortunate to have lived next to major fur trade transportation corridors or major trading or administrative posts (district or department headquarters), extensive archival resources are probably available because traders generated massive records at these places. Native communities that were situated far away from such places may face impossible challenges. In remote areas such as Waterhen, trading companies operated small outposts at best, and record keeping was often minimal and record preservation haphazard. As a consequence, it likely will be difficult or impossible to reconstruct a complete picture of Native economic life for remote communities from archival records. Waterhen is a good example. The single incomplete journal for the 1849–50 trading year happened to cover a time when the local economic/ecological cycle enticed Native people to engage in fur trapping at the expense of fishing. If a longer run of journals had been available, it likely would have shown that there were other times when local conditions favoured fishing over trapping and other activities.

Researching the economic history of the Waterhen area also brought home to me that it is important to make clear to the courts that Native groups had to be economically flexible and opportunistic in order to survive. They had to be able to maximize the gains and minimize the losses they experienced from vacillations in bird, animal, and fish populations and changing economic circumstances. To help the court

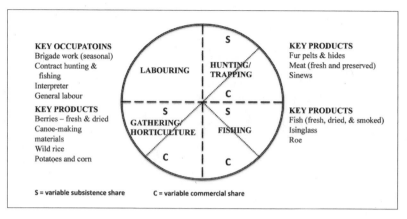

Fig. 20: Post-contact Native economy of the Woodland Ojibwa.

visualize the dynamic nature of Native economies, I developed a model (fig. 20) for my research report for the Public Interest Law Centre.[46] I conceived woodland Native economies as having had four distinctive spheres: hunting/trapping, fishing, gathering/horticulture, and labouring. The relative importance of each sector to the whole shifted over time according to changing ecological or economic circumstances. Likewise, over time the commercial- and subsistence-oriented components of the hunting/trapping, fishing, and gathering/horticulture sectors varied in relative importance.

Although I thought that presenting the economic history of the Waterhen area in this way would help explain to the court why Native people who often sold fish were buying them in 1849–50, I was nonetheless dubious about proceeding with the case. I knew that many other Native communities in Manitoba offered much better prospects of making solid cases for commercial fishing rights on the basis of the existence of extensive documentary records. Fortunately, the Waterhen case did not go forward.

From my perspective as an historian and expert witness, the research done on the Moonias and Treaty 2 claims was very useful. It led me to think about the many problems Native people face in presenting their economic histories to the courts. Having the time and occasion to do so proved to be very fortunte, because I subsequently had the opportunity to confront most of the issues that I had addressed in these abortive claims in the landmark Métis hunting rights case, *Regina v. Powley* (2003).

# CHAPTER 4

# INTERPRETATION OF A TREATY:
# SHARE OR SURRENDER?

In 1989 the Samson Cree Indian Band and Nation of Hobbema, Alberta, and the Ermineskin Band and First Nation filed a breach of Treaty 6 and trust claim against Canada in the Federal Court of Canada (*Victor Buffalo v. Regina*). Their action asked for damages in the amount of $1.385 billion plus interest. The complex lawsuit proceeded in two phases: Phase I concerned historical and treaty issues and Phase II addressed questions of money management. Not counting closing arguments, the litigation took 370 trial days, involved over 25 lawyers and 65 witnesses (including former prime minister Jean Chrétien), generated 15,000 documents and more than 50,000 pages of transcripts, and cost the opposing parties more than $100 million collectively.[1]

By all measures, the suit of the Samson Cree, known as *Victor Buffalo et al. v. Regina,* was the granddaddy of treaty claims in Canada. Indeed, it even surpassed the massive *Delgamuukw* land claim trial in scope.[2] To handle the case, the Federal Court of Canada constructed a high-tech courtroom in downtown Calgary. For me, this high-profile trial stood in stark contrast to my first treaty rights case (*Horseman*), which took place in a sparsely furnished, small, bland courtroom with five people present, including myself and the judge. The lavish *Victor Buffalo* trial raised a critical issue – the mounting costs that plague Aboriginal and treaty rights legal battles. Few First Nations other than the oil-rich ones of southern Alberta can shoulder such massive financial burdens.

One reason the trial was so costly was that the plaintiffs and their legal team believed that historical evidence pertaining to all aspects of Cree history was crucial to their claim. The opening historical segment took up almost half of the court's time (174 days), during which Federal Court Justice Max Teitelbaum listened to the testimony of thirty-five experts. These included Cree elders, who presented their evidence on the Hobbema Reserve, and other witnesses, whose range of expertise represented the academic disciplines of archaeology, Canadian history, economic history, ethnohistory, historical geography, legal history, linguistics, and political science (Table 3). Collectively, the reports and testimony of this eclectic array of experts covered virtually all aspects of western Canadian Native History, the fur trade, early colonial settlement, economic development, treaty making in Western Canada, and Federal-Indian[3] relations after Treaty 6 (1876).

### ISSUES OF TREATY NEGOTIATION AND SETTLEMENT

The treaty rights cases that I have earlier described were cases concerned with harvesting rights, in which the Native people appeared as defendants in criminal actions. *Victor Buffalo* was different. In this litigation, the defendants were plaintiffs in a civil case. A key issue they raised was whether their ancestors had signed Treaty 6 in 1876 in the belief that they were agreeing to surrender their traditional territory to Canada (with the exception of the lands set aside for reserves) or on the understanding that they were consenting to share these lands with newcomers. This fundamental question raised a wide range of issues about approaches to western Canadian and Native history and about the use and reliability of oral sources. *Victor Buffalo* was one of the first major Aboriginal or treaty rights cases after *Delgamuukw* to address the latter concern. The trial made it clear that *Delgamuukw* had not settled the matter as many thought; rather, it had served to intensify the battle over oral history evidence in the courtrooms of the country.

Peter Hutchins and Jim O'Reilly, who were among the first lawyers in Canada to specialize in Native law, led the plaintiffs' legal team.[4] They asked me to address two basic questions: first, how had First Nations' trading relationships with the Hudson's Bay Company over the previous two centuries influenced Cree approaches to and understandings of treaty negotiations in 1876? Second, how did the rapidly changing economic circumstances of the 1870s influence Cree negotiating objectives? These questions were of interest to me for several

Table 3: Expert Witnesses (Excluding Elders)

| Name | Specialization* | Focus of evidence | Days |
|---|---|---|---|
| Prof. Arthur J. Ray | Historical Geography | Pre-Treaty 6 relations with HBC and Canadian treaty-making practices | 4 |
| Joan Holmes | Historian | All aspects of pre-treaty Native history | 6 |
| Bob Beal | Historian | Western Canadian history | 14 |
| Prof. Carl Beal | Economic History | Economic history of Native/ government relations after Treaty as they concerned federal treaty obligations | 3 |
| Prof. James Youngblood Henderson | Law | Legal history | 1 |
| Prof. Doug Sanders | Law | Legal history/Native law | 1 |
| Prof. H.C. Wolfart | Linguistics | Linguistics as it pertains to Cree interpretations of treaty | 4 |
| Prof. Winona Wheeler | Historian | Theory and methods of oral history | 7 |
| Prof. Alexander von Gernet | Archaeology | All aspects of western Canadian Native history and oral history methods | 9 |
| Prof. Thomas Flanagan | Political Science | Western Canadian Native History and historical methods | 9 |

reasons. When I had begun my research into the history of Native participation in the Canadian fur trade in the late 1960s, a lively academic debate was underway about whether First Nations' participation should be viewed as having been primarily of a socio-political or economic nature.[5] In 1978 Donald B. Freeman and I had addressed this issue at length in *Give Us Good Measure*.[6] We acknowledged that the trade had these two dimensions, but emphasized that HBC records demonstrated that Aboriginal people were very sensitive to changing markets. Our findings challenged those who downplayed Native economic motivations in the belief that non-market behaviour was a characteristic that set Aboriginal people apart from the European newcomers. *Victor Buffalo* offered me a chance to revisit the political aspect of the fur trade. My purpose was not to address again the old, oddly persistent debate, but to reflect on the ways in which fur trade diplomatic/political institutions and practices had shaped long-term relations between western Canadian First Nations and the Crown. Questions about how the economic circumstances of the 1870s Prairie West influenced treaty negotiations also attracted me because I had addressed this topic in *The Canadian Fur Trade in the Industrial Age* (1998).

I submitted my report, entitled "The Economic Background to Treaty 6," in June 1997.[7] I emphasized that the Hudson's Bay Company had been the dominant European presence for the Cree and their neighbours in the Canadian West for over two hundred years prior to the treaty. During that long period, the Cree wedded their socioeconomic and diplomatic traditions with those of the English in the course of establishing and sustaining their partnership with the Hudson's Bay Company. The fur-trading institutions and practices that cemented this relationship, particularly the gift-giving and negotiating traditions, and the treaties that Canada had already negotiated to the east in the area of present-day Ontario (most notably the Robinson Treaties and Treaty 3), served as models for treaty negotiations in the 1870s (fig. 21) As a result, the treaties included provisions that had been central features of the classic, pre-1870s fur trade. The key elements were gift exchanges, clothing allowances for chiefs, the presentation of medals at the time of treaty signing, and, in Treaty 6, the formal promise to provide aid in times of famine and pestilence. I noted in my report that the latter clause was particularly important for the Plains Cree in the 1870s, as they had recently been ravaged by another smallpox

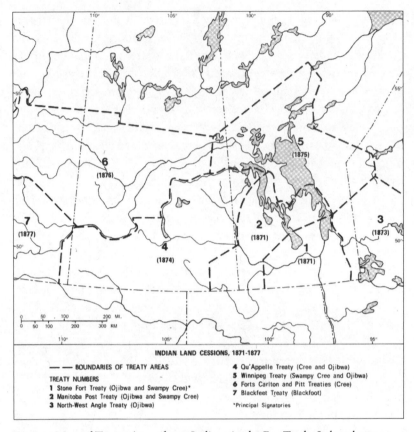

INDIAN LAND CESSIONS, 1871-1877

- - - - BOUNDARIES OF TREATY AREAS

TREATY NUMBERS
1 Stone Fort Treaty (Ojibwa and Swampy Cree)*
2 Manitoba Post Treaty (Ojibwa and Swampy Cree)
3 North-West Angle Treaty (Ojibwa)

4 Qu'Appelle Treaty (Cree and Ojibwa)
5 Winnipeg Treaty (Swampy Cree and Ojibwa)
6 Forts Carlton and Pitt Treaties (Cree)
7 Blackfeet Treaty (Blackfoot)

*Principal Signatories

Fig. 21: Map of Treaty Areas from *Indians in the Fur Trade*. I closed my
1974 monograph with a brief commentary about treaties marking the end
of an era. Interest in the fur trade of the late nineteenth and early twentieth
centuries, and my involvement in claims litigation, led me subsequently to
explore the subject more extensively.

epidemic. Also, they were already suffering from severe food shortages,
with their buffalo hunting days rapidly drawing to a close. The few remaining herds were being decimated by over-hunting.

Of particular relevance to the law suit, my search of the HBC records
had revealed that, from the 1680s onward, First Nations granted the
company access rights to their territories and approval to build and
maintain trading posts. They had not surrendered their lands to the
company. Further evidence of this fact was their outrage when they
learned in 1870 that the Hudson's Bay Company had sold their lands
(known to the Crown and the company as Rupert's Land). Their anger

impeded negotiations for Treaty 4 in 1874 and continued to be an issue in Treaty 6 talks.

### "PAPER TALK": REBUTTALS AND SURREBUTTALS

After my fellow experts and I had submitted our reports, the Crown's two experts, political scientist Thomas Flanagan and archaeologist Alexander von Gernet, wrote lengthy replies. The Crown had retained them as rebuttal witnesses, but did not commission them to do any original historical research, in the belief that such evidence was not essential for the case. In his rebuttal brief, which he submitted in July 1998, Dr Flanagan focused on the reports of those of us who had relied on documentary records and extant historical scholarship.[8] Dr von Gernet addressed the ethnohistory report of Joan Holmes, which dealt with the pre- and post-contact era, but he focused primarily on oral history evidence. His first rebuttal, submitted in March 2000, treated the general limitations of oral history and his second, filed in May of the same year,[9] questioned the validity of the testimony of oral history expert Winona Wheeler. As soon as Dr Flanagan had filed his lengthy rebuttal, Mr Hutchins and Mr O'Reilly, acting for the plaintiffs, asked us to make written replies. After doing so, Dr Flanagan promptly filed a surrebuttal brief, which we all answered. In this way, we became engaged in an intense paper war long before we ever appeared in court.[10]

In our war of "paper talk," to borrow an old Mi'kmaq expression, we contested revisionist and "standard" interpretations of Plains Cree history. We were battling over several basic issues. The first concerned the historical locations of the ancestral Samson Cree. Ms Holmes argued for the plaintiffs that the western Plains Cree had lived in the region, including Alberta, from the earliest times; Dr von Gernet countered for the defendant by arguing that published archaeological and historical research (including my own) showed that the ancestral Samson Cree did not move into the Hobbema area until the early nineteenth century.[11] I was never clear why this issue had been raised, given that no one had ever challenged the Cree right to negotiate Treaty 6 in 1876.

The second issue in sharp dispute was central to the lawsuit because it concerned the question of what the Cree thought they had agreed to in Treaty 6. Witnesses for the Samson Cree, especially Algonkian linguist Chris Wolfart, argued that the Cree would not have understood certain concepts, especially the notion of surrendering the land, because of fundamental differences between English and old Cree (pre-1876).[12] On behalf of the Crown, Dr Flanagan countered with the argument that the Cree would have fully understood the terms of the treaty because by 1876 they had a long tradition of dealing with English-speaking fur traders. Also, he noted that interpreters were present during treaty negotiations, a fact that in his view meant there was no reason to suspect the Cree misunderstood the government's intentions.[13] In other words, according to him, the treaty was – and is – "plain on its face" to both parties.

The debate about interpretation raised interesting questions about the role and competency of the interpreters, the extent to which the dialects of Plains and Swampy Cree and Plains Ojibwa interfered with translation efforts, and our ability, over a century and a quarter later, to determine what the interpreters had said to the Cree when they stated that they had fully "explained" the treaty; the problem we face today is that the translators never described the content of their explanations. Finally, the translation issue raised questions about personal memories. Métis Peter Erasmus, one of the key translators, recalled the event many years later when he was an old man living on a small government pension as a reward for his interpretation efforts.[14] Compounding the problem, his memoirs actually were written by a newspaper reporter who asked him questions about his life. Prior to doing the interviews, the reporter had done research in old newspapers. So, there is uncertainty about what the memoirs represent. This was a major issue at trial.

A third broad historical question that arose in *Samson*, one closely related to the interpretation issue, concerned the oral histories of the Plains Cree themselves about Treaty 6. Through their oral history evidence, the plaintiffs advanced the proposition that their ancestors had agreed to share their lands, not surrender them, in exchange for promises that Canada would provide various social services, most notably education, health care, aid in times of famine and pestilence, and help in making the transition from a buffalo-hunting economy to a farming way of life. The elders put forward these perspectives in their oral histories. As noted, a key object of my brief was to determine whether HBC records and others, mostly government documents, supported the Cree position. An aspect of this was the consideration of whether there were gaps and perhaps silences in the documentary record that left space for Cree historical perspectives.

As the briefs and counter-briefs regarding these various concerns piled higher, I asked Mr Hutchins if there was any need for us to go to court and hash it out again. He said, "There is, unfortunately!" Evidence had to be "tested." This meant that my fellow experts and I had to defend not only our original submissions but also our rebuttals and surrebuttals as well.

### LEARNING FROM A PAST EXPERT

Because I was scheduled as the first expert witnesses to appear after the elders, Mr Hutchins wanted my testimony to serve as the "road map" for the evidence of other experts who would follow me. Accordingly, we spent considerable time preparing a long and detailed set of questions for my evidence-in-chief. It so happened that while we were working on this list, I was conducting research in the papers of anthropologist Alfred L. Kroeber, located in the Bancroft Library at the University of California-Berkeley, about his involvement as the lead expert for the plaintiffs in Indian claims before the United States Indian Claims Commission. Kroeber had kept lengthy notes. So, during the day, I read about Kroeber's meticulous preparations to be an expert; in the evening, I primed myself to be one. This involved commenting on the preliminary 36-page list of ninety questions that Mr Hutchins had e-mailed to me. It was an odd experience, but it gave me a unique historical perspective about the process that I had been drawn into half a century after Kroeber.[15]

My testimony began in Calgary on 3 October 2000. I had arrived on the weekend for final preparations and met the whole team of the plaintiffs' lawyers for the first time. They filled a large boardroom. Mr Hutchins, in a well-tailored blue suit, sat at one end of the long table situated in the middle of the room; Mr O'Reilly, more casually attired, sat at the other end. After introducing me to everyone, he explained the different roles that he and Mr Hutchins would play during my appearance in court. He said it would be his role to raise any objections that had to be made and address any challenges that the Crown put forward. In other words, he would be my "protector" in court. Mr

Hutchins, on the other hand, in a very gentlemanly and respectful way, would lead me through my evidence-in-chief.

After I had been instructed on what to expect, the other lawyers brought up the issues that they anticipated would arise and asked me how I would respond. Owen Young was one of those present. He asked me the most complex questions about the philosophy and methodology of history. We continued our dialogue long after this meeting through e-mail correspondence. He was keenly interested in these topics and was thinking about them as part of his planning for the cross-examination of the Crown's experts. The reason for his interest was that Dr Flanagan had championed the superiority of traditional Western approaches to history that sprang from the European Enlightenment over the more relativistic and poly-vocal outlooks that had arisen from post-modern era of the 1990s.[16]

While we were getting ready for my appearance, I told Mr Hutchins I would like to lead off my examination-in-chief with a short Power-Point slide presentation. I explained that I wanted the judge to be able to visualize the historical context of the treaty. Although I realized that Justice Teitelbaum had more experience presiding over Aboriginal and treaty rights cases than most judges, I suspected he would not be familiar with the history I would be discussing.[17] Apparently, my request came as a surprise to everyone because a slide presentation had yet to be used in Aboriginal rights litigation. Accordingly, Mr Hutchins replied that he would have to raise my proposition with Crown council. After I assured them I would not use my presentation as a Trojan horse to sneak in new material, they agreed to my proposal.

## AN UNUSUAL OPENING PRAYER

I arrived in court on the day the trial reconvened from a long summer recess that had followed the elders' testimony at the Hobbema Reserve in June. In his opening remarks, Justice Teitelbaum said warmly: "It is certainly a great pleasure to see you all this morning. I make the assumption that each and every one of you had a terrific summer, relaxed and prepared yourselves for the next number of weeks before this court; and one must be relaxed."[18] He then observed, "Mr O'Reilly, I see you standing, sir." This time the counsel had not risen to make an objection. Rather, he said: "I would like to ask permission of the Court to have a short opening prayer, if it is at all possible … What I would propose is that five persons, including Mr George Ka-Niptehtew; J.B. Stanley, who is a very respected Elder; Ernest Stanley, and Lawrence Saddleback – Mr Saddleback is a Samson Member – and then Mr John Ermineskin of Ermineskin, would come forward for the prayer ceremony, and they would put some objects in the glass case which is in the courtroom." Justice Teitelbaum and Crown counsel agreed to his request. After the prayer, Mr O'Reilly explained: "Some of the objects which are in the glass case are meant to be [a] medium through which the spirits of the ancestors are called upon to pray for all; the Court, all counsel, the counsel for all sides, and everybody involved in the court process. So, it is meant to be an instrument through which there is universality and not one side of this."[19] With this acknowledgment of Cree tradition, the trial resumed with me in the witness box.

As is customary, Mr Hutchins began my evidence-in-chief by turning first to my *curriculum vitae*, even though attorneys for the Crown had already accepted me as an expert. His object was to highlight my published research that was relevant to the issues I was bringing before the court. In doing this, he had to be careful not to dwell too long on my CV because Justice Teitelbaum had already warned him to be brief, given that my expertise was not being challenged and my CV had been submitted as an exhibit. I have always welcomed the opportunity to begin by going over my career, because it is a relatively stress-free way to acclimatize to a particular courtroom and get a sense of the presiding judge.

In *Victor Buffalo*, reviewing my CV also gave me time to familiarize myself with the high-tech courtroom that had been built especially for the trial. Most striking, and at times distracting, was the monitor placed directly of everyone in the courtroom, including me in the witness box. My testimony appeared instantaneously on these monitors. It was like having a technological trickster who in a flash transformed what I said into a digital document. The catch was that I had to resist the urge to "read myself" as I spoke, because I stopped talking whenever I became too engrossed in reading.

I also learned the hard way that, for the transcription system to function properly, I had to face the microphone in the witness box and speak close to it. As a witness, I found this to be a very distracting exercise because I like to engage judges by facing them as I testify. On numerous occasions, Justice Teitelbaum had to interrupt my testimony to remind me to speak directly into the microphone.

Mr Hutchins began my evidence-in-chief with a series of questions about the importance of context when trying to understand historical documents. In the course of our exchange, I emphasized that Treaty 6 must be understood as having been a product of an ongoing process. As an example of a key source that emphasized this point, I cited Alexander Morris's book *The Treaties of Canada with the Indians of Manitoba and the North-West Territories Including the Negotiations on which they were Based, and Other Information Relating Thereto,* which was published in 1880.[20] As lieutenant-governor of Manitoba, the North-West Territories, and Keewatin, Morris had negotiated Treaty 6 and other Western treaties. In his book, he said that the earlier treaties of Canada, especially the Robinson Treaties (1850) and Treaty 3 (1873) had been his blueprint for Treaty 6.

After completing these preliminary questions about contextualizing and interpreting documents, including maps, Mr Hutchins told Justice Teitelbaum that I wanted to preface the balance of my evidence-in-chief by showing the court a PowerPoint slide presentation that I had prepared. Mr Hutchins began by saying: "Now, I understand, My Lord – I don't know if the Registrar has indicated this to you – but Professor Ray would like to give us a small demonstration ... via Power Point, and I certainly don't understand technology, but there would just simply be some images which would be flashed on everybody's monitor from Professor Ray's machine. Perhaps he can explain the technology better than I."[21] Justice Teitelbaum responded by prompting me, "Just tell me what you are attempting to do, sir." I replied: "I just want to, in very few slides, give you a quick overview of what the general trend of the discussion will be with a few images, so you can [know] – who is [Alexander] Morris, who is [William] Christie,[22] what ... these ceremonies we are talking about look like."[23]

My visual presentation contained nine slides that covered Hudson's Bay Company–First Nations relations, from the chartering of the company to treaty negotiations in 1876. I selected images that I could speak to at length (Appendix 2) and would reinforce the fact that First Nations relations with the Crown (the "Queen Mother," as the Cree expressed it in 1876) began in western Canada through the Hudson's Bay Company, a decade or more after its founding in 1670. Focusing on the political and diplomatic dimensions, I stressed that the ongoing symbiotic relationship had to be renewed regularly through certain practices, such as the smoking of the calumet (pipe-smoking ceremony) and reciprocal gift exchanges. I also emphasized that mutual commitments were symbolized by presents from the company, most notably "captains' coats," and by trading medals. Afterward, I learned through the grapevine that Justice Teitelbaum liked the "show."

### PROBLEMS OF TALKING ACROSS DISCIPLINES

After I completed my presentation, Mr Hutchins began my long evidence-in-chief, which focused on my brief and the hundreds of pages of supporting documents. This went smoothly, but Justice Teitelbaum did make a couple of significant interventions. One of these took place late in my first day on the stand when I was answering a series of questions from Mr Hutchins about the expansion of trading posts into Saskatchewan. To my surprise, Justice Teitelbaum asked: "Sir, these trading posts were set up by the Plains Cree?"[24] I replied: "Set up by the Europeans. When I say 'trading post frontier,' I mean European trading posts. But what I am saying is that often Native traders, for example, with that map[25] following page 1 [of my report], those Keskatchewan [Saskatchewan] Cree, they are going to York Factory, which is a long distance. That is where they do their first trading before the Hudson's Bay Company moves inland. The Hudson's Bay Company doesn't move inland until 1774. A hundred years go by before the Hudson's Bay Company moves inland." Justice Teitelbaum then enquired further: "But the trading post at York was set up by whom?" I realized in these exchanges that I was correct to assume that he did not have much familiarity with the fur trade; I also realized that I was not explaining enough.[26]

Another exchange with Justice Teitelbaum the following day underscored the problem of talking across disciplines, in this instance across the fields of law and ethnohistorical geography. It arose during the course of my discussion of Canada's various goals for the numbered treaties leading up to Treaty 6. I had pointed out that in Treaty 3 the government wanted to obtain the right-of-way it needed to build a railway and telegraph lines. I discussed the fact that First Nations living in the southern part of the proposed Treaty 3 territory were very reluctant to surrender their land, but they were willing to negotiate access rights. I reiterated that this was a long-standing practice in the fur trade.[27]

Unfortunately, when addressing this topic in my written report, I had stated: "Similarly, it is understandable why the Indians were prepared to lease use rights. This was more in keeping with their traditional practices and their wish to share their lands with the new-comers as they had been doing since the late seventeenth century."[28] When we got to that passage in my evidence-in-chief, Justice Teitel-baum wanted to know where the word "lease" came from. He said: "Let's re-go over this part, because with all due respect, sir, I did not understand your reply at all. Please forgive me. Because I have a big mark here on page 70 and 71 when I read it, and I still don't – I thought I would get an explanation of what I read, but I still don't understand it. I would ask you to, please, let's go back over again, and tell me where you come with the term "lease," and how you find the word "lease," and why you use the term "lease," and what made you come to that term. Particularly with regard to telegrams and tele-graphs and lines and everything else, sir. I wonder if you would do that for me."[29] After a lengthy exchange, I explained that I had used the word "lease" to describe situations in which First Nations granted outsiders access to their traditional territories for specific purposes. Often they received gifts or token payments of some sort from the out-siders as an acknowledgment of having granted the right. I apologized to Justice Teitelbaum for having used a word in a way that caused confusion. We agreed that, rather than say "leased access rights," it was better to say "negotiated access rights," and we moved on (fig. 22).[30]

My cross-examination by A.D. Macleod, QC was testy and pro-voked Mr O'Reilly to make numerous and sometimes lengthy objec-tions to his line of questioning. Among the many themes Mr Macleod addressed, one stood out, given the number of questions he addressed to it either directly and indirectly. It concerned the central issue of whether there was any reason to suppose that there could have been any ambiguities in the minds of the Cree about the meaning of the negotiations and the resulting treaty. As noted, I had written and tes-tified that there were reasons, and I and other of the plaintiffs' experts had challenged Dr Flanagan for taking the contrary position.

In his questioning, Mr Macleod zeroed in on several aspects of this issue. One concerned my contention that it would have been unclear to the Cree what the relationship of Canada and the Hudson's Bay Company was to the "Queen Mother." In my opinion, Mr Macleod

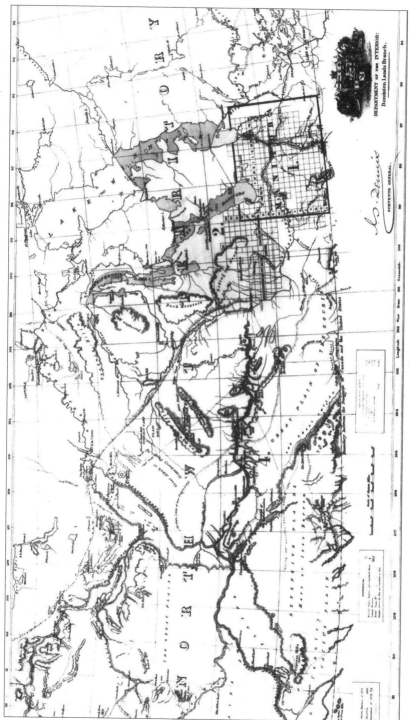

Fig. 22: Map of Western treaty-making to 1875.

attempted to cloud the issue by repeatedly asking me if I disagreed with the proposition that the Cree knew the difference between Canada and the Hudson's Bay Company. I agreed that they did, but argued that this was not the critical issue. More important were the ways these two organizations represented the Queen. I had made the point during my evidence-in-chief that two of the members of Canada's negotiating team symbolized two different links to the "Queen Mother." William J. Christie, the recently retired HBC chief factor for the Saskatchewan District, represented the older tradition, while Lieutenant-Governor Alexander Morris represented the new one, yet to be defined.[31] Canada had deliberately chosen Christie, knowing that the Cree would trust him. I also stressed that the government's accounts of the negotiations, which Morris provided in his book, indicated that Morris always referred to himself as a representative of the "Queen Mother." He did not say he represented Canada, even though the Treaty 6 text says, "The Plain and Wood Cree Tribes of Indians and all other of the Indians inhabiting the district hereinafter described and defines, do hereby cede, release, surrender and yield up to the government of the Dominion of Canada."

Mr Macleod also focused on A.G. Jackes's account of the treaty negotiations. Dr Jackes had been the secretary of Morris's treaty commission, and according to the commissioner, his report was "a narrative of the proceedings taken down, day by day ... [that] embraces an accurate account of the speeches of the Commissioners and Indians."[32] It was for this reason that Morris included it in the book he published in 1880. On the second and third days of my evidence-in-chief, Mr Hutchins had taken me to Jackes's narrative so that I could reiterate my point that it contained "no indication that this surrender language that we just read together in the proposed Treaty 6 was explained to the Crees."[33] Mr Hutchins also had asked me if any of the other documents regarding Treaty 6 talks, which Morris included in his book, suggested that land surrenders were discussed. I replied, "No, they did not."[34]

## A BATTLE OF WORDS AND WITS

Continuing his cross-examination, Mr Macleod attacked my observation through several lines of leading questions and propositions. One of these played on statements I had made in my report, to the effect that the Cree came to the talks as well-informed and tough bargainers. For instance, Mr Macleod kicked off a string of related questions by proposing: "But you make the point, and I take it we are all in agreement here, that the negotiators for the Indian people were well-informed and they were well-informed about many things, including the changes you refer to and also the negotiations of previous treaties?"[35] His objective clearly was to try and lead me to the conclusion that the Cree would have been aware of Canada's goal. Indeed, he moved in this direction several questions later when he asked if I agreed that Canada's intention had been to obtain land surrenders from them. Of course I agreed.[36] He then dwelt on the fact that the "yield and surrender" clause in Treaty 6 was virtually the same as those that were included in treaties 1–4. He proposed, therefore, that the Cree would have learned about it from their neighbours and relatives to the east.

In a series of replies, I argued that Mr Macleod was jumping to an unsupportable conclusion. I noted that, according to Morris's own account, he had announced: "We come to share the land; we come to give you these things on top; we come not to take away your livelihood. That is the message that Morris is telling us he is giving these people." I added: "I do not see anywhere where that language of surrender is used, and I might say, sir, that I find it is a strange language, it is a language foreign to any kind of talk I have seen in trading records and what transcripts we have from Native accounts, it is a rather foreign concept and, to put it frankly, it is rather lawyerly talk, and it is not [the] talk of the country."[37] Mr Macleod was unhappy with my reply. He shot back: "Sir, with all respect, please just listen to the question I am asking you. You didn't answer my question. The tribes are communicating back and forth about the treaty process; they are exchanging information about what is going on?"[38]

And so we battled on over the "yield and surrender" clause. Eventually Mr Macleod produced a copy of the longhand draft of the treaty that Morris had taken with him to forts Carlton and Pitt. Suspecting that I had not seen it, he pointed out to me that one of the few clauses that had not been modified was the one pertaining to surrendering the land to the Crown. He proposed that this proved his point. I replied that, to the contrary, it made my point. All the modified clauses dealt with subjects of great concern to the Cree and addressed topics that had been discussed at great length, according to Morris and Jackes. I stated that my opinion was that the likely reason the "yield and

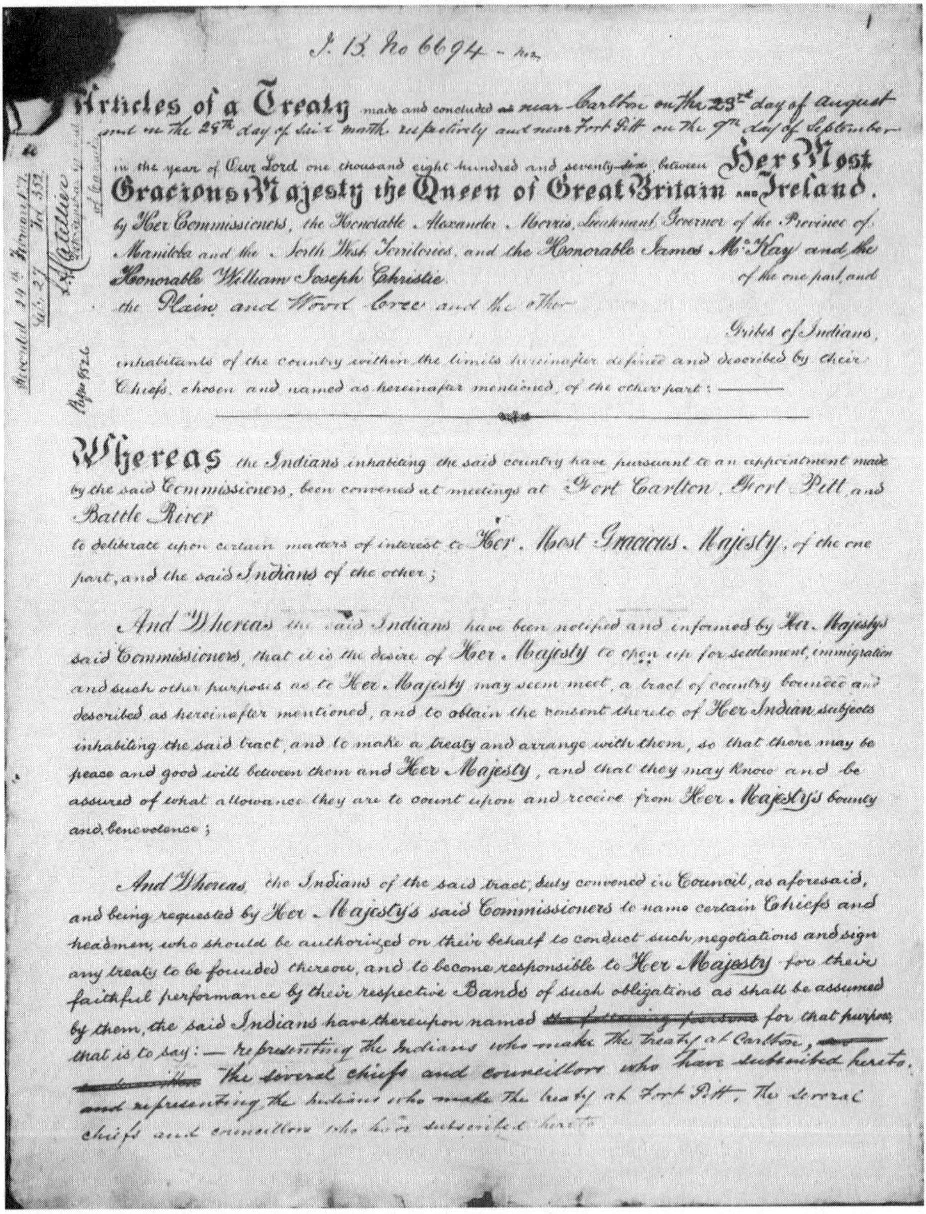

J. B. No 6694 - 1912

Articles of a Treaty made and concluded as near Carlton on the 23rd day of August and on the 28th day of said month respectively and near Fort Pitt on the 9th day of September in the year of Our Lord one thousand eight hundred and seventy-six between **Her Most Gracious Majesty the Queen of Great Britain and Ireland** by Her Commissioners, the Honorable Alexander Morris, Lieutenant Governor of the Province of Manitoba and the North West Territories, and the Honorable James McKay and the Honorable William Joseph Christie, of the one part, and the Plain and Wood Cree and the other Tribes of Indians, inhabitants of the country within the limits hereinafter defined and described by their Chiefs, chosen and named as hereinafter mentioned, of the other part: —

**Whereas** the Indians inhabiting the said country have, pursuant to an appointment made by the said Commissioners, been convened at meetings at Fort Carlton, Fort Pitt and Battle River to deliberate upon certain matters of interest to Her Most Gracious Majesty, of the one part, and the said Indians of the other;

And Whereas the said Indians have been notified and informed by Her Majesty's said Commissioners, that it is the desire of Her Majesty to open up for settlement, immigration and such other purposes as to Her Majesty may seem meet, a tract of country bounded and described as hereinafter mentioned, and to obtain the consent thereto of Her Indian subjects inhabiting the said tract, and to make a treaty and arrange with them, so that there may be peace and good will between them and Her Majesty, and that they may know and be assured of what allowance they are to count upon and receive from Her Majesty's bounty and benevolence;

And Whereas the Indians of the said tract, duly convened in Council, as aforesaid, and being requested by Her Majesty's said Commissioners to name certain Chiefs and headmen, who should be authorized on their behalf to conduct such negotiations and sign any treaty to be founded thereon, and to become responsible to Her Majesty for their faithful performance by their respective Bands of such obligations as shall be assumed by them, the said Indians have thereupon named ~~the following persons~~ for that purpose, that is to say: — representing the Indians who make the treaty at Carlton, the several chiefs and councillors who have subscribed hereto, and representing the Indians who make the treaty at Fort Pitt, the several chiefs and councillors who have subscribed hereto

Fig. 23: First Page of Draft of Treaty 6, showing that the surrender clause had not been altered in the field. The government negotiators modified the other clauses in response to issues the First Nations raised during treaty talks.

surrender" passage had not been modified was that it had not been discussed (fig. 23).[39]

Before ending this line of questioning, Mr Macleod drew attention to *Indians in the Fur Trade* and quoted the following statement: "Between the summer of 1871 and 1876, all Indian claims were extinguished in the grassland, parkland, and bordering woodland areas of the Prairie Provinces by Treaties 1 through 7." After we discussed the fact that the book had been published in 1974 on the basis of research I had undertaken from 1968–70, he asked the reasonable question: "I take it, it was your view at that time that the Aboriginal title was extinguished by Treaties 1 through 7 in the grassland, parkland, and woodland areas of the prairie?"[40] I agreed that was my view at the time based on then-current scholarship. Of course, Mr Macleod followed up by asking me why I had changed my mind. I pointed out that, since that time, a lot of oral history research had been undertaken that provided insights about First Nations' understandings of the treaties. In the early 1970s, their voice on treaty history had been largely silent. Also, for the *Victor Buffalo* litigation, I had undertaken research in Morris's unpublished papers located in the Manitoba Provincial Archives. Mr Macleod then asked why I had not mentioned post-1970s treaty research in the new introduction to the 1998 edition of *Indians in the Fur Trade*. I explained that my objective had been to discuss the development of fur trade scholarship after 1974. The treaties had not been a central focus of the book in the first edition. Rather, I had only mentioned them in passing in the closing chapter.

The other line of questioning in Mr Macleod's cross-examination focused on the issue of translation. A substantial portion of his questioning dealt with the Peter Erasmus's memoirs,[41] but he also dealt with other translators who had been present.[42] On repeated occasions, Mr Macleod proposed through questions and by reading excerpts from various documents that the translators had "explained" the treaty to the Cree.[43] My stock reply was that this is what the record says. However, I also repeatedly noted that neither Erasmus nor the other translators ever said what they had explained. In other words, the documents are silent about the content of the explanations. During re-examination by Mr O'Reilly, I again stressed this point.[44]

## EXPLAINING IT TO THE JUDGE

After Mr Macleod's rigorous cross-examination and Mr O'Reilly's re-examination, I was questioned by Justice Teitelbaum. His purpose was mainly to clarify the "yield and surrender" clause, in particular, the phrase "release, surrender and yield up to the Government of the Dominion of Canada." He thought he had understood me to say that Canada had not been a party to the treaty. I explained:

> What I was trying to respond to, is that in the negotiations, the references are always to the Queen. This is the language of the treaty, but I don't see where in these negotiations that idea is brought across. That is the point I was trying to make. Morris is representing himself as a representative of the Queen Mother. The treaty, of course, we understand the treaty process is with Canada, but it is not clear to me, and I don't think it was totally clear to the aboriginal people, what the relationships were between the Queen Mother, Canada, and the Hudson's Bay Company. That's my point. I am not saying that – obviously the treaty is with Canada, but if you look ... we have been back and forth over all these negotiations. Morris is ... representing and presenting himself, and he is always talking in terms of the Queen Mother.

I thought I had finished after answering the judge's closing questions. I was wrong. Unhappy that Justice Teitelbaum had not fully quoted the "yield and surrender" clause when asking me about it, Mr O'Reilly undertook one more re-examination:

> I must apologize, but I took exception to the way in which that question was being phrased, because I had wanted Your Lordship to continue on that question of the surrender clause, because it had said: "... yield up to the Government of the Dominion of Canada ..." On page 352 [of Morris] for Her Majesty the Queen, and Your Lordship stopped at: "... yield up to the Government of the Dominion of Canada ...." And my respectful submission is that that sentence, that last phrase is vital: "... the Dominion of Canada for Her Majesty the Queen...."

To reinforce the point of my answer to Justice Teitelbaum, Mr O'Reilly's re-examination continued as follows:

Mr O'Reilly: The treaty, if you go back to page 351 [Morris], there was no mention as a party in what is described as the articles of a treaty, there is no mention of Canada. Is that correct or not correct, Dr Ray?

A Ray: Correct.[45]

Mr O'Reilly: When you look at the surrender clause, the fourth line is –pardon me, the third line after: "... do hereby cede, release, surrender and yield up to the Government of the Dominion of Canada for Her Majesty the Queen and her successors forever, ..." So from your point of view, is that a surrender, whatever it is, to Canada or to Canada for Her Majesty the Queen?

A Ray: In the latter case. All through the negotiations, it is always in reference to the Queen.

Mr O'Reilly: And was that explained, that relationship between the Dominion of Canada and Her Majesty the Queen and whether there was an agency or not an agency during the treaty negotiations?

A Ray: We don't know. The record is pretty silent on that.[46]

At last, I was finished.

The trial continued for another two years. The witnesses who followed me revisited the various themes and issues that had been covered in my testimony and evidence, albeit the emphasis of their testimony differed. Of particular importance, Dr Wolfart dealt with the linguistic issues that translators would have faced. He noted that there would not have been words in the pre-treaty Cree language, or "old Cree," to convey the concept of ceding or selling land. Dr Wheeler talked about the ways in which First Nations' oral histories differed from document-based Euro-Canadian history. She was a counterpoint to Dr von Gernet, who questioned the general reliability of oral history evidence and the specific testimony of the Cree elders.

Just over five years after I had testified, Justice Teitelbaum issued his judgment. In the third paragraph of his reasons, which totalled 368 pages, he stated: "While at times it felt like the Court had been sent back to school, the historical information and interpretations

presented were always interesting and, on many occasions, quite fascinating. It would have been all too easy to wander down the many
well-trod avenues, lesser byways, and faint trails of our history."[47] He
then devoted 70 percent of his judgment (257 pages) to a discussion
of the historical evidence. Most of Justice Teitelbaum's text is composed of a list of the experts and a summary of their evidence.[48] He
began his section on "findings" with the caution: "The SCC's decision
in *Delgamuukw, supra*, does not mandate blanket admissibility of oral
history or oral tradition evidence; nor does it establish the amount
of weight that should be placed upon such evidence by a trial judge."
Justice Teitelbaum continued: "The decision merely speaks of 'due
weight.' This does not amount to equal weight, an interpretation which
the plaintiffs seem to suggest. In *Mitchell, supra*, McLachlin C.J. held
that 'due weight' meant that oral tradition evidence is entitled to 'equal
and due treatment.' It should neither be undervalued, nor artificially
constrained to carry more weight than it could reasonably support."[49]

With this forewarning, Justice Teitelbaum proceeded to dismiss
oral histories, explaining, in part, that he preferred Dr von Gernet's
approach to evaluating this line of evidence, which essentially involved
checking it against documentary records, to that of Dr Wheeler's because it was more practical.[50] He explained:

> I prefer the approach advocated by Dr von Gernet over that of
> Dr Wheeler. In response to a question from the Court as to how
> it should evaluate an oral tradition reduced to a transcript, Dr
> Wheeler replied that the Court should seek assistance from
> "local experts" for a full contextual reading (transcript volume
> 157, 21901–2). While Dr Wheeler's approach may suit schol-
> ars, it is simply not feasible, nor is it realistic, for a trial judge.
> The Court cannot embark upon independent fact-finding in-
> vestigations into evidence tendered at trial. The Court must rely
> upon the parties for the evidence and any assistance from ex-
> perts. And while Dr Wheeler offered some interesting insights
> into the nature of oral traditions and oral histories, she did not
> present the Court with any analysis of the oral traditions ten-
> dered at trial.[51]

Justice Teitelbaum also preferred the written accounts of the treaty
talks, including the transcribed memoirs of Erasmus,[52] to the recol-

lections of the elders. This preference meant that he dismissed the Cree contention that their ancestors had agreed to share the land as being after-the-fact invention. He did so without commenting on that fact that such ideas were in accordance with the long-standing pre-treaty practice of sharing the land with the Hudson's Bay Company. His "findings of fact" led Justice Teitelbaum to conclude that the Cree would have fully understood all of the terms of Treaty 6, including the contentious "yield and surrender" clause.

# CHAPTER 5

# WITNESSING ON BEHALF OF
# A FORGOTTEN PEOPLE

While I was involved in *Samson*, Jean Teillet, who is the grandniece of the legendary nineteenth-century Métis leader Louis Riel, asked me if I would be willing to appear as an expert in a Métis hunting rights case involving two hunters, the Powleys, from Sault Ste Marie, Ontario. Steve Powley and his son Roddy had been charged with killing a bull moose near the community without having obtained a hunting permit ("outdoor card") from the Ministry of Natural Resources as required by the Ontario Game and Fish Act (1990).[1] The Powleys did not deny the charges, but they asserted that Section 35 of the Constitution Act (1982) guaranteed them Aboriginal hunting rights as Métis. Ms Teillet, who was just beginning her distinguished career in the field of Native law, was heading up their legal team. She wanted me to prepare a brief and testify about the nature of the Aboriginal economy in the Sault Ste Marie area on the eve of the Robinson Treaties of 1850. Her request was of interest to me in part because it would involve researching the Métis, whom I had originally intended to be the subject of my doctoral dissertation. Also, I was intrigued because the *Powley* litigation concerned the Métis community of Sault Ste Marie, which academic historians had mostly ignored, preferring to concentrate on the buffalo hunters of the Canadian West.[2] These considerations led me to join Ms Teillet's defence team.

## RESEARCHING THE MÉTIS OF THE UPPER GREAT LAKES

The Powleys made their claim at a time when Métis rights litigation was in its infancy. No case had made its way to the Supreme Court since the passage of the Constitution Act in 1982, which recognized the Métis as an Aboriginal People. The court acknowledged this in 1996 in *Regina v. Van der Peet*, which concerned the question of whether the Stó:lō of the Fraser River in British Columbia had an Aboriginal right to fish for salmon for commercial purposes. In its ruling, the Supreme Court elaborated on the doctrine of continuity that it had first enunciated in *Sparrow* by saying that constitutionally protected Aboriginal rights were limited to those practices of pre-contact origin that defined (were integral to) distinctive Native cultures. It recognized that allowance would have to be made for the historical fact that the Métis people emerged after contact. As the Supreme Court expressed it: "It may, or it may not, be the case that the claims of the Métis are determined on the basis of pre-contact practices, customs and traditions of their Aboriginal ancestors; whether that is so must await determination in a case in which the issue arises."[3] The Court added: "Customs and traditions need not have existed prior to British sovereignty or European contact. British sovereignty, instead of being considered the turning point in aboriginal culture, would be regarded as having recognized and affirmed practices, customs and traditions which are sufficiently significant and fundamental to the culture and social organization of aboriginal people."[4] In other words, for the Métis, culturally defining practices that are eligible for constitutional protection include those dating from the period of initial European contact to the establishment of effective British/Canadian control.

Before undertaking research for the trial, I met Ms Teillet in the spring of 1997 in Toronto. At that time, she was an associate in the law firm of Ruby & Edwardh. Over lunch we discussed the historical issues that *Powley* raised in the aftermath of *Van der Peet*. We were joined by renowned criminal, constitutional, and human rights lawyer Clayton Ruby, QC, who was assisting Ms Teillet. Several interrelated questions were paramount from the outset: Was there a distinctive Métis community at Sault Ste Marie before the British asserted effective sovereignty in the area? When did the British establish effective control in the area? Was moose hunting a culturally defining practice of the Métis community before that time? Had a Métis community survived from the latter date to the present whose members continued to earn part of their livelihoods off the land? Ms Teillet wanted me to address the first three questions; she had retained another historical geographer, Victor Lytwyn, to deal with the issue of continuity.

After a lively discussion about the impending case, Mr Ruby expressed his worry that it would be very challenging to find the kind of evidence that we would need to make a convincing case for the defendants and avoid having to resort to cultural "mumbo-jumbo" in court![5] I was more optimistic. I was familiar with many of the fur trading records that were available for the Upper Great Lakes area, having already consulted many of them when I had worked for Francis Thatcher on the Treaty 9 fishing rights case. Also, I had previously undertaken a small research project for the Flying Post First Nation, which is situated approximately 200 kilometres to the northeast on the height of land that divides the waters flowing into James Bay from those flowing into the Great Lakes.[6] This divide marked the northern limit of the Hudson's Bay Company's Fort Saint Mary's District. I had not looked at the HBC records for St Mary's post, however. They proved to be more limited than I had expected.

As my research progressed, it became clear that the location of Sault Ste Marie astride the main fur trade route connecting Montreal to the west was both advantageous and problematic from the perspective of finding documentary records that dealt specifically with the settlement's economy and society before 1850. On the positive side, its location on the "fur trade highway" meant that most of the early explorers and traders of central and western Canada had visited the community. Its situation beside one of the most important Native fisheries in the Great Lakes region – the whitefish fishery at the rapids in the St Mary's River – further enhanced its strategic importance. The Ojibwa had fished there since time immemorial and soon after contact it became a crucial provisioning place for fur traders. Also, travellers had to portage their canoes around the rapids until the North West Company (NWC) built a small canal to bypass them. As a result, from the time of the French regime (1751–60) onward, Europeans operated forts and trading posts at Sault Ste Marie. Passers-by visited them and left eye-witness accounts of the developing settlements. Beginning with the accounts of explorer and fur trader Alexander Henry (the elder) in 1761, they noted that the community had a Métis component.[7]

Having discovered that accounts describing the settlement during the open-water season were numerous, I learned that there were few that told about economic life inland and during the freeze-up season. Outsiders rarely travelled overland during the winter. Even after 1821, when the Hudson's Bay Company assumed control and its agents generated more records, their accounts continued to emphasize life at the settlement and along the river. This emphasis derived from the fact that Fort St Mary's served as a transportation depot for the company. The surrounding district was not a major source of furs for two reasons: fur bearers were not plentiful, and Americans and Métis free traders siphoned off much of the local fur trappings. For these reasons, the company did not maintain the network of inland posts that could have served as monitoring stations.

## BUILDING MODELS OF AN ABORIGINAL ECONOMY

Even though the archival records did not provide the balanced coverage of life in the Sault Ste Marie area that I had anticipated, nonetheless several crucial historical facts about the local Native economy emerged from the various HBC records pertaining to St Mary's and the adjacent districts. These diverse archival sources indicated that the local hunting economy was in dire straits during the first half of the nineteenth century. Aboriginal people often faced starvation during the winter in the forested interior, and Native hunters often had to resort to arctic hare or travel to Michipicoten and Sault Ste Marie for food when game and the local fisheries failed them. The life-threatening food shortages were partly the upshot of the ruinous HBC–NWC rivalry from the 1790s to 1820. The companies' cutthroat competition had fostered the depletion of wildlife throughout the forested lands of central and western Canada.[8] Of particular relevance to *Powley* was the fact that moose populations had been particularly hard hit in the upper Great Lakes region. The HBC records revealed that these animals had diminished to the point that neither the local Ojibwa nor the Métis could rely on them. Even woodland caribou were scarce. Bear were present, and HBC account books showed that there was a modest trade in bear skins (fig. 24).

It was immediately clear to me that this collapse of the moose population prior to 1850 was going to be a contentious issue at trial, considering the nature of the charges against the Powleys. For me it raised yet again the question of how broadly or narrowly Aboriginal livelihood rights should be construed. As I have already noted, this topic first piqued my interest in *Horseman* and had come up in the fishing rights research I had undertaken in Ontario and Manitoba. I thought

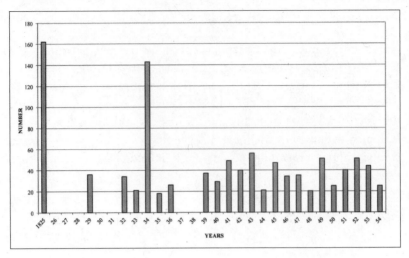

Fig. 24: Bear returns, Hudson's Bay Company, in Lake Huron District.

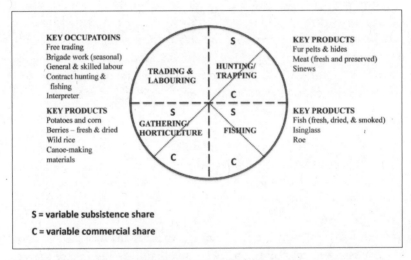

Fig. 25: Métis economy of the Upper Great Lakes.

that the absence of moose in 1850 might give me a good opportunity to argue against the current legal practice of characterizing Aboriginal livelihood rights in species-specific terms. This approach arises from conservation legislation that sets seasons and catch limits for various species of fish and wildlife, but it is at variance with the historical realities of Métis' and First Nations' economic life. I underscored this point in the report that I sent to Ms Teillet on 17 March 1998 by presenting models of traditional Ojibwa economy based on the notion of "seasonal activity cycles."[9] Ethnohistorical geographers have used this conceptual model for many years, and I had used it in my Treaty 2 report (see fig. 20, p. 65). I also included a model of the local Métis economy to highlight its economic diversity and flexibility (fig. 25).

In discussing these models, I noted that ethnohistorian Charles A. Bishop, who pioneered the use of HBC records for the study of the Ojibwa relatives of the Sault Ste Marie Métis, had determined that fisheries were important all year round, but especially during the open-water season.[10] This was the time of the year when the Ojibwa lived mostly in settlements beside their fisheries along the shores of lakes Huron and Superior and the St Mary's River. During late summer and early autumn, they collected berries and wild rice. In the spring, collecting activities included making sugar and gathering supplies for canoe building (raising birch bark and collecting spruce root). Hunting and trapping took place mostly during the late autumn, winter, and early spring. In the latter half of the seventeenth century, the Ojibwa took up horticulture after the Iroquois attacked and scattered their Huron trading partners during the late 1640s. Before that date, the Ojibwa had obtained considerable quantities of dried corn from the Huron in exchange for furs and hides. The various economic activities that the Ojibwa engaged in during their annual cycle meant that they moved over a large territory, even though they spent most of their time at their fishing/horticultural villages (fig. 26).

The economy of the local Métis was similar in many respects to that of their Ojibwa relatives and neighbours; but there were some important differences. Most notably, the Métis economy was more diversified and had a stronger market-oriented component. They were more intensively involved in the fur trade as labourers (seasonal and permanent), especially as voyageurs manning company canoes and boats, as interpreters, and as contract fishers and hunters (Table 4). Their voyageur activities were important for the additional reason that they served to link Métis communities together over broad regions, thereby facilitating the development of inter-regional, or national, self-consciousness. As free traders, they competed with the Hudson's Bay Company and with Americans. I noted in my report that the relative importance of each sector of the Métis economy, similarly to that of the Ojibwa, varied over time according to fish and wildlife cycles as

Fig. 26: Métis farm at Sault Ste Marie in the late nineteenth century.
Typically, these farms were situated on narrow lots extending back from
the riverbank.

well as local and external economic circumstances. These factors also
determined the relative importance of subsistence-oriented activities
compared to those of a commercial nature. Comparable to Métis of
Red River and elsewhere, the families at Fort St Mary's developed
small farms that extended back from the St Mary's River in long
narrow lots. The local economy of the Métis was spatially extensive
and overlapped with that of their Ojibwa relatives who lived nearby
at Garden River and with Métis relations who lived to the north at
Michipicoten post.

### A CHIEF TRADER CORRESPONDS WITH A GOVERNOR

My research also made it clear that Métis who lived in the vicinity of
Sault Ste Marie and elsewhere in Lake Superior country had developed

Table 4: Men Mentioned in St Mary's Post Journals, 1824–25

| Name | Parish* | Capacity | District** |
|------|---------|----------|------------|
| Bienvenue, Amable | | Labourer | St Mary |
| Bon Enfant, Jean | Canada | pork eater^ | St Mary |
| Bosquet, Michel | St Mary | Freeman – contract fish buyer | St Mary |
| Bourgeau, Antoine | | Labourer | St Mary |
| Buchon, Francois | Canada | pork eater | St Mary |
| Cadotte, Antoine | St Mary | Freeman – contract fish buyer | St Mary |
| Chretien, Michel | Canada | pork eater | St Mary |
| Couture, Joseph | St Mary | discharged labourer | St Mary |
| de Lorme, Charles | | Labourer | St Mary |
| Dubois, Joseph# | | | L. Superior |
| Dupras, Amable | Lake Superior | Boatman | St Mary |
| Frichette | | Labourer | St Mary |
| Gaudert, Pierre | Canada | pork eater | St Mary |
| Gingrus, Antoine | St Mary | Freeman – contract fish buyer | St Mary |
| Gingrus, Antoine | St Mary | Freeman – contract fish buyer | St Mary |
| La Fertin, Antoine | Canada | pork eater | St Mary |
| La Tourelle, Michel | Canada | pork eater | St Mary |
| La Valle | | Boatman? | Batchewana |
| La Verduce | St Mary | Freeman – jobber | St Mary |
| Le Mai | | Labourer | St Mary |
| Mandville, Vital | Canada | pork eater | St Mary |
| Martin, Boulez | St Mary | discharged labourer | St Mary |
| Mellorrie, Xavier | Lake Superior | Boatmen | St Mary |
| Perrault, Jean Bte | St Mary | Freeman – labourer | St Mary |
| Pichette, Joseph | Canada | pork eater | St Mary |
| Quebec | | Labourer/boatman | St Mary |
| Ropertin | | Labourer/boatman | St Mary |
| Ross, Clark | Lake Superior | Boatman | St Mary |
| Seccard, Phillipbert | | Labourer | St Mary |
| Topier, Francois | St Mary | Freeman – labourer | St Mary |

^Term for voyageurs who travelled to and from Montreal
*Place of birth or hiring.
**Assigned district.
# Died 1824.
Source: St Mary's Post Journals HBCA B 149/a/1.

a distinctive identity well before 1850 and that they had played an instrumental role in forcing the government to the treaty table.

A key source for this information was the correspondence that took place between Chief Trader William Mactavish, who managed Fort St Mary's from 1848 to 1850,[11] and HBC governor Sir George Simpson.[12] In his gossipy letters to the governor, Mactavish described how the local Ojibwa and their Métis relatives, led by Shinguacouse and Nebenaigoching,[13] petitioned Canada for a treaty to address their concerns about the impact that copper mining and mineral exploration in the region could have on their Aboriginal title. They also used force to back up their demands for a treaty. On 20 November 1849, for instance, Mactavish wrote to Simpson and informed him that earlier in the month an armed party had seized the Quebec Mining Company's property at Mica Bay on the eastern shores of Lake Superior. He told the governor that the perpetrators of the so-called Mica Bay Incident were a thirty-three-man force, rather than a rumoured one hundred, and that twenty-one of them were "half- breeds."[14] Three weeks later, Mactavish again wrote to say that "the latest news is that 2,000 Red River half breeds are to be down to act as allies of Shing-wakonce's, having sent him a wampum belt with a message to that effect this autumn."[15] Although Mactavish expressed doubts about this claim, it does suggest that there was an awareness in the larger Métis world about developments that were taking place in the upper Great Lakes, an awareness facilitated by the travels of the voyageurs between Sault Ste Marie and Red River and beyond.

I found that government records pertaining to the preparation for and the negotiation of the Robinson Treaties also affirmed the existence of the Métis as an Aboriginal People by the eve of the treaty and acknowledged that their concerns had to be addressed. For instance, the summer before the Mica Bay raid, Canada sent Captain Thomas G. Anderson and Alexander Vidal to Lake Superior with instructions to gather information on the region, as a prelude to treaty negotiations. These two men reported back that the "native population" of the upper Great Lakes included "half-breeds" who were closely related to the Indian bands at Sault Ste Marie, Michipicoten, Pic River, and Fort William. Vidal and Anderson thought that the close association of the "Indians" and "half-breeds" would make it hard to compensate one and not the other.[16] In other words, the Métis had a well-developed self-consciousness and notions about their rights. It was a few months after Vidal and Anderson's visit that the Mica Bay affair took place. Mactavish and William Benjamin Robinson, who negotiated the treaties bearing his family name, indicated that the Métis sent very influential representatives to the treaty talks. In all of these respects, the events of 1849–50 leading up to the Robinson Treaties foreshadowed the events that would take place twenty years later at Red River.


A FORTUNATE EXCLUSION FROM COURT

Just over a month after I sent my final report to Ms Teillet, the trial commenced in the Court of Ontario (Provincial Division) in Sault Ste Marie. At the stately old courthouse, Justice C. Vaillancourt, who was attired in scarlet robes, presided in an oak-panelled courtroom that had been restored to its nineteenth-century splendour. A very large official provincial seal adorned the wall behind him.[17] Lawyers outfitted in their black and white robes and Métis elders decked out in their colourful assumption sashes faced him in the front rows. Behind them, the room was filled with other members of the local Métis and First Nations communities. A few reporters also were present. The imposing setting, the opening legal rituals, and those who had come to bear witness reminded me of the ways in which Aboriginal people used elaborate calumet and various gift-giving ceremonies to underscore the solemnity of public proceedings that aimed to facilitate the peaceful settlement of differences and restore order. My chance to be a quiet observer and reflect on the unfolding trial was cut short, however, when one of the two lawyers representing the Crown, Elizabeth Christie, requested that Justice Vaillancourt bar witnesses from attending until after they had been called to testify. He agreed. That meant that I was forced to leave temporarily because Ms Teillet, following in the tradition established by the *Delgamuukw* trial, was leading off the Powleys' defence with testimony from local Métis elders.

Although I was initially frustrated by Ms Christie's successful motion, it proved to be very advantageous for me as an expert. When I left the courtroom, Ms Teillet suggested that I go down to the local library and review my report. She gave me her cell phone and said she would call when the elders had nearly finished their testimony. With her cell phone in hand, I headed off to the Sault Ste Marie public library, which is beautifully situated beside the St Lawrence Seaway. I discovered to my further delight that the library had an excellent archive section that contained documentary records pertaining to the surrounding region, many of which had been unavailable to me in Vancouver. Particularly useful were early maps of the city and surrounding area. I pored over these maps and other records while an endless procession of towering Great Lakes cargo ships floated by a few hundred feet from the archive windows. While I was at work in this idyllic setting, Ms Teillet called to ask me if I would be willing to provide some general background information about Native history and the fur trade in eastern Canada during my evidence-in-chief even though I had not been asked to address these subjects in my report. The reason was that issues had arisen unexpectedly as a result of the unfolding testimony of the Métis elders. This was not an unusual development, as trials often take lawyers and experts in directions they had not anticipated. Considering that the topics she wanted me to tackle were ones I normally dealt with in my Native history survey course at the University of British Columbia, I agreed.[18] Over dinner after my third day in the Sault Ste Marie archives, Ms Teillet reported that the elders had nearly finished their testimony and that it would likely be my turn to appear in court late in the afternoon the following day. She guessed correctly; I was called to the witness stand the next day after the court's two o'clock break.[19]

During the day and a half of my evidence-in-chief, Ms Teillet asked me a series of questions that gave me the opportunity to elaborate upon key aspects of my research without simply repeating my report. Trial judges generally dislike the latter practice. One important issue that she asked me to address was the timing of the establishment of effective European control in the Sault Ste Marie area. I suggested that it could not have been before the merger of the Hudson's Bay Company and the North West Company in 1821, which the British parliament had encouraged, if not forced, to bring order to the lands beyond the settler colonies of British North America. It was also likely that it did not happen after 1850, given the purposes of the Robinson Treaties. Ms Teillet concluded my evidence-in-chief with two key questions. In the first she asked: "Dr Ray, did the Métis as you understand at that time [ca. 1850], did they think they were Native people?" I replied in part: "Yes, they believed they had a Native right and interestingly, the Vidal and Anderson Report agrees that they had a claim, that they were here, they were people that were rooted in the land that had a right. Yes. I think they definitely did." In her following question,

Fig. 27: Métis fishermen at Sault Ste Marie in the late nineteenth century.

Ms Teillet enquired: "One more question, Dr Ray, can you say that hunting is integral to the Métis society here?" In reply, I re-emphasized one of the major points of my report by saying that "certainly at that time it was an integral part of it and I would say that … the trouble I have with a question like that is it segments the economy which is a … which is a distortion of the reality. The economy was based on the right to live off the land, whether it meant hunting, fishing, trapping and the relative importance of any one of those activities in any year over a period of years would depend on the game cycles, economic conditions and so on, so that … to me the hunting right is bundled into those rights"[20] (fig. 27).

## "PROFESSOR DECLARES A PEOPLE!"

What I did not know when I answered Ms Teillet's questions was that a reporter from *The Sault Star* was present that Friday afternoon. The next morning, when I headed off for coffee a copy of the newspaper was laying under my hotel room door. The banner headline proclaimed: "UBC Professor declares the Métis a People!" My first thought was that this headline would make my forthcoming cross-examination very unpleasant. The Ontario government had long opposed the recognition of Métis rights. Indeed, I subsequently received what Ms Teillet described as a "vicious cross-examination." When we resumed the following Monday, Bruce Long, the crown counsel, began in a low-key fashion by picking around the edges of the issues that were of major concern to him. After these preliminaries, he zeroed in on the central issue of hunting game – moose in particular. He asked a series of questions for the purpose of having me restate that there had been no moose or significant caribou hunting in the area for several decades before the negotiation of the Robinson Treaties and to suggest that game hunting was not an integral Métis cultural practice in the Sault Ste Marie area. The following exchange is typical of several encounters we had regarding these interrelated issues:

Q  [Mr Long]. So returning to an earlier point, you said by 1850 the commercial fishing at the lakes was more important because the game, large game I took it to mean, had become so limited, so I take it from that, Sir, that there was at least one generation who grew up without hunting big game except bears.

A  [Me]. Well, I think if you'll excuse me, it's a ... to my mind it's a nonsense question in the sense that ...

Q  I'm sorry?

A  To me, in terms of native economies, the question doesn't make a lot of sense because today we tend to think of fishing, hunting, and not just hunting, you know game hunting versus goose hunting, we ... we break up all these economic activities into separate activities, but the Native people didn't look at it that way and the Metis didn't look at it that way. Hunting was part of living off the land as was fishing, collecting and various other things and the relative importance of these activities would shift over time, but it's ... it's a livelihood off the land issue and at this point in time hunting was, at least for commercial purposes and probably for subsistence purposes, wasn't as important as it might have been, but the other point I made in my report, the other reason why commercial fishing increasingly is important is the markets for it are increasing too. South of the border. It's increasingly profitable to be a fisherman.

Q  Maybe ... maybe you could help me Dr Ray, what was my ... what was my original question?

A   You were asking me about moose hunting.

Q   Alright. Alright, I think I was suggesting to you that given the times that you've described ...

A   Right.

Q   ... and the scarcity of large game, that there was at least a generation who grew up without hunting big game.

A   No, I wouldn't ... I would ... I don't think that's true there's a whole generation. As I said, there's ... you said, I don't know why we got on this track cause I mentioned that clearly bear hunting is going on, so to me the operative point is this is game hunting. I don't ... to be species specific I think is to put an unrealistic limit on our understanding of the Native economy, the way it worked.

Q   I'm not asking about the Native economy. I'm asking more about the situation as far as the availability of game.

A   No, but you said a generation had passed without game hunting and I'm saying it did not.

Q   No, Sir, I'm sorry, if I did I mis-spoke myself. I apologize. I'm simply asking you if it is not correct, given the numbers, and the situations that you've described, that at least a generation grew up without hunting big game, including moose.

A   No, and I'd said no. They hunted big game bear, but moose and caribou do not seem to have been prominent.

Q   Do not seem to ...

A   Have been prominent in hunting.

Q   Do you have any records of them hunting moose in that forty year period that you described?

A   No. But ... no, I don't, but I'm saying, but ... you're ... you're equating they don't have moose, therefore game hunting doesn't occur and what I'm resisting is that implication. That is not what I said. Game hunting occurs but by the nature of the cycle at this time it seems to be more focused on bear, but I will not accept the proposition that a whole generation went by without game hunting.[21]

In several exchanges of this sort, Mr Long focused on the specific issue of the absence of moose hunting in the decade before the Robinson Treaties for the purpose of implying that game hunting had ceased to be a defining characteristic of local Métis when effective British sovereignty was established. In reply, I countered by stressing that earning a livelihood off the land was the defining characteristic. To survive, Aboriginal people had to be opportunistic and flexible in their responses to economic and wildlife cycles. Downturns in moose and caribou populations meant that neither the Métis nor the Ojibwa relied on these animals immediately before or after the negotiation of the Robinson Treaties. It did not mean, however, that hunting was not important to them.

### A LANDMARK DECISION

After seventeen days of trial spread over a six-month period (April–September) in 1998, Justice Vaillancourt rendered a landmark decision on 26 February 1999, in which he acquitted the defendants. The evidence presented at trial had convinced him that a Métis community existed at Sault Ste Marie well before 1815. This predated the establishment of effective European control locally, an event Justice Vaillancourt decided occurred sometime between 1815 and 1850. Regarding the hotly contested issue of defining Métis hunting rights, the judge concluded: "The evidence indicated that the Ojibway and Métis had always hunted and that this activity was a integral part of their culture prior to the intervention of European control." He went on to flatly reject the Crown counsel's approach to the issue:

> Mr Long stressed the fact that moose were scarce if not non-existent between 1820 and 1880 thereby creating a scenario whereby at the time of effective control of the area passing from the aboriginal People moose hunting would not be a part of their culture. I find that to take this approach one must suspend common sense. I take the position that just because a particular species is in short supply or temporarily in a state of great depletion that does not eliminate that particular animal as a hunted species by the aboriginal group.[22]

Justice Vaillancourt added that "the right to hunt is not one that is game specific. The evidence makes it clear that prior to the 1820s that moose would have been part of the Ojibway and Métis diet. In fact, it would appear that the aboriginal societies in the Sault Ste Marie area were opportunistic when it came to hunting animals for their food or otherwise."²³

The defendants and their community were overjoyed with the Justice Vaillancourt's ruling. Ms Teillet grabbed the judgment from the fax machine as soon as it arrived in her Toronto office, read it quickly, and headed downtown to the provincial parliament building where the House was in session. She was eager to get Premier Mike Harris's reaction. So were members of the media, whom she had tipped off. The premier, an opponent of Métis hunting rights, was caught off-guard. In the heat of the moment, he announced on the steps of the legislature that the province would appeal Justice Vaillancourt's ruling all the way to the Supreme Court if necessary. This proved to be the case. The province challenged Justice Vaillancourt's conclusions about the nature of the Métis economy, particularly the assertion that hunting game was an integral cultural practice, and it argued that the evidence did not support the notion that the Métis community of Sault Ste Marie survived to the present day.

The province lost all its appeals.²⁴ Along the way, the Court of Appeal for Ontario took the opportunity to chastise the Ontario government, citing the effects of historical discrimination of federal and provincial governments toward the Métis as evidence that their community had been extinguished:

Not only was the trial judge entitled to take into account the evidence of the severe prejudice and discrimination inflicted upon the Métis: it is my view that it would have been quite wrong for him to ignore it. The constitutional recognition of the existence of the Métis as one of the Aboriginal Peoples of Canada may not be capable of redressing all the wrongs of the past, but it cannot be that when interpreting the constitution, a court should ignore those wrongs. As noted by Dickson C.J. and La Forest J. in *Sparrow*, at 1103, "[f]or many years, the rights of the Indians to their aboriginal lands – certainly as legal rights – were virtually ignored." It is undeniable that past practices, including those of government, have weakened the identity of Aboriginal peoples by suppressing languages, cultures and visibility. It would be completely contrary to the spirit of s. 35 to ignore these historical facts when interpreting the constitutional guarantee. For this reason, the continuity test should be applied with sufficient flexibility to take into account the vulnerability and historic disadvantage of the Métis. The trial judge was entitled to conclude that the Sault Ste. Marie Métis community had suffered as a result of what was at best governmental indifference, and to take the historically disadvantaged situation of the Métis into account when assessing the continuity of their community.[25]

The Court of Appeal's determination was of central importance to future considerations of the identity and extent of Métis communities.

# CHAPTER 6

# DEFINING MÉTIS COMMUNITIES

# AND CUSTOMS

When I agreed to take part in *Powley*, I had no idea that it would lead me to reorient my long-term research agenda toward the historical geography of Métis communities and to become involved in a succession of harvesting rights cases in the prairie provinces. This new orientation occurred because of the nature of the landmark *Powley* decision. As we have seen in the previous chapter, the litigation had provided the test case about Métis rights that the Supreme Court had been waiting for since its *Van der Peet* ruling in 1996.[1]

In the *Powley* decision the Court took the opportunity to make several fundamental determinations. It defined a Métis as being someone of mixed ancestry, who self-identifies as Métis and is accepted by a Métis community. It held that Métis rights are communal and are to be determined in reference to the historical customs and practices of specific communities. It defined the latter in sociological-geographical terms as being "a group of Métis with a distinctive collective identity, living together in the same geographical area and sharing a common way of life." The Court added: "We should not be surprised to find that different groups of Métis exhibit their own distinctive traits and traditions. This diversity among groups of Métis may enable us to speak of Métis peoples."[2] This sweeping ruling raised new questions about the extent of the Métis world in the eyes of Canadian law and made the identification and delimitation of Métis communities central features of ongoing harvesting rights litigation.

In the immediate aftermath of *Powley*, the federal government commissioned a series of reports for the purpose of identifying potential historical Métis communities in various parts of the country.[3]

Through the Office of the Federal Interlocutor for Métis and Non-Status Indians, the Department of Indian Affairs and Northern Development provided "post-*Powley* funding" (2003–10) to the Métis National Council (MNC) for a national historical research initiative. In 2003 I agreed to join the MNC research team and, in collaboration with a former student of mine, Dr Kenichi Matsui of Tsukuba University of Japan, I became involved in a multi-year project aimed at identifying and delimiting the spatial economies of historical Métis communities in the Great Lakes and Prairie Provinces. Because our ongoing research was highly relevant to harvesting rights litigation in the latter provinces, I was asked to appear as an expert witness on behalf of Métis defendants in *Regina v. Belhumeur* (2007) in Saskatchewan, *Regina v. Goodon* (2008) in Manitoba, and *Regina v. Jones; Regina v. Hirsekorn* in Alberta (2010).

### WRESTLING WITH THE TERMINOLOGY OF SETTLEMENT

With the *Powley* decision, the Supreme Court had raised a very knotty question. "Community" is a frequently used word with multiple meanings.[4] It can be used geographically as a reference to a particular place or physical settlement. It can also be employed to describe a group of people who have common characteristics and interact regularly. As noted, in *Powley* the Court implied both meanings. This inclusionary interpretation has resulted in a tug-of-war over meaning in post-*Powley* litigation. Provincial governments have sought to limit the spatial extent of Métis rights by equating communities with physical settlements; Métis litigants, on the other hand, have emphasized the socioeconomic interpretation to promote a more expansive determination of their rights.

The historical literature about Métis is not helpful on this issue. The reason is that scholars have used the terms "community" and "settlement" interchangeably. An added problem is that their employment of these terms has been coloured by persistent evolutionary ideas about Métis culture that can be traced back at least as far as the foundational studies of Canadian historian George F.G. Stanley and French historical geographer and sociologist Marcel Giraud. In his landmark work, *The Birth of Western Canada: A History of the Riel Rebellions* (1935),[5] Stanley interpreted the armed clashes of the Métis with the Canadian state in 1869–70 and 1885 as having involved a half-primitive, half-civilized people defending their way of life against the industrializing and expanding Canada. Ten years later in *Le Métis Canadien*, which remains the most comprehensive study of Métis history to date, Giraud most fully articulated the notion that the Métis were a partly "primitive" and partly "civilized" people.[6] Giraud's employment of the term "settlement" reflected the cultural evolutionary model that underpinned his work. For example, when writing about the formation of the Red River Métis at the beginning of the nineteenth century, he observed that some of these "nomad" freemen established the "nucleus of the Pembina settlement" at the fork of the Pembina and Red rivers. He added that this was "one of the Métis centres of population most dominated by prairie ways."[7] In other words, for Giraud settlements were places where the more sedentary or "civilized" aspects of Métis life were manifested in farming activities and the construction of log houses and other structures. In contrast, he referred to locations where Métis assembled for hunting and fishing as "semi-nomad encampments."[8]

Scholars have subsequently decried the evolutionary cast of Stanley's and Giraud's outlook, but they have not revised their approaches accordingly. For example, it has become common to refer to places where nineteenth-century buffalo hunters pursued their prey during the winter as "wintering sites" or "wintering camps." In contrast, places where Métis engaged in agriculture during the summer months are referred to as "settlements" rather than as "summering places," even though most Métis spent the bulk of their time away from their "settlements." This settlement-oriented perspective has also favoured the development of a "homeland" (settlement) *versus* hinterland (hunting-trapping-trading ranges) notion of historic prairie Métis culture. This outlook is ironic, considering that the prairie Métis of the nineteenth century are most famous for having been buffalo hunters. More important, it has adverse implications for Métis litigants because it implies that their historic communities were closely tied to the land in only a small portion of the territories that they exploited on a routine basis.

I first addressed these issues in *Regina v. Belhumeur*. This case concerned Donald Joseph Belhumeur of Regina, Saskatchewan, who had been charged with illegally fishing on Katepwa Lake in the Qu'Appelle Valley, which is less than an hour's drive (90 kilometres) northeast from his home town.[9] Mr Belhumeur's legal defence team included Clem Chartier, QC, who at the time was president of the MNC, and

Michelle Leclair-Harding. On his behalf they put forward an Aboriginal rights defence that was similar to that of the Powleys. In this instance, the defendant's ancestors included buffalo hunters from the old Saskatchewan and Fort Pelly districts of the Hudson's Bay Company. Mr Belhumeur's kinship connections extended throughout most of the southern part of the province and included many families whose ancestors had played major roles in the western Canadian fur trade of the nineteenth century.

For his defence, Mr Chartier and Ms Leclair-Harding asked me to write a report that provided a general overview of the economic geography of the Métis in the Canadian West before 1870, emphasizing their role in the fur trade. They also wanted me to provide detailed information about the central and southern Saskatchewan area. In my brief, I expanded on the ideas that Kenichi Matsui and I were developing about the natures of historic Métis economic communities. Also, I drew upon the data from the HBC archives that we had been collecting in our ongoing MNC project. In my submission of August 2005,[10] I began with an extended discussion of the historiography of the Métis, highlighting the problems associated with the scholarly use of the words "community" and "settlement." I stressed the importance of consistently differentiating between the two.[11] I also pointed out that a local or regional community could include multiple settlements. As I had done in my brief for *Powley*, I emphasized that Métis economies were highly diversified and included a number of spatially extensive activities, such as hunting, fishing, trapping, trading, and transport work. In the prairie region, the latter activity included employment on canoe and York boat brigades and on cart trains. This meant that no settlement was sustained solely by economic activities that took place within its built-up or cleared area. On the contrary, most settlements were heavily reliant on activities that occurred elsewhere.

Although the Hudson's Bay Company had maintained Fort Qu'-Appelle in the Qu'Appelle Valley near Katepwa Lake, no records from this post have survived apart from the reminiscences of trader Isaac Cowie, who was stationed there from 1867 to 1874.[12] The problem with Cowie's memoir is that he did not begin working on it until a quarter-century later, when he moved to Winnipeg in 1901. So, although the memoir contains some useful information about the local economy in the late 1860s and early 1870s, Cowie did not provide the level of detail that litigation requires. Fortunately Fort Qu'Appelle had been

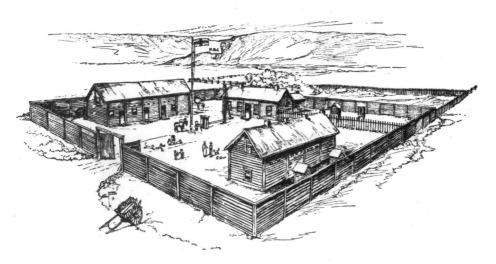

Fig. 28: Fort Qu'Apelle, 1867.

an outpost of Fort Ellice (fig. 28). The latter post had been located farther east near the confluence of the Qu'Appelle and Assiniboine rivers, where it had served as the company's district headquarters for the Swan River District. Consequently, many of Fort Ellice's journals have survived. These records allowed Dr Matsui and me to construct a seasonal cycle of activity for the post for the late 1860s (fig. 29), and we were able to track the movement of the people who were involved. Most of them were Métis. Oliver Flammand and members of his family were among those mentioned most frequently. He served in a range of capacities, including common labourer at the post, camp trader, free trader, hunter, and cart brigade leader. His annual round of activities involved most of present-day Saskatchewan south and southwest of Fort Ellice (fig. 30). Flammand also led a cart brigade to and from Red River.

## WHEN A JUDGE IS INTERESTED IN LOCAL HISTORY AND HERITAGE

The *Belhumeur* trial took place in the historic town of Fort Qu'Appelle in a small courthouse located a few thousand metres from the old HBC fort on the site where Treaty 4 had been signed in 1874. The presiding Saskatchewan Provincial Court Judge, Justice D.I. Morris, was the past president of the Fort Qu'Appelle Historical Society. She clearly

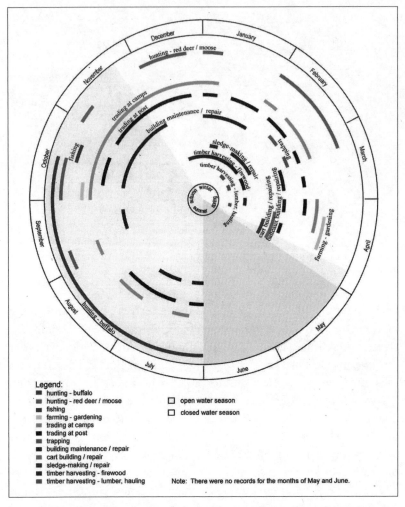

Legend:
- hunting - buffalo
- hunting - red deer / moose
- fishing
- farming - gardening
- trading at camps
- trading at post
- trapping
- building maintenance / repair
- cart building / repair
- sledge-making / repair
- timber harvesting - firewood
- timber harvesting - lumber, hauling

☐ open water season
☐ closed water season

Note: There were no records for the months of May and June.

Fig. 29: Seasonal cycle for Fort Ellice, 1868–69, based on post journal entries.

had a keen interest in local history and was proud of the community's heritage. During the first break in my testimony at trial, she pointed out to me that the popular coffee shop up the street from the court-house was a former HBC store. The museum is located around the corner from the old store, and a portion of the building consists of the last surviving section of the nineteenth-century trading post where Cowie had served.

Following the precedent set in *Delgamuukw*, the defence led off with elders and members of the local Métis community, including the defendant and his relatives. These witnesses talked about their family connections and about the ways they and their ancestors had lived off

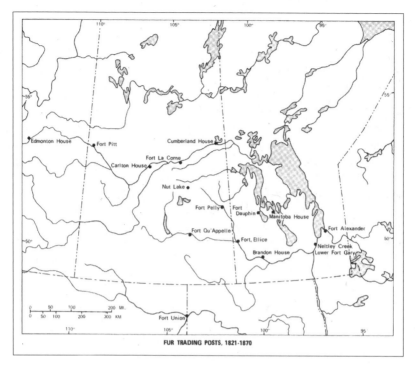

FUR TRADING POSTS, 1821-1870

Fig. 30: Hudson's Bay Company Parkland and Prairie Posts, 1821–71.
Métis rights litigation in the Prairie Provinces led me to revisit the records
of these trading places that I had examined many years earlier for *Indians
in the Fur Trade.*

the land. It was after they had presented their oral histories that I was
called to the stand. Ms Leclair-Harding asked me a series of questions that enabled me to highlight the key findings of my report. These
findings included my discussion of the problems of terminology, the
cultural-evolutionary aspects of scholarship about Métis history, and
my conclusions about how the nature of nineteenth-century Prairie
Métis economies shaped the spatial characteristics of their communities generally and the Qu'Appelle Valley community in particular. I
stressed that HBC data about the movements of the Flammands and
other families made it clear that the Qu'Appelle Valley Métis economy
encompassed most of southern Saskatchewan (fig. 31).

After my experience in *Powley*, I had expected a vigorous cross-
examination to follow my brief evidence-in-chief. I was pleasantly surprised when that did not happen. Apparently one of the reasons that
I was spared the ordeal was that Mitch McAdam, who represented the

Fig. 31: Métis camp near Fort Ellice, 1882.

Fig. 32: Fragment of Old Fort Qu'Appelle. It is part of the local museum.

Crown, was taken off-guard by Ms Leclair-Harding's brevity. Therefore, he had not finished preparing his cross-examination questions. So Mr McAdam asked Justice Morris for a short recess so that he could organize his thoughts. When court resumed, he began by focusing on the problems of the extant historical scholarship about the Métis that I had detailed in my report and evidence-in-chief (fig. 32).

The purpose of his questions was immediately clear. Mr McAdam wanted to make the point that historical interpretations change over time; therefore, there was no reason for the court to place any more weight on my perspective than those of Stanley, Giraud, Gerhard Ens, or the other scholars I had mentioned.[13] I thought this was a smart cross-examination strategy and one that recalled my experience of being qualified as an expert in *Delgamuukw*, when Crown attorneys had argued that experts were not needed because documents were "plain on their face" and the courts were not helped by experts who stated otherwise. While Mr McAdam never expressed this perspective openly, he did not call an historical expert for the Crown even though he introduced historical documents as evidence. In any event, his line of questioning highlighted for me the risks of bringing needed historiographic discussions into the courtroom. After making his point about the relativity of historical interpretations, Mr McAdam's questioning turned to the sources and methods that I had used in my brief. He finished in less than two hours. This was a pleasant surprise. It meant that my entire testimony lasted one day whereas I had been warned that I might have to be on the stand for two or three days.

TESTIMONY OF A MÉTIS FIDDLER AND THE RED RIVER JIG

My shorter-than-expected encounter also gave me the unique opportunity to return to the trial the following day and listen to the testimony of a renowned Métis fiddler Oliver Boulette. He grew up in the small Métis settlement of Manigotagan, Manitoba, which is located on the southeastern shore of Lake Winnipeg. At the time of the trial, Mr Boulette was an executive director of the Manitoba Métis Federation and was spending most of his time in Winnipeg. Mr Chartier and Ms Leclair-Harding called him as a witness to explain and demonstrate the uniqueness of Métis fiddle music. Mr Boulette's appearance served to highlight, sometimes in comical ways, the challenges that courts face as arbiters of aboriginal culture. The *Van der Peet* ruling had forced them to take on this role.

Mr Boulette began his evidence-in-chief with an account how central music had been to him as a child and to all of his Métis relatives. He explained that fiddle music was always a central aspect of celebrations and public gatherings. Ms Leclair-Harding then asked how Métis fiddle music originating from Red River differed from the fiddling styles of other ethnic groups. Mr Boulette replied:

> I'll explain it, is that if you read music formally it almost works out to 16 beats for – for the measure. So you would go one, two, three, four, one, two, three, four, one, two, three, four, up to sixteen, and that would be your first measure, and then the tune would change a bit for the second part and it would be the same thing, but it would almost [always] work out to 16. With Métis music we defy that, we almost defy music, and what we do is we drop off a beat and we may only work out to 15, or we may add one or two grace notes which gives us 16, 17 or 18, and what – what the sound that gives you is it sounds like the fiddle player is playing out of beat, out of time. It defies music. So if you are playing with somebody formally they'll go one, two, three, four, one, two, three, four, and on the even beat they will change the chord, but we will go one, two, three, four, one, two, three, four, one, two, three, four, and when we get to fifteen we will change, and the person that is accompanying with you will be out of time. So how do you overcome that? You have to feel it. (Fig. 33)

He then offered an amusing example of the problems Métis rhythms posed for others:

> I was playing one time for a French dance group which was they're – they're something like River Dance and they're very choreographed and they dance very well but they dance in perfect time, and when they danced to my music they – they couldn't. They got out of time when they got to the 15. And they said, "What's wrong, you're not playing right," and so I explained just what I'm explaining to the Court here today, and they then danced again to my music and they said, "Oh, I know what we

Fig. 33: Former Hudson's Bay Company Store on Broadway St in Fort Qu'Appelle. The judge encouraged me to visit the coffee shop in this building during a break in the trial.

have to do, we have to scuff to – to do that," and Métis people do this all the time without thinking, and what a scuff is, is a hit with your heel that picks up the note. And so Métis dancers, they don't have to think about this, it's in their blood and it's in their heart, so when they dance they – they will pick up that beat if it's less or if it's more. So it's – it's fluid and it's fun to watch people learn it and they kind of get mixed up in doing it, but it's a natural for Métis people and it comes automatic but they don't notice it. So that's the best way that I can explain it. I could maybe demonstrate on the fiddle just a little bit later.[14]

Ms Leclair-Harding then asked Justice Morris if Mr Boulette could demonstrate his discussion by playing his fiddle. The judge promptly replied, "Of course!" This provoked a lengthy objection from Mr McAdam:

Your Honour, I – I'm going to raise to my feet and object at this point. Certainly I – I – I've sat and listened to the testimony this morning from this individual, I haven't objected so far. I realize that he's come a long way to provide information to the Court. I really don't see the relevance of the evidence. The issue before the Court concerns the existence of an Aboriginal right to fish for a Métis individual that lives in Regina, has some ancestral connections to Fort Ellice and other places. It doesn't concern an Aboriginal right with respect to playing the fiddle or Métis music or any of those sorts of things and the Crown certainly isn't going to challenge or dispute that – that those are important cultural aspects of Métis life and – and would qualify as Métis rights under the test laid down by the Supreme Court in the *Powley* case. Of course those are issues that aren't ever going to get litigated by the Court because we'e not going to run into somebody being prosecuted for an offence for playing the Red River Jig or anything like that. I think much of the testimony that this witness has given has been hearsay, it's things that were told to him by other people.

Mr McAdam continued his objection by saying that playing the fiddle in the courtroom raised an issue of decorum, an opinion that recalled Chief Justice McEachern's opposition in *Delgamuukw*, when Gitxsan elders asked to sing traditional songs as evidence. Mr McAdam also expressed the opinion that fiddle playing posed potential problems for any appeal that might arise:

To actually have him play a song for us, this is – this is a courtroom, this is – this is a court of law, we're here to deal with legal issues, it's not a concert. And, quite frankly, the other concern that I have is how does this all appear in the record if this matter goes on appeal. I know that my friend has initially asked the witness to get out his fiddle and show the fiddle to the Court. I doubt very much that she's going to tender it as an exhibit and so how does – how does an appeal court even know what was shown or – or what it looked like. Maybe it's not significant whether an appeal court sees it or not, but if it isn't significant or relevant to an appeal court then it isn't significant or relevant to you. And I think the same thing goes for any song that my friend wants this witness to play. I don't know how that's going to get recorded. It's certainly not going to be able to show up in a transcript.[15]

## A JUDGMENT IS DELIVERED

Justice Morris then asked Ms Leclair-Harding to reply to Mr McAdam's objection. She responded by noting that witnesses already had testified about other aspects of Prairie Métis culture, such as the Michif language. She reiterated that music was a key component that linked settlements and communities together, and emphasized that the distinctiveness of Métis music could not be fully appreciated without hearing it played. Justice Morris, who seemed keen to hear the Red River Jig, overruled Mr McAdam's objection. Regarding the question about how the fiddle could be entered as an exhibit, Justice Morris decided that Mr Boulette should describe his instrument in detail before playing it. This was a sensible solution, considering that no one had provided a photograph of the fiddle or brought a camera to take one.

In accordance with Justice Morris's instructions, Mr Boulette resumed his testimony by giving a detailed description of his fiddle (fig. 34). Being a consummate storyteller, he used this as an opportunity to talk about the history of Métis instrument making and tuning:

By way of description, Métis people also built their own violins. I – I have a violin back home that whatever wood they could use they made these things, and the one that I have is made out of poplar wood. This one here is made out of maple with a – with a spruce top, but the – the Métis would use whatever. You would hear the expression that guitars were made out of cigar boxes. Well, Métis people would – would – would take a knife and carve and make these things as well. So they weren't – they didn't – they didn't have Wal Mart where you could go down the street and purchase these things so they made them and, of course, the strings at that time were catgut, that we have steel now, so they were able to – to – to make these things after they were introduced to their families. The violin is tuned by many different ways and – and people would just tune it the way they felt, but the Red River Jig was one where the top string was tuned to give – to give the music a drone sound, and people would say it was almost like a bagpipe sound. What I would like to play for the Court is the Red River Jig, the tune that I explained, and the A part is this part here ...[16]

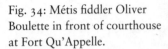

Fig. 34: Métis fiddler Oliver
Boulette in front of courthouse
at Fort Qu'Appelle.

Ms Leclair-Harding ended Mr Boulette's evidence-in-chief by
asking him a series of questions that allowed him to explain to the
court why he chose the Red River Jig and describe some of the other
kinds of songs fiddlers played:

Leclair-Harding: Thank you. The – you've played the Red River Jig
and you've explained a portion of it. In terms of the Red River Jig,
you talk about the fact that it was part of – it was developed in the
Red River. Do you know, was it played anywhere else other than
in Manitoba?

Mr Boulette: It's played all across the Métis homeland. It has no borders. Where there are Métis people there are Métis fiddles and I
think you can find a fiddle, and a lot of people do, in a closet of
an uncle or an aunt or a grandfather would play the Métis fiddle.

Leclair-Harding: In terms of music, you played the – the fiddle and you talked a little bit about songs earlier and I think you indicated to the Court that there was songs for celebrations and stuff. Could you talk a little more about that?

Mr Boulette: Some of the tunes were named after events or situations … another Métis tune is Whiskey Before Breakfast.

Leclair-Harding: How did it get that name?

Mr Boulette: Crooked Stovepipe, a person must have been looking at a stovepipe, and that would be an event one. There were many animal names as well. You would have Caribou Reel, Buckskin Reel, all around the animals in the fur trade. You would also have tunes named after places and I heard the name used Fort Ellice, there's a name named after the forts, places that people were, Lower Fort Gary, Fort Ellice, and they talked very much about also the work that they did. There's – there was Lucky Trapper's Reel, Fur Trader's Reel, so a lot after the fur. So they were named after the events and their way of life that they – they lived.[17]

Mr Boulette's lively and highly entertaining testimony made it clear to me how much I missed when acting as an expert in Aboriginal and treaty rights litigation. I have been barred from hearing the testimony of most of the aboriginal elders who have appeared in cases that I have testified in because usually I appeared after them.

Justice Morris issued her judgment a year after the trial. Regarding the problem of "community," she noted that Chartier and Leclair-Harding had contended that the rights at issue were those of the whole Métis nation and, more particularly, the regional community encompassing the whole parkland/grassland region. In reply, Mr McAdam had argued that this definition was too broad for the purposes of the *Powley* test. He countered with the suggestion that the Court adopt a much narrower definition following the example of Saskatchewan Provincial Court Justice J. Kalenith in *Regina v. Laviolette* concerning the Métis of Green Lake, Saskatchewan.[18] Justice Morris accepted Mr McAdam's argument. She concluded: "I am satisfied that the evidence shows that the 'regional community' is the Qu'Appelle Valley and environs which extend to the City of Regina." Justice Morris also accepted that Mr Belhumeur had ancestral ties to this historical and contemporary community and therefore dismissed the charges against him. The Crown did not appeal. Her decision was in keeping with the

Fig. 35: Author with lawyer Michelle Leclair-Harding
in front of courthouse after testifying in *R. v. Belhumeur*
at Fort Qu'Appelle. The monument in the background
commemorates the negotiation of Treaty 4 in 1874 on
the grounds of the current courthouse.

common practice of the courts to limit the scope of their decisions to
what is essential to deal with the issue before them. Making a determination about whether the historical or contemporary Qu'Appelle
valley community extended beyond Regina was not required in dealing
with the charges against Mr Belhumeur. Therefore, Justice Morris did
not do so. The Crown did not appeal (fig. 35).

# CHAPTER 7

# DEFENDING THE ABORIGINAL
# RIGHT TO HUNT

*Belhumeur* was the first of three Métis harvesting rights cases in the Prairie West in which I appeared as an expert witness. The other two, *Regina v. Goodon* and *Regina v. Jones and Hirsekorn*, revisited many of the same historical issues. In these trials I again worked with the legal team of Jason Madden and Jean Teillet. *Goodon* raised the specific legal question of whether the defendant, William Goodon, a descendant of the early nineteenth-century Métis leader Cuthbert Grant,[1] has an Aboriginal right to hunt in the Turtle Mountains, located fifty kilometres to the south of his home in Brandon, Manitoba (fig. 36). The defendant had been charged with killing a ring-necked duck without a licence in the Turtle Mountains in contravention of the Wildlife Act of Manitoba.[2]

The brief that I presented in *Goodon* was similar to the one I had submitted in *Belhumeur*.[3] However, the thrust of Ms Teillet's line of questioning during my evidence-in-chief had a different emphasis from that of Michelle Leclair-Harding. A key reason was that Crown counsel for Manitoba had in this case retained an historical expert, Clint Evans. Accordingly, Ms Teillet aimed some of her questions at issues Dr Evans had raised in his submission.[4]

One of these issues was the use of primary and secondary sources by academic historians. While primary records are generated by contemporary observers, secondary records are publications based on those sources. In the introduction to his brief, Dr Evans had stated: "My report is based on an analysis of primary source documents, most notably the unpublished archival records of the Hudson's Bay Company. I have adopted this approach partly because I prefer to ground my work in the

Fig. 36: "Running Buffalo," a sketch by Paul Kane. Typically, Métis and First Nations buffalo hunters also took wolves, trapped furs in wooded areas, and hunted other game animals whenever buffalo were scarce locally.

historical record rather than in the writings of other historians and partly because [the] existing literature (secondary sources) about the Métis in the pre-1870 era of the southwestern area of present-day Manitoba is both thin and, in some cases, of dubious quality."[5]

Ms Teillet led me through my sources and a discussion of the historiography concerning the Métis so that I could point out that it is accepted scholarly practice to begin a research project with a review of the relevant academic literature. Likewise, it is common practice to include such surveys in the published results to give readers the context they need in order to determine how theoretical perspectives and methodologies influenced research directions and conclusions. Historiographic context also makes it is easier for the reader (or listener) to determine whether the final results confirm current knowledge or break new ground in terms of the data uncovered and interpretations offered.

After having me make clear that my report drew heavily on both primary and secondary sources, Ms Teillet asked me specifically, "Are the secondary sources on Métis in southern Manitoba voluminous, or thin, or how would you look at them?"[6] I replied that it was a somewhat difficult question to answer for two reasons. On the one hand, it is unclear what territory is being referred to. I said that if one searches for academic books and articles having the words "southern," "Manitoba," and "Métis" in the title, there are few works. On the other hand, if we accept that the Red River and Assiniboine River basins are part of southern Manitoba and include studies of Métis from those places, the literature is vast; scholars have long focused on the Red River Métis.[7] In this way, Ms Teillet's opening evidence-in-chief questions immediately addressed a major claim that Dr Evans had made to justify his approach.

### ISSUES OF VOICE AND SILENCE

Ms Teillet then proceeded to ask me a number of questions concerning voice and silence in primary record. Regarding voice, I had noted in my report that most of the records pertaining to the Métis were written by "outsiders," or non-Métis observers. Métis wrote very few journals or memoirs. Whether outsiders mentioned the Métis depended on the kinds of relationships, if any, they had with them. My key point was that the failure to mention the Métis in a particular record did not necessarily mean they had not been present. I noted that silences in documentary records about the Métis are especially problematic in the late nineteenth and early twentieth centuries for several reasons. The fur trade economy, in which the Métis had played crucial roles, yielded to the wheat economy in the parkland/grassland regions; the Métis faced increasing discrimination as a consequence of the armed conflicts of 1870 and 1885 and the waves of immigration that followed; and the Métis increasingly were pushed into an underground economy by provincial conservation legislation that did not make allowances for their Aboriginal harvesting economy.[8] As I mentioned in my written submission and during my evidence-in-chief, these problems can make it difficult to rely solely on the documentary record to establish that there is continuity between Métis of the past and contemporary Métis communities, as the precedent of *Powley* now requires.

Ms Teillet then asked me a series of questions about the points I had made about the ways in which evolutionary perspectives had coloured the writing of Métis history. Here, we covered the same ground as in the *Belhumeur* trial. She also asked a series of questions about the historical issues raised by the terms "community" and

"settlement." Ms Teillet's objective again was, in part, to address Dr
Evans's report. He had adopted the Crown's perspective of equating
community with settlement and argued that from the mid-nineteenth
century onward, visitors to the Turtle Mountains, most notably George
Dawson and John Palliser, did not observe the physical presence of
any Métis settlements, or remains of former ones, along their trav-
erses.[9] Therefore, Dr Evans argued that these hills lay beyond the
range of any Métis communities by the time Canada assumed control
over the region in the late nineteenth century. To counter this perspective, Ms Teillet devoted many questions to the parts of my report
where I discussed the different types of settlements that the fur trade
generated and the spatially expansive nature of the regional Métis
economies associated with them. In that discussion, I had noted that
some of the larger settlements included segments of Métis and non-
Métis communities; in contrast, only Métis were present at some of the
smaller ones.[10] As in *Belhumeur*, I noted that regional Métis communities included multiple sites.

In the course of my evidence-in-chief, we also spent considerable
time dealing with the issue of "Red River myopia," or the scholarly
practice of viewing the Prairie Métis world from the perspective of the
Red River settlement. In particular, she had me address the notion that
the Turtle Mountains had been the "wintering site" or "camp" of the
Red River Métis before 1860s. In my answers to her questions I noted
that the Turtle Mountains are a large, mostly wooded, low plateau
area (the plateau extends 32 km north-south and 64 km east-west)
that should be thought of as a region rather than as a specific place.
The size of this physical feature or ecological area meant that Métis
hunters could resort to the Turtle Mountains yearly without returning
to the same sites.

## WINNIPEG: WINTERING SITE OF SUMMER COTTAGERS?

While reiterating my evidence-in-chief, I also stressed that it made
little sense to think of the Turtle Mountains as a wintering place unless we thought of Red River and other Métis farming places as "summering places." In making this argument, I was echoing the sentiment
of a local historian from Boissevain, Manitoba, located on the northern
flanks of the hills, who stated that the tendency among academics to
think of the Turtle Mountains as a historical wintering place made as

much sense as today thinking of Winnipeg as the wintering place of summer cottagers. It was especially dubious to think of the hills as a winter site before the 1860s because the summer buffalo hunts also took place in the vicinity. This meant that many Métis from various places in southern Manitoba (the confluence of the Assiniboine and Red River, the lower Assiniboine River, and St Laurent on the southeastern shores of Lake Manitoba) and Pembina, North Dakota, would have spent as much, or more, time every year in the Turtle Mountains and environs as they spent elsewhere. On the basis of this reality, I also recommended in my evidence-in-chief that repeated use of the area should be regarded as a defining characteristic of permanent use and occupation.

After Ms Teillet finished two days of questioning me, the attorneys for the Crown, Elizabeth Thomson and Rod Garson, asked for a day's recess to prepare their cross-examination. They assured the Court that this break would enable them to complete their questions in half a day. Justice Combs agreed. I took advantage of the break to visit the library at Brandon University. I wanted to re-examine the maps and journals of the Hind, Dawson, and Palliser expeditions in anticipation that these accounts would be crucial, given their importance to Dr Evans's conclusion that there were no Métis settlements/communities in the hills when these men made their visits.

As it turned out when the trial resumed, I had misjudged what the thrust of the cross-examination would be; as a consequence, I was over-prepared for Ms Thomson's brief cross-examination, which to everyone's surprise did not last the whole morning. She opened by asking me, "Are you familiar with, sir, a standard reading for undergraduate history courses called *What is History* by E.H. Carr?"[11] She then cited the passage from Carr that stated, "The selection and presentation of historical fact is intimately linked with and is largely inseparable from interpretation," and asked me to comment on it. Clearly, Ms Thomson was following a path similar to Mr McAdam's in *Belhumeur*. Her purpose in citing Carr was to suggest that history was open to multiple interpretations of equal validity. Ms Thomson had two good reasons for advancing this perspective. First, it served to place Dr Evans and me on an equal footing, even though his doctoral degree had not been concerned with any topic in the field of Native history; nor had he ever published in the field. Second, it served to play up Dr Evans's apparent reliance on primary sources pertaining to the Turtle Mountain area, whereas I had consulted secondary sources, especially the work of Gerhard Ens.[12] Ms Thomson's intent was made abundantly clear by a series of follow-up questions about sources. For example, she asked me this leading question: "So primary sources then are really, in effect, in terms of any source, the best source that you have to try and piece together the history?"[13] Besides serving to support Dr Evans's approach, it also was an example of yet another appeal to the notion expressed in *Delgamuukw* that documents are "plain on their face" and that the trial judge is as able as anyone else to interpret them.

## EXTENT OF THE MÉTIS COMMUNITY

It was then Justice Combs's turn to ask few questions. He asked me for my opinion of Ens's book *Homeland to Hinterland*. I replied that I thought that Ens's work was well researched.[14] The judge then closed by turning to a central issue of the trial. As he explained: "Well, I guess, I guess I'm interested in knowing, one of the issues, obviously, that I'm sure has been explained to you, that I need to determine is whether or not there was a Métis community in the Turtle Mountains prior to European control."[15] After eliciting my assessment of the sources that are relevant to that topic, including Ens's monograph, Justice Combs asked whether it would be "fair to conclude that a good portion of, of Manitoba would be part of the Métis community [before 1870]?"[16] I made a lengthy reply to this crucial question:

> I have a pretty good idea in my mind how these different communities overlapped and how – you know, I, I do think that there was a regional [community] – there's the local communities and there's a regional community where they all overlap and it's clear that southern Manitoba – given, given the focus of the Manitoba Métis on the herds that I've just talked about [between Turtle Mountains and the Cheyenne River], it kept bringing them together, not just in the wintertime, because there's been a lot of focus on this winter hunt and we've seem to have almost forgotten the summer hunt but …

I continued:

> So that they're – they're coming together on a – you know, it's

– these communities are coming together at least twice a year for extended periods of time and they're also – again, I, I said I'm not a genealogist but – it's well known in the literature that these – that the families are interconnected and so on. So yes, I see a decided – decidedly a community that would at least run from the, the White Horse Plains, round the Red River and down to the Pembina-St. Joseph area, and then southwest and including what is now a good chunk of what's in the States, in the area between the Missouri River area and the Turtle Mountain area.[17]

After this answer, the court adjourned. Both teams of lawyers subsequently called other historical experts to testify. After Ms Teillet and Mr Madden had called Frank Tough and Gwynneth Jones for the defence, Ms Thomson and Mr Garson called Dr Evans. The evidence and testimony of these experts focused on the period after 1850, especially the post-1870 era. Dr Tough and Ms Jones presented an array of documentary data indicating a Métis regional community that encompassed the Turtle Mountains and which had persisted after 1870 even though the buffalo ranges no longer reached the area. Oral histories and genealogies linked the Métis who live in the region today to the historical community.

Just over three years after I had appeared in Brandon, Justice Combs issued his judgment. He concluded:

Within the Province of Manitoba this historic rights-bearing community includes all of the area within the present boundaries of southern Manitoba from the present day City of Winnipeg and extending south to the United States and northwest to the Province of Saskatchewan including the area of present day Russell, Manitoba. This community also includes the Turtle Mountain area of southwestern Manitoba even though there is no evidence of permanent settlement prior to 1880. I conclude that Turtle Mountain was, throughout much of the nineteenth century, an important part of the large Métis regional community.[18]

Justice Combs also accepted that hunting was an integral aspect of Métis culture. Accordingly, he acquitted Mr Goodon. The province did not appeal.

## CHALLENGING A PROVINCIAL WILDLIFE ACT

The case of *Regina v. Hirsekorn and Jones*[19] yet again questioned the right of Métis to exercise their Aboriginal harvesting rights locally. This case involved two Métis hunters from Medicine Hat, Alberta. Garry Hirsekorn had shot a deer for food near Elkwater, Alberta, approximately 32 kilometres southeast of Medicine Hat in the Cypress Hills portion of Treaty 4 territory. Ron Jones had killed an antelope for food near Suffield, Alberta. This is within Cypress County, approximately 50 kilometres northwest of Medicine Hat in the Treaty 7 area of the province. Both men were hunting for subsistence purposes in accordance with the Métis Nation of Alberta (MNA) Action Plan for community hunts. Their actions, however, violated the Wildlife Act of Alberta.[20] Once again, the Métis defendants, backed by the MNA, asserted Aboriginal harvesting rights. Their claim raised two basic historical questions that the court would have to resolve: Were the lands of this region of Alberta included within the hunting ranges of any historical Métis community? If Métis hunted in the region, did they do so prior to the assertion of effective control in the area either by Britain, as represented by the Hudson's Bay Company or by Canada after 1870? Addressing this question required the court to determine when effective control was achieved (fig. 37).[21]

My involvement in *Hirsekorn and Jones* was very similar to my participation in *Belhumeur* and *Goodon*. I presented a revised and expanded version of the report that I had submitted in those cases and covered all the same issues in evidence-in-chief and cross-examination.[22] Most of the additions I made to my report were based on the ongoing research Keniche Matsui and I had undertaken for the MNC project and on additional work the MNA had commissioned for this trial. However, since the company had not maintained any posts in southern Alberta for an extended period prior to 1870,[23] all the new research had focused on the North Saskatchewan country and the Athabasca–Peace River country to the north. So the key challenge that I faced as an expert for the accused was that the Cypress Hills were far away (over 400 km) from the North Saskatchewan region, and therefore lay well beyond the gaze of most company traders.

Fortunately, the Fort Edmonton journals for the late 1860s and early 1870s contain considerable information about the movements of First Nations, Métis, and others who travelled to and from the post.

Fig. 37: L to R: Author, Jean Teillet, and Jason Madden, Courtroom, Medicine Hat, 9 September 2009.

By this time, Métis people had well-established settlements at the post and nearby at Lac Ste Anne, Big Lake, and Victoria. It is clear from the intensive interactions of Fort Edmonton with these places, as revealed in the extensive post journals, that there existed a multi-settlement regional Métis community (the "Northwestern" Métis), whose buffalo-hunting sphere included the grasslands to the south-southeast as far as the Cypress Hills. Considering that the latter area had become the last refuge of the bison by the late 1860s and 1870s, this was not surprising. The fact that by this time, Métis from the Qu'Appelle Valley and Manitoba were also converging on the region suggested that an amalgamation of the hunting spheres of regional communities was underway.

## REVISITING THE BLACKFOOT, THE MÉTIS, AND THE BUFFALO

The trial was held in the Provincial Court of Alberta courthouse in Medicine Hat, in the old downtown area on the banks of the Bow River. Ms Teillet and Mr Madden again represented the defendants.

Table 5: Fort Edmonton Hinterland, 1871–73*

| Place | Number of Contacts | Purpose Services, trading, missionaries, visiting, timber, firewood, root collecting |
| --- | --- | --- |
| Big Lake/"Pines"/ St Albert | 160 | transportation |
| Victoria | 135 | Services, trading, missionaries, visiting |
| Pigeon Lake | 98 | Fishing, missionaries |
| Lac St Anne | 93 | Fishing, services, trading, visiting, missionaries |
| The Plains | 93 | Bison hunting and trading |
| Fort Carlton | 58 | Brigades and correspondence |
| Rocky Mountain House | 50 | Brigades and correspondence |
| Lesser Slave Lake | 30 | Brigades and correspondence |
| Fort Assiniboine | 24 | Brigades and correspondence and services |
| Lac La Biche | 22 | Brigades and correspondence and services |
| Jasper House | 20 | Brigades and correspondence |
| Fort Pitt | 20 | Brigades and correspondence |
| Red River | 12 | Brigades and correspondence and visits |

*Determined from the Fort Edmonton Post Journals, 1871–73, PAMHBCA B
1 The journal entry for 4 March 1871 indicates that the post's fishers set nets there.

Thomas Rothwell from the office of the provincial Attorney General represented the Crown. He had developed a novel theory of the case with the help of Dr Evans. This was the idea that the Métis had not hunted in the area in question before the early 1870s because it been part of Blackfoot territory. According to Mr Rothwell, the Blackfoot had fiercely defended their territory against all intruders, including the Métis (Table 5).

Ms Teillet again led my evidence-in-chief and covered most of the topics we had dealt with in *Goodon*. In addition, she asked me a lot of questions that addressed Mr Rothwell's theory of the case, in particular his static view of Blackfoot history and his notion that this First

Nation had exclusively used and occupied its traditional territory. To address these ideas, Ms Teillet asked me about themes that had been central to *Indians in the Fur Trade*, particularly the subjects of trade, warfare, and migration in the plains region after European contact. For example, she asked, "Can you describe whether these people are all friendly or whether they're all at war?"[24] In a lengthy reply, I noted that there was an ebb and flow in intertribal relations with alternating periods of peace and war. Citing information that Isaac Cowie had provided in his memoir,[25] I noted that Blackfoot relationships with the Hudson's Bay Company, the Cree, and Métis varied regionally in the early 1870s. The Blackfoot were hostile toward the company and its trading partners in Saskatchewan; by contrast, in North Saskatchewan River country they had more peaceful relationships.[26] Cowie had explained that the reason for the difference was that First Nations and Métis from Saskatchewan, who obtained their arms at Fort Carlton and company posts in the Swan River district, had been encroaching on Blackfoot territory in pursuit of the dwindling buffalo herds. The Blackfoot resented this incursion. Along the North Saskatchewan River, members of this First Nations and their allies traded at Rocky Mountain House and Fort Edmonton. The Blackfoot had also intermarried with some Métis families from this area, such as the Birds and the Munros.

In my report, evidence-in-chief, and re-examination, I also noted that groups sometimes negotiated rights of access to their neighbours' territories. As an example, I cited HBC trader Anthony Henday, who was on a trading expedition in 1755 from York Factory on the western shores of Hudson Bay to Blackfoot territory. Henday reported that the Blackfoot allowed his Cree travelling or trading companions to hunt for their food on Blackfoot territory, but they were barred from trapping furs.[27] This Blackfoot practice of allowing outsiders access to their traditional territories for trading purposes, which was common to other First Nations, continued throughout the post-contact era. This permission also allowed the visitors to sustain themselves by harvesting for subsistence purposes. Marriage alliances were another way of gaining access to the resources of a neighbour's territory. On this basis, some Métis, such as the Munro and Bird families, gained these rights.[28]

In reply to a series of Ms Teillet's questions, I discussed in detail how the progressive depletion of the bison herds meant that by the late 1860s and 1870s the North Saskatchewan Métis hunters no longer

Fig. 38: Fort Edmonton, 1871. Red River Cart and York Boat in the foreground. In the Prairie region, work in the transport sector associated with cart and boat brigades was important for Métis communities.

could reliably hunt for buffalo locally. The Fort Edmonton records indicated that in the 1820s they had been able to do so on the Stoney Plains west of the fort and in the vicinity of the Vermilion River to the east.[29] Afterward, they were forced to shift their focus ever farther afield to the south and southeast. I mentioned that the problem with the Fort Edmonton journals for the 1860s and 1870s is that they were not very specific about precisely where buffalo hunting took place. Particularly troublesome was that the meaning of journal references to "the plains" shifted over time.[30] In the 1820s, it referred mostly to the Stoney Plains to the west of the fort, but by the 1860s, the plains clearly were seven or more days away to the south-southeast. One specific reference mentioned that the hunters were "on the outside of the Hand Hills."[31] I concluded that this would have placed them in the vicinity of the lower Red Deer River near its confluence with the Bow River (fig. 38).[32]

Not surprisingly, our discourse focused on "wintering sites" in the plains region because the Cypress Hills were one of them. Ms Teillet and I also talked at length about the range of Métis free traders who usually operated at these places. To address this question, I revisited

Cowie's memoir. In company with Saskatchewan Métis and their Assiniboine and Cree allies, Cowie camped during the winter of 1867–68 in the Big Sandy Hills, which are not far from the Hand Hills, and he spent the winter of 1872–73 in the eastern Cypress Hills. He mentioned that there were Métis free traders in the area and Blackfoot lurking nearby. We also discussed the fact that during the nineteenth century the Cypress Hills were not the exclusive domain of Blackfoot and their allies. As I had noted in *Indians in the Fur Trade*, the eastern portion of the territory lay within the range of the Assiniboine and their allies. Cowie reported that his Cree informants said that as long as they could remember, the hills, called "Me-nach-tah-kak" in Cree, had been "neutral territory" because no tribe had managed to gain control of them.[33]

After Ms Teillet had finished her evidence-in-chief, the court took a brief recess. During that time the serious, but good-natured, Mr Rothwell asked me if I would be willing to autograph his copy of *Indians in the Fur Trade*. He said he feared that after he had finished cross-examining me I might not want to do so. I assured him I doubted that would be the case, and I agreed to his request.

Mr Rothwell began his cross-examination by revisiting the issue of sources. Along the way, he asked the seemingly inevitable question: "Are primary sources preferred?" He returned to this topic from time to time to note the primary sources that I had not used. Parts of his cross-examination reminded me of my experience in *Delgamuukw*, when the Crown lawyers who were questioning me introduced documents they clearly did not understand. In *Jones* and *Hirsekorn* the same thing happened when Mr Rothwell challenged me about my failure to use the 1870 Canadian manuscript census. He also wanted to use this census return to suggest that there was no Métis community at Rocky Mountain House. His tactic led to a lengthy and at times amusing encounter. It also demonstrated the common evidence-in-chief strategy, which I had experienced at length in *Delgamuukw*, of using the questions to introduce evidence that the opposing trial lawyer wants to put on the record and catch the expert witness off-guard in the process. Mr Rothwell began by introducing the census record:

Mr Rothwell: So, Dr Ray, this [census document] is a – if you unfold it here, is a ... from January 1st, 1870 ... census.

A. Ray: Right.

Mr Rothwell: And you'll see at the top, it says, "Saskatchewan District" there?

A. Ray: Right.

Mr Rothwell: And if you'll look at the – what's it – attached with it is a typewritten version. This is from the Genaille [Glenbow] Archives.

A. Ray: Right.

Mr Rothwell: And so if you look at the top, you can see that it lists French half-breeds, and English half-breeds, and whites?

A. Ray: Right.[34]

He then turned his attention to the information that the census contained about Métis communities in central Alberta, drawing attention to the fact that no Métis were enumerated for Rocky Mountain House:[35]

Mr Rothwell: And you can see that when you look at the communities on here, that for St. Albert, it shows a significant number of French half-breeds.

A. Ray: Mm-hm.

Mr Rothwell: Almost a thousand half-breeds there in 1872.

A. Ray: Right.

Mr Rothwell: But, if you look at Rocky Mountain House, it doesn't show any half-breeds being there.

While he had been introducing his document and making these points, I was actually studying the text itself. I quickly noticed a number of peculiarities. I began to raise them in my replies and soon realized that Mr Rothwell did not understand the document and knew nothing about its context. This gave me the opportunity to make it clear that this record was not "plain on its face":

A. Ray: But, what – there is something odd about that though. Rocky Mountain House doesn't identify any ethnic backgrounds. It just gives a lump sum figure on the right-hand column. It doesn't identify whites, it doesn't identify English half-breeds, French half-breeds. It doesn't identify any Native groups either. So, they haven't differentiated. Do you know … do you know why that is?

Mr Rothwell: No, I don't. I –

A. Ray: – well, you presented – you presented the document, so I – I thought you understood it. Do you – do you know were all these – this has a date of January 1st at the bottom. Were all these censuses done at the same time of the year?

Mr Rothwell: I – I don't know that, Dr Ray. The – the point I'm making is, is that you agree with me that this is a census, and it provides some – some information, right?

A. Ray: But what you've given me, you've given me information, but you don't know what it means, and I don't know what it means, since I don't know the context. I don't know who took this census, I don't know what questions they asked, I – to me, it's useless –

Mr Rothwell: But, as a –

A. Ray: – without a context.

Mr Rothwell: – as a historian, Dr Ray, if you're trying to determine use and occupation of habitation sites, if you looked at this census material, would you – would you not look at other dates, or would this not cause you to make inquiries, to try and determine why they're not set out?

Ray: You're asking me why I didn't analyse the information on this record that you just gave me? I'm – I'm – I'm a little bit confused as to where this is going.[36]

At this point Mr Rothwell attempted to shift the discussion away from the shortcomings of the census document to one aimed at faulting me for not having used it. I resisted his effort:

Mr Rothwell: You never looked at this document, did you, sir?

A. Ray: No. And obviously if I was going to look at this document, I'd have to know a lot more about how it was made, to use it.

Mr Rothwell: Would you agree with me that looking at census records from the period 1871, 1872, for this region, might help answer the question?

A. Ray: … it also would tell me, I – I – I – I can't help looking at amazement at Lesser Slave Lake. It would tell me also that if I was going to try to use these – these records, they're – they're more problematic than the HBC records, because look at Lesser Slave Lake. You know there's a big Metis population there.[37] They're not – they're not showing. There's something really weird about this census.

Mr Rothwell: And didn't you tell us when documents are weird, or something's out of the ordinary, that would cause a historian to say, Well, they're not recording the Metis there. I wonder why that is.

A. Ray: That – well, I did – I did – we did talk a bit about [it]. We could – I don't know if you want to get into the under-representation of Metis and records, and often why that can occur. But, I – I – well, anyway, to me, this – this – this does raise lots of questions, and I suspect when I go back to Vancouver, I'm – I'm very – actually very interested in this record now, as to – as to why it's not representing people who are there. Anyway ...

Mr Rothwell: So, you'd agree with me that it would be useful to look at these kinds of records?

A. Ray: Yes.

Mr Rothwell: Okay. Thank you, Dr Ray.

Mr Rothwell clearly wanted to break off our exchange at this point, but I wanted to continue highlighting the problems of the record he was trying to introduce:

A. Ray: And I didn't think you'd agree with me. That's why I also need to know the context of them, because otherwise we can't use them. But, what is this – there is a memorandum on the bottom. Let's see if – just having a quick look at that. See, the Stony's[38] not included above as they trade more or less with Touchwood Hills, Swan River District. Well, the – given this – this numeration of French Metis population where you can't – am I allowed to ruminate on these a little bit, since I just – they've just been presented, or are we going to move on?

Mr Rothwell: Well, perhaps some of that might be better in redirect, Dr Ray.

A. Ray: Okay. Okay.

Mr Rothwell: But, you would agree with me that this is like a gap, right? That this census presents a gap showing that, you know, for some reason, whether it's right or wrong, it would cause a historian to want to investigate further.

A. Ray: Yes. And for the 1870s period, yes. Certainly that census needs investigation.

Mr Rothwell: [I] Propose to mark it as an exhibit.

At this point in our exchange, Ms Teillet and the Justice Fisher intervened:

Ms Teillet: I – I cannot agree to that. Dr Ray's never seen it before. He said he's never looked at it. He would – it's – he said that he – it's not useful to him. I see no reason – a possible use for this document, through this witness.

The Court: Mr Rothwell?

Mr Rothwell: Well, the document's not being tendered to establish whether there is Metis or not. It's – it's being put in, Dr Ray said that now he thinks it would be interesting, and it does warrant further investigation, and he's quite interested in it, and that it does cause a historian to ask questions. And it's relevant to his report where he says there is Metis at these communities, and here is a census report from the period of time in question. He said he didn't look at it, and that's fair. I didn't expect him to say that.

Justice Fisher: But, I – I guess the problem I have with it …

Mr Rothwell: … is, number one, where does it come from?

Ms Teillet: Mm-hm.

Justice Fisher: Who made it, and does it really give us a – an indication of – of a true census at that time of the year? I – I mean through Dr Ray, I – I think it is problematic in the fact that he cannot speak to it, because he –

Ms Teillet: Mm-hm.

Justice Fisher: – he does not know where it came from, he – he basically does not understand it, I – I do not think.

A. Ray: Well, I – I don't understand the gaps in it.

Justice Fisher: Right. So, I have some difficulty with it, Mr Rothwell, putting it in through Dr Ray.

Mr Rothwell: All right. Your Honour, I'll – that's fine. I don't need to mark it as an exhibit.

Justice Fisher: All right.[39]

So, in the end Mr Rothwell withdrew the census.

### DEBATING ISSUES OF UNCERTAINTY

In addition to battling over the 1870 census records, we also had an exchange about the fact that I had not used the HBC records for Rocky Mountain House or Chesterfield House. I explained that Dr Matsui and I had looked at the surviving post journals from both establishments, but found that the Rocky Mountain House records yielded little of the detailed information we were looking for, while those for the short-lived Chesterfield House post barely spanned the two trading years of 1800–02 and 1822–23. In this instance, Mr Rothwell was not really interested in why we had not used data from Chesterfield House. He wanted to talk about why fur traders had failed twice in their efforts to establish a permanent post in Blackfoot territory. For him, this failure constituted proof that the Blackfoot had blocked all intruders from their territory.

To establish this point, Mr Rothwell began his questions about Chesterfield House with this proposition: "So, you would agree with me there's no fur trading posts in Southern Alberta between the 1830s and the mid 1870s? Is that fair?" After I agreed with him, he asked another leading question: "But if we go back to 1800, Dr Ray, isn't it true that three companies did try and establish posts where the Red Deer [River] flows into the South Sasktachewan [River]?" He then asked: "Why did they fail?"[40] I replied: "Well, there were a lot of reasons. First of all, they – they were resisted by the – the Native people of the area. And it was a lot harsher country than they were anticipating. And there were a whole variety of reasons. So, they basically had to beat a retreat." In the series of exchanges that followed, he dwelt on the hostile reaction the fur traders had received:

Mr Rothwell: And there was actual hostilities, and –
A. Ray: Yes. There was –
Mr Rothwell: – violence –
A. Ray: Yeah.
Mr Rothwell: – visit – visited upon these people, wasn't there, sir?
A. Ray: Yeah. Exactly, there was.[41]

Of course, Chesterfield House dealt with an earlier period. Métis movements in the late 1860s and early 1870s were of much more crucial concern. So, it was inevitable that the issue would arise concerning Métis access to Blackfoot territory on the eve of Canada's acquisition of Rupert's Land in 1870. Through his questions, Mr Rothwell wanted to make the point that it was uncertain from the record precisely where the buffalo herds were and that we could therefore not be certain that Métis buffalo hunting took place in Blackfoot territory. He raised this issue in reference to an entry in the Fort Edmonton journal for 4 July 1871 that I had quoted in my report. The entry stated: "Three Blackfoot came in this evening, in advance for a small party that are coming in ... They reported that peace still exists between the Blackfoot and Cree tribes, and that they, with the St. Albert hunters [Métis], are all camped together in the midst of the buffalo herds." I asked Mr Rothwell what his point was in citing this quotation. He replied, "Well, my point is, sir, we don't know where the buffalo are, do we?" The reason for my query was that this quotation raised issues about the permeability of Blackfoot territory and their complex relationships with the North Saskatchewan Métis. I pursued these topics in the exchanges that followed:

Mr Rothwell: We could guess, but we don't know where they are.
A. Ray: But, what – what – what I found particularly interesting about this – I'm going back to your – our earlier discussions about the impermeability of – or the presumed impermeability of the Blackfoot territory to Metis, et cetera, et cetera. Here, the Metis are said to be camping with the Blackfoot, within the buffalo. Now, either this is an impermeable boundary, or it isn't. And it seems to me that it is not. It's probably one with varying degrees of impermeable – impermeability, depending on the nature of the relations that are existing with these groups at different times. But, you –
Mr Rothwell: But, this could be at the Battle River, couldn't it, Dr Ray?
A. Ray: It could be at the Battle River, it could be – it could be a lot further in the Handhills.
Mr Rothwell: But we don't know, do we?
A. Ray: We don't know. You don't know, I don't know, for sure. But, we do know the Blackfoot and the St. Albert Metis are together.
Mr Rothwell: Yes, we do.
A. Ray: We also know that the Metis from St. Albert go to trade with these people. We also know that these Metis get invited to come to their camps.
Mr Rothwell: But we can't conclusively say if this is in traditional Blackfoot territory, can we?
A. Ray: Well, I would assume that the Blackfoot tended to hang around their traditional territory, but – [42]

After lengthy sparring over various aspects of Métis access to Blackfoot territory in the early 1870s, we concluded:

Mr Rothwell: ... there's a difference between trading with someone in their territory, and settling in their territory, or using resources from their territory?

A Ray: That's right. But, my only point would be that if you're – if you're trading in the territory, and we know they were, you're allowed to harvest – feed yourself when you're there. That's – we've been around that one, too. You don't want me to beat that to death again I'm sure either.

Mr Rothwell: Well, you've been around it with your counsel, but –

A Ray: Okay.

Mr Rothwell: – you may have to go around it with me.

A Ray: Okay. Like those [Métis] car[t] tracks in the prairies, right? They run pretty deep sometimes.

Before wrapping up, we returned to the subject of where Métis hunters from the Fort Edmonton area would have been hunting bison from the late 1850s to the early 1870s. This was to be expected, given that it touched on a core issue of the trial, and it led to some good-natured, if pointed exchanges. Mr Rothwell began by returning to the section of my brief where I had cited James Hector's passage in the Palliser Expedition report where he commented that the post's hunters already had to travel up to 250 miles in search of the herds. As noted earlier, I had concluded that this would put them somewhere between the Bow River and the Cypress Hills. Through a series of questions, Mr Rothwell had me affirm that Hector did not specify the places where the hunts took place.[43] We then turned to the issue of the most probable locations:

Mr Rothwell: So, it doesn't actually say between the lands between the Bow River and the Cypress Hills, does it?

A. Ray: Right.

Mr Rothwell: It says, ... up to 250 miles.

A. Ray: – I was thinking about that last night, so I got out good old Google maps, and I was trying to figure out now what would be within that range? And Medicine Hat I think comes in at 270 miles, as the crow files. And the Handhills, at about 140; something like that, as the crow flies, converting your kilometres to miles. So, he's talking about a huge range here, and I think you've established from your commentary [that] in the 1850s, they're not going to go right into the heart of Blackfoot territory, so they're going to skirt it, heading towards I would assume at least the Assiniboine end of – of the hills would be possible, would you not agree? I mean that would be a possible part of the range, and we know where the Bison are retreating to.

Mr Rothwell: Well, I – I think we're reversing roles here, sir.

A. Ray: Okay. Well, ... –

A. Ray: – sorry about that.

Mr Rothwell: – I'll take it as a compliment, but – so – so, Dr Ray, when you wrote this, it wasn't until last night that you calculated how far 250 miles would take you?

A Ray: I knew it was a good far distance south of the Hudson [Bay Company Post] of – [Fort Edmonton] – I didn't bother to think about it in terms of – of present day place names. But, it doesn't surprise me that it brings it into the range of Medicine Hat – well within the range of Medicine Hat.

Mr Rothwell: Be on the fringe though, right, sir?

A Ray: Yeah. On the fringe, yeah.[44]

Mr Rothwell continued this line of questioning for some time, making the point along the way that a 250-mile arc from Fort Edmonton covered a huge area, which extended eastward as far as old Fort Pitt on the North Saskatchewan River and into southwestern Saskatchewan. When he asked me why they wouldn't have hunted around Fort Pitt in 1870, which was safer, I made a lengthy reply:

A. Ray: Well, Fort Pitt's totally marginal for buffalo hunting by that time. It's become sporadic. I mean, it – I think you'll agree – ...

A. Ray: But, we did have that map of bison migration. You saw that, where – the retreat of the buffalo herds. You wouldn't [...] to me, it would be nonsense to travel 250 miles east of Fort Edmonton into an area equally depleted of game. You wouldn't – you wouldn't go 250 miles west, because you'd be going up the North Saskatchewan. It's not buffalo country. So, you know, like when I think of the possibilities, the possibility, to me, would be – well, they're not going to go east, they're not going to go west. They're going to go some 250 miles, they're going to go south. I take your point, the Blackfoot were defensive of their territory, so I – I'm – I'm not arguing that they're going south – south west into the heart of Blackfoot territory. They're more likely heading south east, on the fringes, towards the eastern parts of the Cypress Hills. That's all I'm arguing. Just given [...] the other references that are out there [...] I agree with you. I can't say there's no doubt that's exactly where they went. I'm telling you, given all the places it's unlikely they went, what are we left with the options for them to go? I mean, –

Mr Rothwell: Right.[45]


As my time on the stand drew to a close, the "250-mile question," became the topic of some light humour. When Mr Rothwell finished his evidence-in-chief, Ms Teillet began to take it up again in her redirect by returning to the Palliser Expedition report. With humour she began:

Ms Teillet: Your Honour knows where we're going ...
Justice Fisher: This is the 250 mile area.
Ms Teillet: That's right.
Justice Fisher: Ms Teillet, go ahead.
Ms Teillet: – I'm here, we're all dug in on this. We might as well dig deeper.[46]

At this point, she had second thoughts and decided not to dig deeper after all. When Ms Teillet and Mr Rothwell were finished, Justice Fisher announced that he had no questions for me. This prompted Ms Teillet to remark: "You don't – ask about the 250 mile[s]." After he said he was not going to, she replied, "Why not; everybody else did?" Justice Fisher answered: "Because everybody else has, but [a] most interesting historical – let us call it a review, which I found extremely interesting." With those remarks, my testimony in *Jones* and *Hirsekorn* was finished. I appreciated Justice Fisher's closing comment and it reflected, for me, the positive atmosphere in the courtroom that he had established from the outset. It was in marked contrast to what I had had to endure in *Delgamuukw*.


A STEP BACKWARD


Sadly, after the trial had concluded, but before Justice Fisher rendered his judgment on 1 December 2010, one of the defendants, Mr Jones, passed away. This meant that the litigation only concerned Mr

Hirsekorn, who had hunted in the Cypress Hills. Justice Fisher ruled against him. He determined that there had not been an historic Métis community in central and southern Alberta before Canada asserted effective authority in the region.[47] To come to this conclusion the judge had to invent some historical facts and revert to pre-*Powley* reasoning. For instance, to conclude that there were no permanent Métis settlements in central and southern Alberta he said these people were only "occasionally" present at Rocky Mountain House, Fort Edmonton, and Lac St Anne (among the twelve locations he mentioned). In fact, from before the 1820s they were continuously present in the former two places, and after the early 1840s had a continuous presence in the latter location following the establishment of a Catholic missionary in 1842. In equating the presence and extent of Métis communities with physical settlements, Justice Fisher reverted to a pre-*Powley* approach that does not take into account spatially extensive economic activities.

Justice Fisher reasoned further that the Métis did not hunt buffalo in southeastern Alberta, even though that was the last refuge for the Canadian herds. He based this conclusion largely on the notion that the region was part of Blackfoot territory and that the latter people fiercely defended their homeland against incursions by all outsiders. In support of this idea, Justice Fisher stated in his "finding of facts" number 63: "The area which later was part of Treaty 7 was called 'terra incognita,' meaning 'earth unknown,' from 1800–1859 by George Simpson, governor of the Hudson's Bay Company.'[48] This loose paraphrasing of the governor failed to take into account the two major qualifications that Simpson had made in his observations that are central to the litigation. What the governor actually wrote was that the area had been: "until lately almost a terra incognita except to the Company's people stationed in it as the warlike character of the powerful plains tribes prevented strangers venturing among them in small parties but now that the Red River people travel in large bodies they do not hesitate to penetrate the plains in any direction."[49] Without these two qualifications Governor Simpson's remark would have suggested major ignorance on his part to the company's long history in the region. As early as 1755, HBC trader Anthony Henday visited the region with a party of Cree and Assiniboine. As was discussed at trial,[50] the Hudson's Bay Company built the short-lived posts of Chesterfield House at the confluence of the Red Deer and South Saskatchewan Rivers (1822–23) and Old Bow Fort (1832–34) on the Bow River. Furthermore, partly on the basis of information obtained from the

Hudson's Bay Company, London-based cartographers Aaron and John Arrowsmith began mapping the region as early as 1795.[51]

Of greater concern is Justice Fisher's conclusion that even if there had been a Métis community whose buffalo hunting range reached to the Cypress Hills before the early 1870s, the practice of nomadic hunting would not have continued to the present because it would have ended with the collapse of the bison herds. This reasoning is a step backward, considering that in *Powley* the Supreme Court of Canada ruled against taking a species-specific approach to Aboriginal harvesting rights. Justice Fisher's ruling does not take into account that First Nations and Métis buffalo hunters also trapped and pursued other animals, particularly in locales such as the Cypress Hills. In any event, if Justice Fisher's logic were applied to the Prairie First Nations relatives of the Métis, they too would be deprived of their aboriginal and treaty "nomadic hunting" rights. Time will tell if the decision will stand. The MNA has filed an appeal asserting that Justice Fisher made errors in law and facts.

# CHAPTER 8

# "TO EDUCATE THE COURT"

I have often reflected on my conversation with lawyer Ken Staroszik that started me on my twenty-five-year journey as an expert witness. I particularly recall his telling me that I would be there to educate the court. He did not mention that it would be a strange classroom or that my "students" would approach and use history very differently. Neither did I anticipate, when I began, that I would become interested in the history of the Aboriginal and treaty rights litigation and eventually feel as much like a participant observer as an expert.

## THE COURTROOM AND THE CLASSROOM

The courtroom is unlike any university classroom and poses unique teaching challenges. There is only one "student" – the judge, who sits at the head of the room, flanked on one side by a "witness-stand" that faces the "jury-box" on the other. Because juries were not involved in any of the trials in which I took part, these boxes were always empty. Legal teams face the judge at tables directly in front of the judge's seat. The problem for me was that the witness stands, which served as my lecterns, never faced my "students." An additional difficulty was that none of the stands could be comfortably occupied for any length of time. On the contrary, all of them seemed to have been intended to torture their occupants, and they quickly became discomforting physical distractions for me.

A further challenge for me in my efforts to engage the presiding judge was the way in which proceedings are conducted. When someone

Fig. 39: Don Monet's sketch of the *Delgamuukw* courtroom.
Usually the witness stand is an isolated feature. Monet did
not sketch the jury box, which was to the left of the lawyers
as they faced Justice McEachern.

asks you a question your natural response is to face him or her in
reply. Given the layout of the courtroom, I found myself looking away
from the judge and toward the lawyers, thereby putting the judge at
the margin of the conversations (fig. 39). Eventually I realized that
responding this way was a bad idea because I had no way of knowing whether the judge was engaged. Beginning with *Powley* I changed
tactics to deal with this problem. Since then I have made a conscious
effort to face judges whenever I answer lawyers' questions. Often I have
had to stand as though I was in front of a lecture theatre to do so. Witness boxes made this difficult, however; I was expected to speak into

a microphone so that the court-recording service could produce a verbatim transcript at the end of each day. Even in the high-tech *Victor Buffalo* courtroom I had to lean way over to be close enough to the microphone to be recorded properly. Justice Teitelbaum's frequent reminders to do so tested my ability to keep to my train of thought.

Most of my "students" were not present by their own choice. Rather, they attended because the case arose within the jurisdiction of their respective courts.[1] The exceptions were Chief Justice McEachern, who was administrative head of the Supreme Court of British Columbia and made case assignments; Justice Teitelbaum, who overruled the plaintiffs' petitions that he recuse himself; and Justice Vaillancourt, who volunteered.[2] In other words, very few of the judges I faced had come to "class" out of a desire for education; rather, they were there to make findings of "facts" that were relevant to settling the dispute brought before them. Nonetheless, many became curious about some, if not all, aspects of the local Aboriginal and fur trade history that was presented to them. My task of engaging the judge-student was probably easier than it was for many other experts because all the judges seemed to have an interest in the history of the fur trade. This did not surprise me, considering that the subject still has romantic appeal to most Canadians. Also, it links the histories of Canadians of European ancestry (the backgrounds of all the judges I faced except one) with those of Aboriginal heritage. In *Delgamuukw*, for example, Justice McEachern clearly related to trader Brown's narrative.

Even though some of the judges I addressed were familiar with aspects of local community history (which seemed to be the case in all the Métis trials), none of them knew much about the complex ethnohistory that was relevant to the cases before them. Also, they were unaware of the diverse natures of the disciplines and methodologies that contributed to understanding that history. Indeed, most ethnohistorians do not have the expertise to deal with the range of evidence judges are expected to master. This lack of familiarity with the subject meant that my fellow experts and I faced formidable challenges as "educators." We had to lead trial judges from secondary school levels of historical knowledge about Canada and about First Nations and Métis defendants and plaintiffs to advanced university graduate understandings in an unreasonably short period of time.

The drawn-out *Delgamuukw* and *Victor Buffalo* trials were not exceptions in this regard. In *Delgamuukw*, for example, experts spent just over eighty trial days[3] of conflicting testimony (excluding the extensive testimony of the elders) attempting to educate Justice McEachern about the pre- and post-contact history of the Gitxsan-Wet'suet'en. I was allocated only four of those days. Along the way, even the most basic concepts had to be explained. For example, ethnoarchaeologists had to define what they meant by the term "hearth."[4] In the even more massive *Victor Buffalo* trial, Justice Teitelbaum received a fifty-eight-day crash course spread over two years on the Native history of the Western Interior of Canada[5] from the time of initial contact (mid- to late seventeenth century) to the present day. The material was presented to him through conflicting testimony supported by reports, rebuttal, and surrebuttal briefs. During the five days that I was present, Justice Teitelbaum seemed to be overwhelmed by the avalanche of historical evidence. For example, he asked me whether the Hudson's Bay Company or the Cree had built the trading posts in the Canadian West. In my thirty-five years of university teaching no student ever asked me a question as basic as this one. The complexities of the *Delgamuukw* and *Victor Buffalo* trials suggest to me that tribunals of judges would have been more appropriate, albeit they would have added substantially to court costs.

### JUDGES BURIED IN DOCUMENTARY EVIDENCE

The practice of burying judges in masses of historical evidence, much of which is of marginal, if any relevance, often further hampered my efforts and those of my fellow experts to teach history in the courtroom. This sandbagging of evidence takes place primarily for two reasons. First, as discussed earlier, opposing counsel are permitted to tender evidence only during the trial phase of litigation. Consequently, they are loath to hold back any ethnohistorical evidence that they suspect might address issues arising at trial or on appeal. The historical "invention" by the courts that occurred in the *Horseman* appeal is an example of why this is an understandable concern. Second, lawyers are not willing to allow their experts, or those of opposing counsel, to follow the standard scholarly practice of merely providing footnote or endnote references to the primary and secondary sources they have consulted. Instead, lawyers expect experts to provide substantial, if not complete, copies of all of the sources they cite. In *Victor Buffalo,* for

Fig. 40: In massive trials such as *Delgamuukw* and *Victor Buffalo*, trial judges are inundated with a wide range of ethnohistorical evidence. Although *Delgamuukw* is commonly remembered as a case in which oral and written histories clashed, in fact, Hudson's Bay Company records reinforced what the elders said about their traditional tenure scheme.

instance, I had to supplement my ninety-seven-page report with three massive appendices that contained whole or partial copies of eighty-eight documents. My surrebuttal briefs included similar appendices. Other experts documented their reports in a comparable manner. In this way, we effectively moved the archives into the Justice Teitelbaum's courtroom, where he had to confront it. The other judges I encountered wrestled with the same problem to varying degrees (fig. 40).

Considering the sheer magnitude of the conflicting and varied evidence, which often was presented orally and in supporting documents at trial, it is not surprising that my judge-students sometimes had difficulty digesting it and therefore made basic fact-finding errors. This happened in the *Delgamuukw* judgment, for instance. Even though I and others had discussed the fur trade at length on the witness stand, Justice McEachern mistakenly stated in his summary findings of fact that "the fur trade in the territory began not earlier than the establishment of the first Hudson's Bay Company posts west of the Rockies ... by Simon Fraser in 1805–06."[6] In fact, Fraser worked for the archrival North West Company, which had prevented the Hudson's Bay Company from expanding west of the Rocky Mountains until after 1821, when the two competing organizations merged.

When summarizing my evidence in his reasons for judgment in *Victor Buffalo*, Justice Teitelbaum stated: "Contact [in the Treaty 6 territory] during this time would involve small groups of Cree travelling to York Factory shortly after the HBC post was founded in 1670."[7] In this instance, he confused the date of the first establishment of a post near the outlet of the Nelson River on the western shores of Hudson Bay with the year that the company had been chartered – 1670. Accordingly, Justice Teitelbaum concluded that the commencement of the post-contact era for the entire plains region was *circa* 1670. In fact, the Hudson's Bay Company did not build a post on the western shores of Hudson Bay until 1694.[8] So, it is highly unlikely that significant contact began in the Treaty 6 area before the late 1690s.[9]

### RHETORIC OF THRUST AND PARRY

Another strange aspect of being an educator in the courts was that I had to work through at least two intermediaries – the lawyers who retained me and those who opposed them. In *Delgamuukw*, there were two teams in opposition: one representing the province and the other the federal government. The other trials involved only one opposing team. I had to conduct my "seminars" in response to these lawyers' questions rather than follow carefully crafted sets of lecture notes. During my evidences-in-chief, the lawyers' questions aimed to elicit responses from me that highlighted aspects of histories that were relevant to, and ideally supported, their theories of the respective cases.[10] Usually, they had developed these theories without previously consulting me. In doing so they were merely following customary practice. Normally experts are not retained until after a statement of claim, and often a revised statement as well, has been filed with the relevant court. Typically these statements are based on a lawyer's hypothesis of the case. During cross-examination, opposing counsel followed with questions that aimed to "test" the evidence. Inevitably they pursued lines of questioning that were intended to catch me off-guard, throw doubt on my credibility, raise issues that undermined my lawyers' propositions, and offer ways of introducing new evidence after trials had commenced.

From these cross-examination practices I learned that it was necessary to develop courtroom survival strategies, especially in drawn-out and highly confrontational trials. *Delgamuukw* taught me that lesson the hard way. Although Mr Adams had forewarned me that I would be given a hard time in this trial, it still came as a rude shock when Mr Willms launched his cross-examination very aggressively. I quickly realized that I had to create breathing room for myself so that I could think about questions that I knew were forthcoming. Sometimes this strategy had consequences that in retrospect are amusing. For example, Mr. Willms's cross-examination strategy involved asking easy questions to give me a false sense of confidence, before following up with tough ones. In one of his "easy questions," he asked me about the Hudson's Bay Company's Made-Beaver standard, which expressed the prices of all trade goods and commodities in terms of the value of a prime winter beaver pelt. Anticipating the tougher question that was going to follow and wanting time to think about it, I gave a long dissertation on this HBC trading custom. Eventually Mr Willms objected to my ongoing answer; Mr Adams then rose and objected to his objection, pointing out that I was merely answering Mr Willms's question. In one of his few interventions, Justice McEachern halted the sparring between these two lawyers to ask me if all the detail that I was providing was really necessary. I reiterated what Mr Adams had said and continued on until the coffee break.

Courtroom practices and strategies of this nature, which are associated with the various dimensions of presenting and testing evidence, had the consequence that, with the exception of *Spade and Wasseykessic*, when I wrote my own evidence-in-chief I was never able to present coherent sets of ethnohistory lectures or conduct a focused "seminar."

Another limitation I had to deal with in my role as an expert witness-educator was that I could not make the points I thought were important unless lawyers asked me opportune questions. Although I sometimes made suggestions to my lawyers about the framing of questions while I prepared for my evidence-in-chief, as I did with Peter Hutchins in *Victor Buffalo* and Jean Teillet in *Goodon*, it was never permissible to do so once cross-examinations began. As I mentioned when discussing *Delgamuukw*, experts are prohibited from talking to their lawyers about the case while they are being cross-examined. I noted that in the *Goodon* trial I had taken advantage of the one-day break between my evidence-in-chief and cross-examination to "bone-up" in the Brandon University archives. I found several points that I wanted to make about the Métis landscape of southern Manitoba as portrayed on maps from the Dawson and Palliser expeditions. Once the trial resumed, however, I was not able to do so because opposing counsel only asked me questions about historian E.H. Carr's philosophy of history and I could not prompt Ms Teillet to ask me the questions in a redirect. So, I left the courtroom very frustrated.

## CONFLICTING APPROACHES TO THE USE OF HISTORY

While learning my way around the courtroom, I also came to appreciate that the judicial and scholarly communities employ history very differently. Scholars do not provide finality to historical interpretation. Rather, it is now widely, if not universally accepted in the academy – as the battle of experts in *Victor Buffalo* showed – that our perceptions of the past are linked to the present because they are socially constructed and connected to current concerns.[11] An analysis of the ethnohistorical literature regarding Aboriginal people in North America makes this clear. Succeeding generations of academics have deployed different theoretical and methodological frameworks, thereby continually altering our understandings of Native history. In this way, scholarship has helped to keep the Aboriginal past alive in the academy and connected to its present interests.

Courts, on the other hand, use history to bury the past rather than to continually revisit it. Judges use their findings of historical "facts" to resolve disputes arising from contested pasts so that opposing parties in litigation can move forward. Given that courts must provide resolutions in a timely fashion, they may have to invent historical "facts" for decision-making purposes, as the the appeal courts did in *Horseman*. Supreme Court of Canada Justice J.J. Binnie acknowledged this reality in 1998, when he responded to criticisms from the academy (including one from me) about the way trial judges, especially Justice McEachern, had used Native history to make their decisions.[12] Justice Binnie pointed out to these critics that "the law sees a finality of interpretation of historical events where finality, according to the professional historian, is not possible. The reality, of course, is that courts are handed disputes that require for their resolution the finding of certain historical facts. The litigating parties cannot await the possibility of a stable academic consensus."[13]

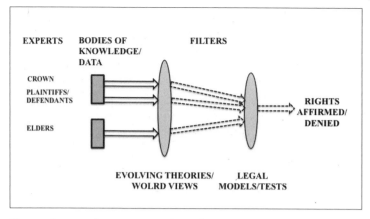

Fig. 41: Interpretive process in claims litigation.

The result is that historical evidence enters claims trials from the dynamic context of the academy into the seemingly less dynamic world of the law where judges are seen to treat the past as belonging to another realm of time, a realm that can be separated from the present and understood on its own terms. While this may be the common operating assumption, in fact, courts imagine pasts (formulate models) that suit their needs. In this way judges' views of history are, in fact, very rooted in the present. Their models have been and are constructed in reference to extant jurisprudence and/or legislation rather than in consideration of past or current academic discourses.

The voices that are privileged also shape the judge-students' perceptions of the past. Until *Delgamuukw*, courts gave little weight to First Nations and Métis viewpoints as expressed in their oral histories. On appeal, the Supreme Court of Canada faulted Justice McEachern for paying them little regard. Since that ruling, judges have had varied responses to oral history evidence. In *Victor Buffalo*, Justice Teitelbaum mostly discounted the lengthy oral histories of the Plains Cree plaintiffs; in the Métis cases, with the exception of Justice Fisher in *Hirsekorn and Jones*, however, the judges took them into account. In these ways, claims litigation is an ongoing exercise that filters Aboriginal pasts through multiple sets of academic and legal models, or lenses, to affirm or deny Aboriginal and tribal rights (fig. 41).

An understanding of the courts' objective in using history helps explain why some judge-students were not interested in debates about the nature of history.[14] Again, Justice Binnie offered a terse explanation of why this should not be a surprise. He said that judges search for – or make – findings of "facts" that address the current relevant case law. This means that those of us who are academics have to play a role in the courtroom that is different from the part we are accustomed to playing. We are not in court to present evidence to "test" legal models, which would be in keeping with scholarly practice: instead, were are asked to present "facts" and interpretations to demonstrate whether claimants' histories meet the legal tests those models require.

## DESTABILIZING THE ACADEMIC CONSENSUS

A key problem, and one that Justice Binnie did not consider in his commentary, is that rights litigation research destabilizes the "academic consensus." In Canada, a key reason for this is that, up until the land title suit of the Nisga'a of British Columbia in *Calder v. Regina* (1973), both the legal system and academic scholarship concerning Aboriginal people largely supported their dispossession and economic marginalization. Particularly important to the colonization process were notions of property originating with English philosophers, most notably John Locke,[15] as well as evolutionary models of cultural development[16] and nation-building historical narratives that glamorized Canada's treatment of its Aboriginal people.[17] Ever since the *Calder* case, which launched the Aboriginal and treaty rights litigation era in Canada and was the first to involve anthropological or ethnohistorical experts,[18] Aboriginal people have repeatedly had to challenge this colonial legacy by bringing new research findings to the court. My fellow expert witness-educators and I, appearing on Native people's behalf, have had the obligation to assist in this. Those who have appeared in opposition on behalf of the Crown usually have reiterated the older narratives, some of which are still worthy of consideration, whereas others are out of date.[19]

In all the trials that I have discussed, the judges had to make choices between older outlooks and claims and research-based revisionist perspectives. The former featured peer-reviewed literature of earlier times and, therefore, presumably still bore the stamp of scholarly approval; the latter, in contrast, highlighted findings that had yet to be subjected to academic peer review. *Delgamuukw* and *Victor Buffalo* were probably the most glaring examples of trials in which

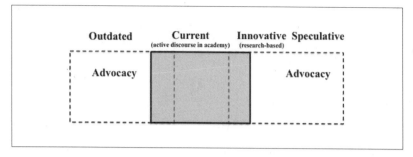

Fig. 42: Judges are presented with an array of interpretive models, ranging from those long-abandoned in the academy, through innovative ones based on new research, to those that are purely speculative. Outright advocacy lies at the extremes.

judges had to make this kind of choice. In the former trial, Justice McEachern favoured the antiquated scholarship partly because he thought it had not been "tainted" by the claims process. What he did not know (none of us did in fact) was that the intellectual framework behind some of the scholarship that was most crucial to the Crown's defence against the Gitxsan-Wet'suet'en had been moulded by U.S. Indian claims research thirty years earlier.

Older scholarship appealed to the courts for an additional reason. It suggested resolutions to the disputes at hand that were less disruptive to the current economic order, which is the legacy of colonialism. In *Delgamuukw*, for example, it suggested that the tenure system described by trader Brown was not Aboriginal in origin, but an invention in response to the arrival of Europeans. In *Victor Buffalo*, traditional scholarship suggested that government negotiators had dealt entirely honourably with the ancestors of the Samson Cree and made it clear to them that they were surrendering their ancestral land to Canada. I noted that prior to Treaty 6 talks Lieutenant-Governor Morris had already misled Native People about the sale of Rupert's Land during Treaty 4 negotiations.

## EDUCATOR AS EXPERT OR ADVOCATE

The range of scholarship and evidence that is available to experts makes it difficult to be clear where the boundary lies between acting as a professional expert-educator and being a mere advocate (fig. 42). At times it takes a lot of effort not to be drawn over the line. I found this was especially so during evidence-in-chief, when I was sometimes asked questions that I had not anticipated, and during cross-examination, when opposing council was pressing hard. At these times I was being asked to reach conclusions "on the fly," and had to make an intentional effort to pause, take a breath, and get my bearings. To achieve the latter I often asked myself if I would subject to peer review the interpretation and supporting evidence that I was about to tender in court. This rough guideline helped me determine whether my response would be that of an academic professional or an advocate. From the outset this approach has led me to publish the significant aspects of my claims research in academic articles and monographs, beginning with *Horseman*.[20]

## EXPERT WITNESS AS EDUCATOR: WHO IS QUALIFIED?

The battles that take place in court over ethnohistorical evidence and interpretive frameworks raise an additional question: who is qualified to teach in the courtroom/classroom? Regarding the issue of qualifications, clearly the expert witness-educators who were involved in the trials I have discussed possessed very disparate credentials. Some of them had gained their knowledge of Native history through active research and publishing agendas. Like me, they were research-based teachers in the academy who brought to the court their in-depth understanding of the history that was relevant to the litigation at hand.[21] This type of expert witness-educator had earned a doctoral degree (the research degree of the academy), held full-time university teaching and research positions, appeared in court only occasionally, and did not depend on claims work for an income. Because of the complex nature of ethnohistory, the domain of these witnesses' expertise was often limited to a few Aboriginal groups, to a small geographical area, or to a narrow range of topics, methodologies, and lines of evidence.

Perhaps the best examples were the experts whose research was based on archaeological, ethnographic (oral interviews), and linguistic fieldwork. Collecting data of this nature is time-consuming and geographically focused, and often depends on the establishment of close working relationships with a First Nations group. Most academics who are engaged in this kind of research are unwilling to appear on behalf of the Crown, either out of loyalty to their informants or because they fear their testimony will jeopardize future research prospects. Ethical issues also arise, leading some of these scholars to refuse to work on the Crown's behalf. Their reluctance occurs because universities and professional associations typically require scholars to make assurances that their research will not harm their subjects. The adversarial nature of the courtroom/classroom raises the question about whether it will be harmful to oppose Aboriginal claimants/defendants.

One unfortunate result of this potential conflict of interest has been that federal and provincial governments have often been unable to retain the most appropriate experts. In particular, the Crown finds it virtually impossible to retain academic experts who have close ties to the Aboriginal communities that are involved in litigation. Lawyers who represent the Crown therefore commonly do not have access to oral history evidence before trial. This leaves them little choice but to treat this line of evidence in an adversarial fashion, as happened in the high-profile *Delgamuukw* and *Victor Buffalo* cases.

The other group of experts who have appeared in the trials I have discussed are those who did not hold full-time university appointments and were not publishing scholars, but made their livelihood primarily from consulting work. Most of them did not have doctoral degrees.[22] Some of these full-time consultants had no prior in-depth familiarity with the history of the First Nation or Métis community that was the subject of the litigation. In other words, they were generalists who moved from case to case. Very few of these roving consultants ever publish their claims research, or subject it to other types of peer review.

The highly varied background of expert witnesses means that the trial judge-students receive their history lessons from "educators" of very uneven credentials. Some have in-depth knowledge of dimensions of local history that was based on long periods of intensive study; others offer perspectives with little depth, based on quick readings of the readily available primary and secondary sources. This unevenness leads to questions about the ability of the judge-students to assess the credentials of their "educators" and evaluate, or weigh, their presentations. As we have seen, the assessments begin when a trial judge decides whether to accept an individual as an expert. Judges base their decision on the presentation of the witness's CV and any challenges from opposing counsel. Occasionally this process can be time-consuming, especially if the field of expertise is unfamiliar to the court. My appearance in *Delgamuukw* is an example. As I noted, when I appeared the field of historical geography had yet to be accepted by the courts as a field of special expertise. Once a judge has given an expert the stamp of approval as an ethnohistorical expert, other courts usually do likewise, even though the litigation before them may involve evidence that is unrelated to their specialty.

It has been my experience that judges give roughly equal weight to the testimony of experts with highly varied backgrounds – people whom the academic community would consider to hold sharply different qualifications. My experience is that judges usually discount the testimony of historical experts only when they blatantly display biases in their interpretation. Also, judges have shown little concern about experts who appear in court routinely but rarely, if ever, subject their court submissions to peer review in any of the usual forums provided by the relevant academic associations.[23] In my opinion, there are three reasons why judges tend to value historical experts roughly equally. The first is the common underlying notion that anyone can be an historian. The second is the lingering notion that documents are mostly "plain on their face."[24] The third is the belief that historians are essentially clerks, whose primary role is bring to the court's attention those documents that historians deem to be relevant.[25] As we have seen, in *Delgamuukw*, Justice McEachern valued me as his guide to the massive HBC archives.

As problematic as the courtroom may be as a classroom, and even though judges approach and use history differently than is my practice, the reality is that, in the end, it is the judges who in their reasons for judgments write the ethnographies that matter most to Aboriginal people. Rights are recognized or denied on the basis of judges' perceptions.

However flawed and inefficient the education process in the courtroom might be, there is no question that Aboriginal people have made major gains since the landmark *Calder* decision of 1973 and the Constitution Act of 1982. Along the way, Aboriginal people have used the courts as places for the public witnessing of their histories and stories even though they feared, as the Gitxsan-Wet'suet'en did, that the courtroom experience could be a painful even humiliating exercise.

One of the most satisfying aspects of the process for me as a participant, however, has been the appreciation that elders and community
members have expressed to me for my willingness to take part. These
expressions, which necessarily came after my testimony, made the very
stressful aspects of being an expert witness-educator so worthwhile
(fig. 43).

Fig. 43: Author being presented with Métis national flag and beadwork
in appreciation for appearing in *R. v. Belhumeur*.

# APPENDIX 1

Delgamuukw Exhibit No. 964: District Reports of Hudson's
Bay Company
Chief Trader William Brown 1823[1]

The Babine Tribe of Indians who inhabit the country North West of
Stuart's Lake, and are considered as belonging to the Establishment of
Fort Kilmaurs, by the best information I have been able to procure
amount to two hundred Married Men, or thusly, and are divided as
follows. The two Villages of Nahtellcuz and Thachy,[2] (which are about
twenty miles asunder, at the former of which our present establishment
[Fort Kilmaurs] is situated) contains twenty four Married Men, twenty
six Married Women, seven young men, fifteen young girls and widows
and twelve Boys. Caspine[3] is the principal Chief of these two Villages.
After him the followers [who] are considered the most respectable
being heads of families and possessors of particular tracks of country,
which they claim an exclusive right to: Oo lad, himself of the village of
Tachy Sawbuck, Squee, Sotuaq, Titeza and Chiliclue. The others are
more or less related to some of these eight and may be considered as
their followers but they have little or no control over them, as every
one as far as I can judge considers himself his own master.

Caspine is a man in his prime, and a tolerable good hunter and
I believe much attached to us, but is too simple and Childish for a
Chief. He is particular for a mean beggarly way of asking for almost
everything he sees and extremely thoughtless and extravagant in his
demands for Debt.

Ool lad is now becoming an old man. Is a tolerable good hunter,
but is in general always naked,[4] either by losing his property at play,
or by making feasts for his deceased Relations.

The Residents of the Village of Nasschick amount to thirty four
Married men but there are a great number of Strangers who generally

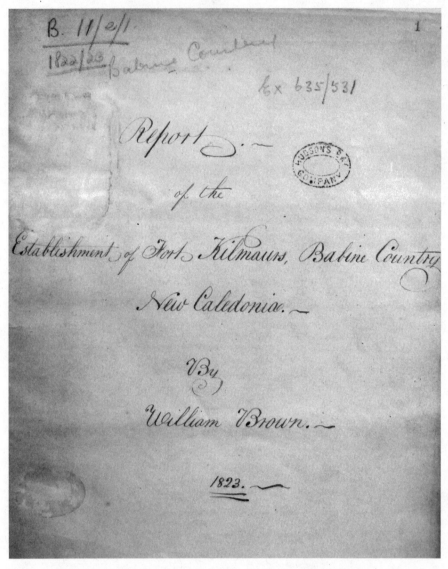

Report.

of the

Establishment of Fort Kilmaurs, Babine Country

New Caledonia.

By

William Brown.

1823.

Fig. 44: Cover Page of William Brown's District Report for 1823.

resort there, on account of the Salmon being commonly plentiful. The Principal Chief is Ack Koo Shaw, and after him How chete ta ku, Nan kaa, Cub bah, and several others, who are possessors of Land and heads of families. But none of them have any particular characteristics to distinguish them from the rest of their Country men.

Ack-koo-shaw is a deep designing, cunning Old Man who will let no opportunity slip of turning every thing within his power to his own advantage. His advanced age renders him unfit for the Laborious parts of the chase, but still he is generally possessed of the greatest part of the furs of his followers.

Hot-set,[5] the largest and most populous of the Babine Villages,[6] is situated on the Banks of the Ochilcho or Simpson's river, which is one days March in summer, and three in winter to the West of this Lake. I have had various accounts of the Number of Indians who reside here, Judging from which I believe the following will be nearly the truth. From one hundred forty to one hundred and fifty married Men, an Equal number of Married Women, and from one hundred and sixty to two hundred Young Men, Young Women, Widows, Widowers, and children, of these there are twenty chiefs of different gradations and sixty seven Married Men whom they dominate Respectably as being heads of Families and possessors of lands. The following is a list of the Chiefs according to their Rank and as they are placed at their feasts. But having seen little of them I can say nothing as to their Character:

Oss. Him I sent the present to.
Smuggltuim
Quilt-No
Hook-ah-tut
Kie less. Son of the first.
Matt
Killough-cune
Met-tee-ik
Une-fluck. A woman Chief-ess
Choled-soap, or Ubel-cune
Killough
Ute-an-non
Cheigh
Koo-ock
Mee-im

Coughlet
Jack-kay
Tzee-one
Use-tah
Coute-sa-u

It is impossible to say what might be the amount of furs received
by the company from this tribe, as it was not a great amount of them
who visited the Establishments, they being in dread of the Indians,
who inhabit the country between them and the different Settlements,
on which account the greatest part of the Babines of the Lake traded
their Furs with the Indians of the Portage, and Fon du Lac of Hakaseley,
unless when people came from St. James in the winter to trade with
them. Those of the Simpson's river carried part of their furs to the Establishment of Fraser's Lake, or traded them with the Indians of Stellah.[7]
But as far as I am able to judge by the information I collected both last
winter and this, three fourths of the furs procured by the Indians of
Simpson's River, were carried below and traded with the Indians of
the Sea Coast. Last summer they made a more advantageous trade
than usual so that when I was at Ack-Koo-Shaw's village in the beginning of January, the most of the Indians of that quarter were talking
of carrying their furs below [the] ensuing season. They wished to make
it appear there was an European Settlement at the Atnah Village[8] at
the Forks.[9] But by dint of enquiry and questioning one and then another at different times I ascertained there are no European Settlements
either there or at the sea. There being only a trading Vessel which cruises
in those seas, and when she approaches the Land for the purpose of
trade she commences firing and the Natives on hearing this put off in
their Canoes and barter such furs as they have. With the property they
receive in this traffic they mount the River and trade the furs of the Indians of the Interior, by which they derive 'handsome profits to themselves.' The goods these people bring as far as I have seen or could
learn are of the coarsest kind, by which they make it appear they give
great bargains while they are only imposing on them with trash. The arms
they trade are old Muskets, Bayonets, and pistols, with large Crimson
powder sometimes mixed with fine Beads. Their leather people here
speak most of as being good and cheap.

This traffic I would suppose might without great danger or difficulty be in a great measure put a stop to, if it is checked in the bud.

But if the Natives of the seacoast are allowed quietly or any length of time to collect the furs of the Indians of Simpson's River and those between that and the sea, they will ere long extend their Views, and make their excursions longer. So that in a short time I would not be the least surprised to see them share, the trade of not only this Lake, but of Stuart's Lake, and Fraser's Lake also.[10] The distance from the Forks to the sea being so short that they make three trips in the course of the summer. This with the spirit of traffic which exists amongst all the Carrier tribes, would render the thing perfectly easy, were they not to come higher than the entrance of this Lake, or even the Forks where then now come to. In fact, I learned from Quitt-No that when the Little Chief of Stellah (this place is within twenty miles of the settlement of Fraser's Lake) heard the Indians recount the advantageous trade they had made he informed them that him and his people would carry their furs to the same Market [the] ensuing summer. If he does so, his example will very quickly be followed by others. To prevent which it will be necessary to adopt such measures as will entirely put a stop to that trade unless the company wish to have themselves opposed by a band of Indians destitute of both property and principles.[11]

I would have gone there this winter to try what could be done, though the party I had was by far to weak for such a service, still I resolved to visit that, until I ascertained provisions were so scarce there, that I would not be able to find subsistence for the few people I could take with me. This being the case I sent by the Little Chief of Stellah, who was at Ack-Koo-shaw's Village while I was there, one pair Indian Stockings, a Garrah Shirt, and some other small articles, in a present to the Principal Chief, to induce him to use his influence to prevent his people from carrying their furs below, at the same time intimating that I would visit him next fall, when I hoped all his people would have their furs collected to trade with me. I have since understood that when he received the present, he assembled his people, shewed it to them, and made a long harangue. The purport of which was, 'that they would make good hunts this Spring and carry their furs to this establishment During the summer' – but none of them on any account to trade with the Indians of the Sea Coast.

On the 23rd of Feby one of the Chiefs arrived from them with between forty & fifty skins, and informed me that he was sent by the principal Chief who had gone below to the Atnah Village to collect all his young men, with the intention of going off a hunting, and coming here in the summer. After which they meant to go a hunting again, to prepare for us visiting them Next fall.

They are so much taken up with the idea of White People visiting their country, that I am of opinion it will for a time at least put a stop to the trade of the Sea Coast. But if the means cannot be afforded next fall to gratify them in that point I much doubt little need be expected from them. However as far as the arrangements depend upon on one I will endeavour to have them completed by that time that if the people can be spared they may be detained as short as possible.

I do not suppose it will be prudent to go there with less than two or three Gentlemen,[12] and from twenty five to thirty men, as there is to be a great feast, and besides the Babine Tribe, all the principal Indians who inhabit the country between these and the Sea Coast to be assembled on purpose to make a general Peace,[13] at which they particularly want us to be present. Those Indians who are in the habit of trading with them will be there also; we will have an opportunity of ascertaining what will be the best method of putting a stop to their traffic. If the people arrive in good time from head quarters, I would suppose this number of Gentlemen and men may be dispensed with, without in any great degree injuring the other Establishments, as their services will not be required for any length of time. Should this be the case and we find we are not able to make an arrangement to stop the trade of the seacoast, the most effectual way in my opinion to do so, will be to form an Establishment at the junction of Simpson's River and McDougall's River.[14] This was the idea I formed in the early part of the winter, and intended to apply for the means to do so ensuing fall, but from information I have received since, it appears to me better to let this lie over for the present, and direct our Views to another quarter where the trade made be extended more advantageously and perhaps open a way to the formation of an Establishment there or further down at a future period, As I will state in its proper place. The Grand obstacle to the forming an Establishment at the Forks is that the greatest part of McDougall's River from this lake to its junction with Simpsons River[15] is not navigable – it being impeded with Rapids and the Rocks on each side is high and perpendicular as to render it impossible to make Portages. So it will be necessary to go over Land, which by the different accounts I have received may be a distance of between Seventy and Eighty miles. This account of McDougall's River I have had it frequently confirmed this winter, by different Indians whom I particularly requested to examine it.

The Indians of this Establishment have done little this year, so that the returns will not greatly exceed seven Packs. They being prevented by starvation from making as good hunts as usual during the Summer, and the few furs they did procure were either traded at St. James or with the Indians of that Establishment. On my arrival in the fall they had not a Pack of furs amongst the whole of them. The cold season setting in soon after, which in conjunction with an erroneous Idea they had formed, of receiving goods when once a Fort was in their Country whether they had Furs to give for them or not, kept them loitering about the Village, without exerting themselves [as] they might have done. But from the spirit of Rivalship which at present exists amount them, I expect they will make a good hunt [the] ensuing season. If they were once arranged with the necessary implements for hunting, I suppose the Returns will amount to between twenty five and thirty Packs, But this will not be for this two or three years.

These Indians Received as little Debt as possible, still it was necessary to let them have some as it not infrequently happened that an Indian was in absolute want of an article to enable them to go a hunting and had not [the] wherewith to pay for the whole of it, which made it our Interest to advance them a few skins. By the Debt book there are at present two hundred & ten skins due the Company by forty three different Indians so that it does amount to a great deal to each individual.

The General Character of the Babine is similar to the other Carrier in New Caledonia. They are Kind and hospitable to strangers, which may be considered as the only good feature in their Character, for they are Dishonest, Passionately addicted to Gaming, Licentious, Lazy, Indolent, and in their private habits Dirty and Immoral in the extreme, and if not kept properly in check, on our first outset amongst them, will prove the most turbulent and dangerous tribe in this quarter. I had only occasion to come to a rupture with them once and then they would have had the temerity to attack us with arms, had it not been for the interference of the Chief, though at that time I had nine men in the Fort and they did not much exceed that number.

There are two Atnah Villages situated on the Banks of McDougall's River, about forty miles below where it falls out of this Lake. Which according to my information contain two hundred and thirty one grownup Men. The manner I received this account was a follows. The Indians of this place having gone there on a Visit in the beginning of March I desired one of them "to go into the first Lodge, and cut a small piece of wood for every man that was in it, then proceed to another and do the same thing until he had done so in all the Lodges in the Villages. These pieces of Wood to keep carefully and bring to me." On his return he delivered [to] me the small pieces of Wood, which amounted to the number above mentioned and stated "that he had done exactly as I had desired him." There is another Village, at the Forks which is stated to be more numerously inhabited, with several others along the Banks of the River, which increase in population as the approach the sea. According to [a] report this Country abounds with Beaver and other animals of the Fur kind. But the inhabitants are impressed with the idea that the Beaver is an unclean animal, and as such unfit for food, from which cause they never kill them. Martens and Sifflues[16] they sometimes hunt on purpose to make Robes of their Skins.

These people are a wretched miserable set, little superior to the Brute creation. Their sole occupation is to procure a subsistence, which is easily done, as the Salmon are abundant in the River. Their shoes are made of the skins of these fish, with a Sefflue Robe[s] compose the dress of the greatest part of them. By the statements of the Indians who were there, axes and other Iron works seemed to be what they were mostly taken up with. They remarked that the Babines were well dressed, and signified that they would wish to see White People, but were shamed to go to them as they had no Furs, which they understood was what they were fondest of.

It is probable if there was an Establishment amongst them, they might be induced to become industrious, and hunt. But I do not think it would be altogether prudent to settle there, until we are better acquainted with them. Which might be accomplished by Visiting them and prevailing on some of them to Visit the fort, by doing so they would begin to feel they were in want of many things to supply themselves with which, it is probable they would turn their attention to hunting, to procure [the] wherewith to purchase them.

They are much dreaded by the Babines of the Lake, and are considered by them as a Brave and daring set. Private disputes amongst themselves are generally settled by fighting with knives. Their method is to lay hold of each other by the hair, with the left hand, and with the Right to cut or stab until one or commonly both are killed. I have seen several of their Knives, which are made of a piece of Iron hoop. Some of them have a handle of wood and others are pointed at both ends –

and held by the middle, all of them I have seen had a strong line attached to them on purpose to tie around the hand [so] that their opponent might not be able to wrench it from them. Besides knives, they are possessed of a great many Muskets, Bayonetts [sic], and spears. When the Indians of this place were on their way there, they were met by a party of twelve who had each a Musket and spear, coming up to the Lake to revenge the death of a Relation, who had either died or was killed there a considerable time past. But they were induced by presents to abandon their design and return.

While the Indians of this place was at the Atnah Village the Principal Chief of the Siccanies[17] of the Prairies, and four of his country men arrived there, to whom Caspine made a present of his Shirt and some other articles and entered into an arrangement for him to come here on the first snow [the] ensuing fall. By the different Indians who were then present, (I learned) the following information concerning these people.

The Siccanies of the Prairies are numerous nation, who inhabit the country to the North of McDougall's River, which principally consists of extensive Plains.[18] It abounds in Moose, Carribeau [sic], Beaver and other fur bearing Animals, the two former they hunt for their subsistence, and to cloath [sic] themselves, and the latter as an article of trade. They speak the same language, and have the same habits as the Siccanies on the other side of the Height of Land. They live by the chase and never for any length of time remain on the same place, But are always moving about for the purpose of hunting. They never work the Salmon save for a short time in the spring when they kill some of the large kind for present use. At times they visit the Atnah Villages on the Banks of McDougall's River to trade Salmon when they are unfortunate in the chase. In the fall of the year they are in the habit of hunting the Beaver in the Vicinity of Bear or Webster's Lake and requested the Indians to Visit them there on the fall of Snow, and they would accompany them here with their furs.

There is an extensive Lake, not far from Webster's Lake, out of which falls a very Large River.[19] At the place where this river discharges itself into the Pacific Ocean, there is an Establishment where they trade their Furs, but it is now two years since the Chief was there. This I suppose to be a Russian Settlement, as they describe them as being extremely severe upon the Indians, which is the general Characteristic of the Russians all along the North West Coast. [I] Endeavoured to ascertain what kind of property these people have for trade, But all I could learn was, "they sold Muskets and coarse Powder, and the Chief had a piece of Strouds[20] of an inferior quality, which he had received from them."

I received three or four Beaver Skins of their Killing, which were stretched according to the directions of those with whom they trade, which is long and Narrow. Martens and Small furs they split. But Caspine shewed them the manner we wished the different kinds of furs arranged which they promised to attend to, and collect all they could, to bring with them Next fall. The name of the Chief is Atzen-nah or gunah [unclear].

It appears to me this is the best place in this quarter to attempt extending the trade, as the Country abounds in Beaver and the Indians are Industrious and in the habit of working them. How to get there will be the most difficult point. I am of opinion the Most likely Route to answer this purpose will be by Finley's Branch,[21] and then I would suppose it will be necessary to have an Establishment on each side of the height of Land, as the Portage will be too long to carry across. It is possible that part of the expenses of the Settlement on the east side would be liquidated by the Siccanies of the Portage[22] resorting there. After passing the height of Lands and becoming acquainted with the Country, a way may be opened to form an establishment in the River, to cut off the trade of the Sea Coast. If it is found this traffic cannot be put a stop to in another shape, as also to form settlements amongst some other tribes, which are at present unknown to us. To gain a knowledge of these Siccanies or any other adjacent tribe I will use every means within my Power, and any thing that appears to me to be of the smallest consequence to the concern will be regularly forwarded, for the inspections of those connected with it.

The most part of the foregoing is taken from Indian Report[s], which was the only source of information, which was open to me, I therefore do not give it as facts, but as what appeared to me to be facts from examining and Comparing the different statements which I received. This being the case I hope I will be excused, if any of the circumstances related, or conclusions drawn are wrong, as my wish was not to deceive but to convey information which might be useful.

Wm Brown
Fort Kilmaurs
April 3rd, 1823

Report
of the Babine Country and Countries to the
Westward
By
William Brown, C.T.
April 1826[23]

The most easterly and southeasterly point of the Babine lake is about
sixty miles to the north West of St. James, and is divided from the St.
James or Stuarts Lake by a Portage of twelve miles. The lake lies nearly
north West and South East – is about one hundred fifteen Miles in
length and from two to fifteen in breadth with very few islands, is in
general deep, with no sunk rocks and very few sandbanks. The country in the vicinity is rugged and uneven (but there are no Mountains
close to it of any great heights) intersected by a number of small lakes,
swamps and rivulets where Beaver are numerous. The shores in some
places are bold and rocky with little wood particularly in the South
east: in others the land rises gradually from the edge of the water and
is covered with strong wood, principally pine and poplar, for several
miles below the fort, the hills are covered with grass and a few bushes
of willows, the woods at some former period having been destroyed
by fire. There are very few Fish in this lake considering its extent,
and the number of small rivers which flow into it from Lakes in the
vicinity where fish are abundant: the principal are trout,[24] white fish,
carp and Loche[25] – but they are so scarce that they will not repay the
trouble and expense of nets to look after them. For the month of July
Salmon fry are numerous and a very considerable number of them are
taken by the natives (both in nets and Nowauts) particularly in the
upper end of the Lake, these are succeeded by the salmon from the Sea,
which are in general numerous, but they soon get bad after entering
the Lake: with Holland twine nets a good many might be caught, but
considering all the expenses attending the taking and curing them I
believe it is cheaper to purchase them from the Indians than to work
them further than a sufficiency for the daily consumption of the place.
Our establishment is about eighty miles from the Portage and thirty
five from the River below, situated on the north shore of a large Bay
which stretches for a considerable distance to the northwest – a small
river [?] falls into the head of the Bay, where those Indians who do not
hunt in the spring resort to work the carp, but they have not been
wrought there several years.

Of the Babines of the Lake

There are three villages on the banks of the lake which contain about two hundred and fifty souls including Men, Women and Children, of these there are Seventy who are capable of hunting, but not above half of that number kill any thing worth mentioning, part of them being deterred on account of having no lands and the others from the natural indolence of their disposition. These villages are as follows:

These three villages are as follows. Ratches[26] situated at the entrance of a small River on the south shore about sixty miles from the Portage: this place was formerly the resort of a numerous band of Indians, but they have dwindled away of late years to four families and a few stragglers who occasionally reside there. The salmon mount this River in great numbers and are killed with much less labour than at the fisheries of the Babine river: they are far inferior in quality which in some seasons (particularly when they are scarce) causes the natives to go below[27] and procure their winter stock.

Oollad is the principal of this village, he is now an old Man, but still kills a few furs particularly Martens – of the other three two of them are good hunters, but they are so much addicted to gambling that in general for three fourths of the year they are naked and unable to stir out of their lodges.

The village of Nah tell cuss is situated on a small Island, with in a quarter of a mile of our Establishment – this is the residence of Caupin [possibly Caspin] and his followers with a number of others belonging to different bands – the whole amount to twenty four families. Caupin is now in his prime and would be a tolerable good hunter, if he was not of such an indolent and lazy disposition: his followers are few (he not being the principal chief of his Tribe) and over them he has but little control, for if he had more influence he would be both more troublesome and expensive.

Chilclue, Clikiss, Ashshow, Sawbuck and Squee are reckon'd the most respectable after Caupin, they being heads of families and possessors of lands in the neighbourhood, the first is a tolerable hunter, and is one of the most decent and respectable Men amongst the whole of the Babine nation. Clikiss hunts a few furs, but he is of such an avaricious disposition that it is hardly possible to trade them: his passion prompts him to believe that he will not be sufficiently paid for what he has and under this impression he very often makes caches of them in the Woods, where not infrequently they are either destroyed or stole by his Countrymen.

Ashshaw and Sawbuck kill a few Beaver, but Squee never ventures further in the way of hunting than the snaring of Rabbits.

The Village of Nasschick is situated twenty miles to the South west of the Fort, it is the residence of Ackkooshaw, Cabbah, and Houchite tahkee with their followers, who amount to thirty five married Men.

Ack koo shaw is the principal Chief of the Indians of the Lake and is possessed of the most influence which he in general uses to his own advantage, still he is of great Service to his Country Men by preventing them from carrying their disputes (which are not unfrequent) to a length that might prove fatal to those concerned. He is now an old Man which renders him unfit for the more laborious parts of the chase: however he is generally possessed of more furs than any of his followers, these he either gains at play, or receives in presents or trades from others.

Cabbah belongs to the same tribe as Caupin of which he is the principal chief, he is also an old Man, whose hunting days are nearly over, still he gives to the Fort from twenty to thirty skins yearly, part of which he kills himself and part he receives in presents from his young Men.[28]

Hou chete tah kie is an inferior Chief connected with the tribe of Ack koo shaw having no independent band of his own. His lands are very extensive and are the best stocked with Beaver of any in the vicinity of the Lake, of which he is particularly careful neither killing too many himself nor allowing any other to do so, he generally gives into the Post from twenty to thirty skins in the course of a season.

Tin nu wed, Tulsu, Nandelkaa, Atcliss, At tow an, Piss can nahlah, Tel a ben elk tak and Soguin are reckoned the most respectable Men of the village, as being possessors of lands, they all kill a few furs, but seldom exceed from ten to fifteen skins in the course of the Year.

Of the Babines of Simpson's River

The village of Hotset situated on the Banks of Ochil cho or Simpsons River is about eighty miles to the South west of our Establishment, and is the most populous of all of the Babine villages, it being the principal residence of all of the Indians of that quarter. Judging from my own observations and the different accounts I have had of these people, I do not suppose their number can be less than Seven hundred and fifty including all ages and Sexes, of these I should imagine Two hundred are capable of hunting. They reckon Twenty Chiefs of different gradations and Sixty seven married Men whom they denominate respectable as being heads of Families and possessors of lands. The following are the most noted amongst the Chiefs, and those with whom we have had the most dealings.

Oss [is] the oldest and principal Chief, but neither seems to be so much respected nor to have so much influence as some of the others of less note. From what I have seen of him his character appears to be a mixture of meanness and stupidity. He might give about twenty skins in the course of a year if there was a Post in his Country or regular trading voyages made there twice a year, but no dependence can be placed on his coming to the present Establishment to trade, though he has sometimes visited it.

Smuggle tuem the second chief appears to have much more influence than the former, arising in a great measure from possessing a volubility of tongue and being a thorough adept in cringing and flattery, but these pliant qualities are accompanied by too much levity to be depended upon and too much avarice to be of any real Service. The former making his word or promise of no value, and the latter rendering any permanent good that might be derived from him too expensive, he may collect between twenty and thirty skins in the course of a Season, but no reliance can be placed on his coming regularly to the Post as he trades with the Atnah, the Indians from the Seacoast, or any other with whom it may suit his convenience or he can make the best bargain.

Quilt No, the third Chief, this man is a better hunter than either of the two former, but like them can not be depended upon to trade constantly at the Post. He had his followers generally kill in the Spring about a Pack including small Furs. He is more feared than respected by his countrymen, having more than once dipped his hands in blood.

Matt, the sixth chief, this man has a surly, rough and savage disposition, but has so far proved himself more honest in his dealings than any of the former. He is tolerable hunter and has for these two Years constantly traded at the Fort; in his transactions with us he is sometimes sullen and difficult to please, but has never shown any other bad propensity. However, with his own Countrymen as also with the Atnahs (amongst whom in years of scarcity he resides) his brutal disposition frequently involves him in quarrels in the course of which he has killed and maimed several.

Cho led Sop, the tenth chief, according to seniority, this Man appears to be of a quiet steady and peaceable disposition, and possesses considerable influence amongst his Countrymen, he generally trades at the Fort. What he kills himself and receives from his followers commonly amounts to between twenty and thirty skins in the course of the Year, of the other fifteen who are considered Chiefs none of them seemed to me to be of any great consequence further than amongst those of their own family and even with them their authority appeared to be very limited: they may in the course of the year between what they kill themselves and pick up amongst their adherents collect from ten to twenty skins each, which they in general trade with the Atnahs their neighbours or the Indians from the Seacoast. I have tried all in my power to induce them to come to the Fort but without success, principally on account of the want of leather, as they will not part with their furs for anything else, and ever since I was there in the Fall of 1823 our stock of that article has been so very scanty, as not only to prevent us from making trading voyages to their Country but even of supplying those who come to the Fort, which has proved a serious loss to the concern, as two thirds of the Furs procured by them have found their way to the Seacoast.

These Indians have much more the appearance of Hunters than any of the other Carrier tribes, they being in general tall and clean made which may in great measure arise from their being accustomed to hunt and to live upon animal food from their manner of working the Salmon with the scoope [sic] net or spear, they can not lay up a sufficient stock to serve them for the Season, but are obliged either to have recourse to the chase or else to their neighbours. However on examining the River it appeared to me that there were many places where it might be barred with little or more trouble than many other Rivers in the Country which the natives of the Country are in the habit of barring: was this done they might in General take a sufficient number of Salmon with less labour than the few they now take: when spoken to on the subject they seemed to be of the same opinion, but they have been so accustomed to their present method, that none of them could be prevailed upon to make the attempt. Everyone excusing himself by saying, that if he was to begin none of the others would assist him. Two years ago [1824] a large mass of Rocks fell into the River, about a days journey below the village,[29] since which time they have wrought the salmon at that place, where I understand they killed last fall about sufficient to serve them for the Winter.

The Lands of these people are extensive and well stocked with beaver, Martens, Fishers, Musquash etc. Had they an Establishment on them, I should suppose that after being supplied with the necessary implements for hunting they would make about Twenty Packs yearly, for now poorly as they are equipped they kill at least half of that number: but from the few Salmon they take in comparison to their number it would be impossible to find subsistence amongst them. Another formidable obstacle is the Land carriage and state of the road, therefore the best and only method that can be adopted by which the greatest proportion of their furs will be secured for the present establishment is to make two trading voyages there in the course of the year, the one in July and the other in the latter end of November, but even then a considerable part would be traded by the Indians below and I am doubtful that a voyage there in the summer would be attended with more expense than the Trade could support, as it would be necessary for people to remain inland for that purpose, and without going there then, the greatest part of their Spring hunt (which their principal one) would find its way to the Seacoast.

## Of the Water communication between the Babine Lake and the Sea

In going to the Country of the Atnah this Spring we followed the River all the way from the Babine lake to the Village of Chil do call, which gave me a much better opportunity of seeing it there last year from the Mountains, and I am glad to find (contrary to the opinion I then formed) that it is navigable as far as we went, and by every information I could procure, the navigation improves the further you Descend, a Canoe moderately loaded when the water is not too high, could go from our present Establishment to the Upper Atnah villages in three days, from there to the Forks in Three more and from the forks to the Sea in six making in all twelve days, allowing five days to come up the current for one to go down, the [return] voyage even then would not exceed two months and a half, so that this is certainly the shortest water communication that exists between Western Caledonia and the Sea,[30] but it would not answer for sending in the Returns of the Establishments on the other side of the Babine portage as all the Furs procured at them during the winter and Spring would have to be sent to the Babine country by trains, for the Water in the Babine River would be too high to descend before the lakes would open to send them by Canoe.

## Of the Atnahs in the Babine River

The two principal Villages of the Atnahs who inhabit the upper parts of the Babine River are Weep sim and Chil do call: they are five miles asunder and about one hundred and fifteen miles to the West or perhaps rather to the North west of our Establishment; there are a number of other villages within a short distance of them, where the different bands reside particularly during the Salmon season: but the above two places is where they assemble to make their feasts and perform all ceremonies of a general nature.

These Atnahs are a numerous race, last Spring I saw at the villages of Weep sim about Three hundred Men none of whom were past their prime, all the old men, Women and Children (on hearing our approach) had fled to the Mountains under the mistaken notion that we were coming upon them to make war. This Spring I went down to the village of Chil do call but did not see so many Indians at the whole of the villages as in the preceding year (a considerable number being at a distance in their Winter encampments) from which I conclude that all the young and active Men belonging to the different villages (attached to the above two) were then assembled, taking these as the number of Men capable of carrying arms, I do not suppose that part of the Nation amounts to fewer than a thousand individuals.

There are three Chiefs, Needchip, Sojeck and Quem, the first is the Principal and from what I have seen of him the best. He is no hunter, but seems very anxious to please, and is very hospitable and generous with what he has, his manner is altogether different from that of the other two, they being a couple of sneaking mean characters who would wish to take all, but give nothing: they appear from their conversations to be much attached to the Traders from the Seacoast.

There are five more Atnah villages which are described as large and populous, the first is two days march below Chil do call and the second is at the Forks which is two days march further; the other three are below the forks and are each two days journey asunder from the upper of which there is a track over Land to another Large River where the Nation called Ute sin nah reside. These people are reported to be hunters, and to procure a good many furs, which they carry to the entrance of the River, and Trade with the Russians, who are said to be established there.

The different statements I have received regarding the People who inhabit the Country between the Atnahs and the Sea are various consequently not to be depended upon, one account is that there is only one Nation called Keespallotes,[31] who extend all the way along the banks of the river to the coast, and that their principal village at the entrance of the River has the same name, other accounts state that there are three distinct Nations between the Atnahs and the Ocean who all speak different Languages.

The information I received regarding the Siccannees [sic] of the Praire [sic] and stated in my report of 1823 is not to be relied upon, they being described there as a numerous nation, inhabiting a Country consisting of extensive Plains and abounding with Beaver and large animals, whereas by accounts I have had of them since, they are only a small band of vagabonds, who are excluded from the society of all other Indians on account of their crimes and reside principally in the mountainous Country lying between the Babine River and Bears lake.

The Atnahs were represented to me in a very unfair and unjust light by the Babines from whom I received the character given of them in my report of 1823. From what I have seen of them since, they are much more industrious and ingenious than the Carriers, as appears from the workmanship displayed in the construction of their Villages, their arrangements for fishing, etc. However in other respects their character, manners and Customs are nearly similar. They are in the constant habit of burning their dead, and making feasts for them afterwards at the time they deposit the bones. The women have the lower lip pierced and a piece of wood inserted in the incision, these pieces of wood are in general much larger than those used by the Babine Women, many of them exceeding two inches in length and one in breadth. This absurd custom seems to have come from the Coast. Both Men and Women have the nose pierced and a long shell passed through it. They receive strangers with the same show of hospitality as the Carriers and have the same appearances of generosity in making presents. They are also addicted to Gaming, but I do not think to such a degree for I saw none of the young men naked as they are to be seen in every Carrier camps, they having in general good siffleux [groundhog] Robes and Leggings of Carribeau [sic] skins. In point of morals and chastity I am inclined to think that a further acquaintance with them will shew [sic] that they are a little superior to their neighbours the Carriers, whom they also much resemble in their ideas regarding medicine and being bad friends amongst themselves which keeps them in a constant state of anxiety and alarm.

From my own observations and the different questions I put to them I do not think there are many Beaver in their Country, it being in my opinion too mountainous. Ouo em acknowledged that on his lands there were few or no Beaver, Needchip and Sojeck on the contrary said that there were a great many small lakes and rivers in the lands belonging to them, where Beaver were abundant, but that they did not know how to work them. That there are Beaver in their country seems very probable, it being higher up the River adjoining to the Lands of the Sicannies and Babines, where the Mountains are not near so high nor rocky, and all the rivulets and vallies which appear from the Main River are in general wooded with small Poplars. Martens by all accounts are numerous throughout and are I believe the principal Furs to be expected from prosecuting the Trade of that Country, of these I think a considerable number might be procured, provided we could secure all they kill.

## Of the Traders from the Seacoast

It does not appear to me that we are able to cope with these people by making derouines [extended trading visits] into the Countries they are in the habit of visiting, unless we sell our property so cheap as to prove prejudicial to the trade of Western Caledonia, and even then we will not be able to secure one half of the Trade, for we do not meet on an equal footing, as they receive goods at a low rate from the Vessels which frequent the Coast, and though these articles generally speaking are old and [of] little worth (particularly the arms) still when compared with any thing we can give at the same prices, they appear great in the eyes of Indians who have no knowledge of the intrinsic value of property, to which may be added they work their own crafts coming up the River, understand the languages and are at no expenses for provisions, nor anything else, Consequently can afford to give a high price for what Furs they receive, and then have what will appear to them handsome profits, besides they have recourse to means which would not do with us. For instance on their arrival at a village they ascertain (if they do not know previously) who have Furs and the amount of them, on which they go to the persons lodge blow a parcel of swans down upon his head (which is reckoned a mark of great honor both amongst the Carriers and Atnahs) and then commence dancing and singing a song in his praise, after which they make him a present and treat him with something to eat, when he according to the custom of the country, makes them a return present of his Furs, which if not equal to what he has received he adds siffleux robes and dressed skins to make up the value.

It would appear that the vessels which visit the entrance of the river bring a better assortment of goods than formerly, as the Atnahs had a number of three and four point blankets and some very fine dressed skins with plenty of ammunition both in cartridges and otherwise, while at the same time the Traders from the Coast seem as if they intended to extend their trading excursions, as they seldom used to come higher than the forks of the Babine and Simpsons River and very frequently not so high. But last Fall they came as far up as the Upper Atnah Village and traded the whole of the Furs and siffleux Robes that Natives had to dispose of, so that when I was there in March, all that I could collect amongst them was only thirty Martens and a little Beaver coating and that at a very high rate, which induced me to return from Chil do call in place of going to the Rocks as was my first intention.

It appears to me that the only effectual method to put a stop to this Traffic to protect Western Caledonia from the inroads of these People and to secure the trade of both Rivers to the Concern, is to form an establishment at the Forks of the Babine and Simpsons River, by which such Furs as are not procured there will be got at either Kilmaurs or Francis lake. If some such measure is not adopted to check them the evil will ere long become of a serious nature. For they are yearly extending their voyages, and there is not a doubt but they will continue to do so while they can procure Furs and are not opposed, they have now made their way as high as the Upper Atnah village, and have only to make one stretch more to reach this Lake. As to Simpsons River they have had the greatest part of the Furs of that quarter for these some years past, which they either procured by these Indians meeting them at the Forks or by the means of the Atnahs (who act as agents for them) going there and trading them.

Were it thought advisable to settle a Post there, it would require to receive its supplies from Farrie's River by sea which it is probably might be done without incurring much extra expense by means of the Vessel employed to trade along the coast, as she could bring the Outfit to the entrance of the River, and there exchange it for the Returns which could be brought there at a certain time as might be agreed on: should the water then be too high to return, the party might perhaps be employed for a time to advantage in assisting the Trade along the coast to the northward by accompanying the vessel to the mouth of some of the large Rivers, and ascending them in quest of Indians, besides the party on their way up and down the River in going to and from the Forks could have an opportunity of collecting all the Furs the Natives had in their possession, but the principal reason for preferring this route is the distance being too great to send the outfit from Stuarts Lake and then take the Returns from the forks to that place on trains, which last would have to be the case if it was attached to Western Caledonia: for though the Outfit could be sent by open Water it would be too late to bring back the Returns in the same manner on account of the drifting Ice in the River, and I am even doubtful if it could be done with trains, as it is but a short time in the Winter that it is possible pass with them by the river, so that the only route that could be depended upon would be over the mountains, which if not altogether impracticable is the next thing to it.

In the event of an establishment being formed at the Forks, it would be necessary to attach the one now in the Babine Country to it, both on account of the Indians of Hot sett, and to have greater force to go up and down the River, for these Indians can with much more facility be supplied from the Forks than any of our own Establishments, as it would be easy from there to make a trip to them in the spring and arrange them previous to their going a hunting, as also another on the arrival of the people in the Fall, and by us being between them and the traders from the Coast we would secure all they killed. So that it is reasonable to suppose that when they found that they were regularly supplied with their necessaries, they would make greater exertions to procure Furs than they now do. But if the two Establishments are not connected together, they will give a great deal of trouble. As they will be running between the two, in the hope of getting property on debt in place applying themselves to hunting to procure wherewithal to pay for it. And by joining the two together the expenses will be much lessened, as the numbers of Men that will be necessary to insure safety going up and down the River could bring in both Outfits, and as they will arrive at an early Season, one part of the Men can proceed on with the one for the Babines of the Lake, while the others make derouines to the Indians of Simpsons River after which they can assemble at the Forks and visit the nation called Utte sin nah or any other Indians who may have Furs. Was such an arrangement to take place the present establishment in the Babine Country should be removed to the small Lake, where the Indians work the Salmon, by doing this the returns could be sent off in the Spring before the Ice broke up in the Lake or the Water rose: If the post was there the Indians of Nass chick (who are the most numerous) would make much better hunts than they now do, and Provisions could be procured with both less trouble and expense, there being plenty of both trout and salmon in the Lake from the month of February until it breaks open, and it would be so far removed from the Establishment of Stuarts Lake, that there would be no trouble with the Indians going between the two places. An Establishment at the Forks would require two Gentlemen and ten or twelve Men, there with the men now required to bring in the Babine outfit I should imagine would be a sufficient force to keep the Indians in awe along the River. Having thus to the best of my knowledge stated the resources of this tract of Country, and the means which seem to me the best calculated for securing them to the concern, it remains with the Governor and Council to determine as to the importance of the one and the expediency of the other.

Comparative Statement of leather yearly allowed for the Trade since established Fall 1822

| Outfit | Number of skins received | Number of skins sold to servants | Number of skins expended general use | Number of skins expended for the trade |
|--------|--------------------------|----------------------------------|--------------------------------------|----------------------------------------|
| 1822   | 235                      | 8                                | 0                                    | 227                                    |
| 1823   | 187.5                    | 8.5                              | 0                                    | 179                                    |
| 1824   | 46                       | 10                               | 12                                   | 24                                     |
| 1825   | 91                       | 30                               | 0                                    | 61                                     |
| Total  | 559.5                    | 56.5                             | 12                                   | 491                                    |

The returns of this place not increasing as might have been expected can be ascribed solely to the small quantity and inferior quality of the Leather that has been allowed for these last two years. The supply of prime skins, such as are calculated for the trade of this quarter, not being a tenth of the number required for the Indians of the Lake alone, consequently it was in vain to make derouines to those of Simpsons River as the result could only have been to incur expences, and receive nothing, and what is worse we would most probably have got ourselves involved into a quarrel with them, for they will not part with their Furs for any thing but leather, and when they saw us in their Country without the article they were in want of there is not a doubt they would be dissatisfied and give us as much trouble as possible. There was only one band of them came to the Fort in the Summer, and when they found that we had not leather to supply them, they became so turbulent that it was with some difficulty we kept them in check without having recourse to arms: in spite of all we could do and every thing we could offer them in the way of trade they went off with their Furs giving us to understand that they would dispose of them to the Traders from the Coast. On reaching Simpsons River they spread the report all over of our having no leather which prevented any of their Countrymen from visiting us. They had a great feast in the Fall when, such of their furs and they could not barter with the Inians of the Lake or Atnahs for leather, they gave away in presents at the Feast in place of that article. An idea may be formed from the following circumstance of how partial they are to dressed leather, and how necessary such an article is in our Commerce with them. When I went there the first time in 1823 several of the Chiefs made me presents of Furs, in return for which I made them what I considered very hard some presents, consisting of cloth, blankets, shirts, etc., but the following day they brought back the whole and informed me that it was not to receive such articles as these that they had given me their Furs: one of them [Smuggle tuem], from whom I had received about Twenty Skins, I had given two yards red strouds, one Gurrah Shirt,[32] one awl, one fire steel, one gun flint, two needles, two hanks thread, two yards gartering, ten ball, one half pound Powder, one pound shot and one sixth pound Tobacco, requested me to take back the whole again and give him a dressed skin in the place, on which I took the articles and in their stead gave him two Middling Moose skins as an equivalent for his Furs – And the same arrangements I was obliged to make with the others, after which they were all well pleased.

It may be remarked from the above statement of Leather, that the quantity allowed for last year, was much less then this, still the returns did not fall off, but it is to be considered that a great part of the stock of the former year remained on hand, which supplied the Indians of the vicinity in the spring and early part of the summer, so that the deficiency only effected [sic] their fall hunts, and prevented us from visiting those of Simpsons River, where last spring the case was very different for the Indians went off to make their hunts with the knowledge that there was no leather at the place, and as might be expected did not exert themselves. On ther return their was still no Leather, the consequence is a great many of them did not give us their furs, but went and played them with their country men in hopes of gaining what they were in want of, and thus they remained playing till the arrival of the Salmon, every one striving to get possession of them in place of going a hunting: when their Stock of salmon was secured and they still saw that we had not wherewith to supply them, they instead of a Fall hunt went to the Feast at Simpsons River and by their return the Season was over so that the Indians of this place did not in the course of the Fall kill Ten beaver amongst the whole of them.

. Leather is an article that is absolutely required at all the Establishments amongst the Carriers in Western Caledonia, but at none of them half so much as in the Babine Country, neither can it be disposed of at any of them to the same advantage, not one sixth of what is sold at Stuarts lake is for Furs and not above one third at Frasers lake: what leather the Indians of these places purchase is generally speaking to make shoes, leggings, etc., consequently skins of an inferior quality is more likely to satisfy them providing they got them cheaper: with the Babines it is different, the leather they buy is not for present use, but to be put carefully apart until the death of a relation, when each skin is cut into three or four pieces and given away in presents at the burning of the bodys: or when they make the Grand feast finally to deposit the bondes and ashes, then the skins are given away whole it being considered on these occasions as of great importance to have fine large white skins. It is therefore very seldom that a Babine finds fault with the price but the quality, as he will readily give ten Beaver for a large prime skin, whereas he will not give the half for one that is small or inferior.

With a plentiful supply of leather (and the Trade of Simpsons River properly followed up) there is every reason to expect an increase of one third in the returns, but if the same trifling supplies are continued, there is greater reason to expect a decrease than an increase, for it is just as reasonable to believe that the Northern Indians, or Cree would exert themselves if they were only furnished with silk handkerchiefs and fine Callicoes in place of Cloth and Blankets, as it is to suppose the Babines will do so when supplied with the latter articles in place of leather. In fact it is only a very few individuals that it is possible to prevail upon (at such times as they have no feasts to make) to part with their Furs for either cloth or Blankets, these goods being mostly all disposed for Salmon and other Provisions.

To manage the business of this place to advantage, it would require from three to four hundred skins yearly, and at least three fourths of them of the best quality, with such a supply little else would be necessary except guns, traps, Ice chisels, Beaver nets and ammunition while good Returns might be relied upon.

The trading so many Salmon for the general use of the district as has been done for these last three years has proved prejudicial to the returns and caused a very great extra expense, as it put the Indians in possession of a great quantity of property and supplied their wants, without the trouble of hunting Furs, while the Salmon on hand reckoned nothing in the balance, but I presume this custom will be discontinued, as the one half of the salmon that was formerly required (on account of the winter transportation) will now be sufficient. From the manner the Indians are at present situated in regard of their Feasts and the probability of the Salmon arriving early (which they invariably do every fourth year) so as to enable them to procure their Winter stock and go a hunting before the cold sets in, there is every probability of their making good returns, providing there is leather to supply them when they come to the Fort in the latter end of May or beginning of June, but if this is not the case I am doubtful that little more need be expected from them than their Spring hunt.

Of the number of Men required for the Establishments
As far as I can judge this Establishment would require a Gentleman and Ten Men to conduct the business, that is a Gentleman and three Men to pass the Summer and seven men to take out the Returns and bring in the Outfit, as the latter would be very bulky on account of the great quantity of leather required, and it does not appear to me that the place can be considered in a state of safety with only a Gentleman & two men. From the Indians of the Lake little danger is to be apprehended, it being only from those of Simpsons River should they come to the fort in large bands and then not be wherewith to supply them, as in that case they are very likely to make some disturbance when they see few People, particularly as they know that if they should commit any depredation they can soon get beyond our reach by going amongst the Atnahs where they will be supplied with their necessaries by the Traders from the coast in exchange for what furs they procure.

Should it be intended to make a trading voyage to Simpson's River in the summer, three men more will be required to Remain Inland, and to go there or to the country of the Atnahs in the fall or winter, one or two Gentlemen and a few men will be required to assist during three voyages, as there will then be a greater number of Indians assembled at the different villages.

## Of the Climate, Soil and Vegetable Productions

The climate in this quarter is much milder than at any of the Establishments which I am acquainted with on the East side of the Mountains: some years rain in the Winter is not unfrequent, and in Summer the heat at times is really oppressive, the lower end of the Lake is generally fast in the latter end of November, but the upper end which is much wider and more exposed seldom before the first of January, and last Fall not till the 25th. The time of opening varies in the same manner, the earliest since we have been here was the last Spring when it was free of ice on the 27th April, and the latest in the Spring of 1823 when it did not break up until the 24th of May.

Owing to the rocky and broken surface of the country there are few places where any thing of Soil is to be met with, and there are commonly low points on the borders of the Lake and small spots in the Vallies [sic], there it is generally a black mould of from four to eight inches in thickness, principally composed of decayed vegetables and resting upon a bed of brown or bluish coloured clay.

The different species of timber to be met with here are nearly similar to those on the other side of the Mountain as are also the different kind of berries, excepting the last there are very few vegetable productions which the natives of this quarter use. The only ones I know is the cypress bark, the fern root, and another round white root of the size of a Musquet Ball, which is comprised of small grains not unlike a Raspberry, with the ... of two or three different plants (which they eat in their raw state) the names of which I am unacquainted.

We have planted a few potatoes every year since the place was Established, but they were always very much injured by the post in the early part of the season, and produced little, until last summer when they did very well, so that from a keg of very inferior seed which was planted the latter end of May, I suppose there would have been fifteen in return had they been allowed all to remain until they came to maturity. Barley yields a good crop and ripens well, but it is generally injured by the squirrels and mice, so does Pease [sic] but they are subject to the same evil. Turnips grow well also radishes and greens, but

Onions and Carrots never came up, whether the fault of the Seed or the soil I can not say: with care and attention a very good kitchen garden might be made which would yield tolerable returns at least two out of every three years.

List of Indians who are indebted to the Concern with their General place of residence and Character

| Number of Indians | Names | Amouunt of debt [skins] | General place of residence | Character and remarks |
|---|---|---|---|---|
| 1 | Ack koo shaw | 9 | Nass chick | The principal Babine Chief |
| 2 | Ane nah cut chan nalte | 3 | Nah tell Nah cuss | A useless devil |
| 3 | Ash shaw | 4 | Hotset | Seldom comes to the fort, what furs he procures he generally trades with the Indians from the coast. |
| 4 | Ash shaw | 5 | Nah tell cuss | Kills a few beaver |
| 5 | As tum | 1 | Hotset | A young lad |
| 6 | Ash lah cah | 2 | Simpson's River | An indifferent hunter, who in general trades what he kills with the people from the coast |
| 7 | At cliss | 5 | Nass chick | No beaver hunter |

| Number of Indians | Names | Amouunt of debt [skins] | General place of residence | Character and remarks |
|---|---|---|---|---|
| 8 | At tee tow | 5 | Simpson's River | A worthless vagabond who is continually drifting from place to place doing mischief. Killed an Indian at Stellah September in 1825 |
| 9 | At tow an | 5 | Nass chick | Another worthless character |
| 10 | Belt sa loce lick | 6 | Nah tell cuss | A quiet inoffesive man who hunts a few beaver & Marten |
| 11 | Bey eigh | 1 | Nass chick | Not great things |
| 12 | Bug ale | 1 | Nass chick | Similar to the above |
| 13 | Caupin | 20 | Nah tell cuss | Chief: see remarks regarding Babines of he lake |
| 14 | Cabbah | 18 | Nass chick | Chief: see remarks regarding Babines of the lake |

| Number of Indians | Names | Amouunt of debt [skins] | General place of residence | Character and remarks |
|---|---|---|---|---|
| 15 | Cab bal lo | 7 | Nass chick | Sometimes hunts but cannot be depended upon |
| 16 | Cad dell | 1 | Nah tell cuss | A lad. Son to Caupin. |
| 17 | Chew ete | 2 | Nass chick | A wandering useless fellow |
| 18 | Chil cow awn | 12 | Simpson's River | Can hunt but has been in a bad state of health for past two years. |
| 19 | Chan tin can nock | 12 | Simpson's River | A fellow of no repute |
| 20 | Chic clue | 13 | Nah tell cuss | A good Indian |
| 21 | Chat zou | 15 | Nass chick | A useless lazy vagabond |
| 22 | Chitt laz zee | 2 | Nass chick | The same as above |
| 23 | Chip can nock | 2 | Simpson's River | Seldom visits the post, trades with the coast Indians, or Atnahs |
| 24 | Choled sop | 18 | Simpson's River | A good Indian |

| Number of Indians | Names | Amouunt of debt [skins] | General place of residence | Character and remarks |
|---|---|---|---|---|
| 25 | Chow an | 2 | Tatchy | A young lad, and good hunter when he choses to exert himself |
| 26 | Chim bin yai | 12 | Tatchy | A tolerable hunter but much addicted to gaming, which very frequently deprives him of the means |
| 27 | Chin ze ol lah | 15 | Nah tell cuss | A tolerable hunter but extremely lazy |
| 28 | Claw bucks | 4 | Nass chick | A most worthless character – son to Ack koo shaw |
| 29 | Clin uzzal | 2 | Nah tell cuss | A good fisherman but no hunter |
| 30 | Cune pats | 2 | Simpson's River | Seldom comes to the fort, generally trades what he kills with the Indians of the coast. |

| Number of Indians | Names | Amouunt of debt [skins] | General place of residence | Character and remarks |
|---|---|---|---|---|
| 31 | Cuts zay | 15 | Nass chick | A tolerable hunter but requires to be kept in awe |
| 32 | Dit chin neigh lan | 6 | Simpson's River | Gains more furs at play than what he kills in hunting |
| 33 | Echelle | 29 | Nah tell cuss | A good hunter, but great Gambler which generally kept in a state of nakedness |
| 34 | Eh had day | 3 | Nah tell cuss | Not much worth |
| 35 | El taw wee | 6 | Nass chick | Kills a few beaver yearly |
| 36 | Goose tah | 5 | Nass chick | A quiet man, but a poor hunter |
| 37 | Haize | 5 | Simpson's River | A fellow that no dependence can be placed upon |
| 38 | Hai its | 7 | Nah tell cuss | A more expert gambler than hunter |

| Number of Indians | Names | Amouunt of debt [skins] | General place of residence | Character and remarks |
|---|---|---|---|---|
| 39 | Hool chaa | 7 | Nah tell cuss | Can hunt but is not to be depended upon |
| 40 | Hool less | 4 | Nass chick | Kills a few beaver |
| 41 | Hon chete (tah kie) | 15 | Nah tell cuss | An inferior chief & tolerable hunter |
| 42 | Jyas ul tah | 4 | Tatchy | A poor looking creature, but not a bad hunter |
| 43 | Killough | 3 | Simpson's River | The whole of these people [43–7] kill Beaver, which they in general trade with the Atnahs or Indians of the coast, and seldom ever come to the fort. This only when trading voyages are made into their country that any can be expected from them. |

| Number of Indians | Names | Amouunt of debt [skins] | General place of residence | Character and remarks |
|---|---|---|---|---|
| 44 | Killough cune | 4 | Simpson's River | Ditto |
| 45 | Kill yul | 3 | Simpson's River | Ditto |
| 46 | Kill yail or Jackay yai | 3 | Simpson's River | Ditto |
| 47 | Kimins skit | 3 | Simpson's River | Ditto |
| 48 | Lacqua | 3 | Simpson's River | These three men [48–50] are hunters but for these two years have traded what they killed with the Indians from the coast. |
| 49 | Lee ien | 1 | Simpson's River | |
| 50 | Leigh | 1 | Simpson's River | |
| 51 | Mah tid zy | 25 | Nah tell cuss | An excellent hunter but extremely addicted to play |
| 52 | Mah tuik | 4 | Simpson's River | Processes a good many furs but has never visited the establishment |

| Number of Indians | Names | Amouunt of debt [skins] | General place of residence | Character and remarks |
|---|---|---|---|---|
| 53 | Matt | 15 | Simpson's River | A tolerable hunter & trades constantly at the fort |
| 54 | Nad zell | 6 | Simpson's River | A useless fellow who knows better how to steal than to hunt |
| 55 | Nah hout nin | 1 | Nass chick | Hunts a little |
| 56 | Nan delk kaa | 13 | Nass chick | Kills a few skins but is rather trouble-some in his demands for property |
| 57 | Neist tee pap | 15 | Nah tell cuss | A good marten hunter |
| 58 | Nigh an | 15 | Nah tell cuss | A good for nothing boy |
| 59 | Nit ol lay | 10 | Nass chick | A good Atnah interpreter but a poor hunter |

| Number of Indians | Names | Amouunt of debt [skins] | General place of residence | Character and remarks |
|---|---|---|---|---|
| 60 | Noose tell | 7 | Simpson's River | Processes a good many furs which he in general either trades at Francis Lake or with the Indians of the coast |
| 61 | Nough let | 4 | Nah tell cuss | Too lazy to do any good |
| 62 | Ool lad | 15 | Tatchy | Kills a few furs |
| 63 | Oss | 11 | Simpson's River | Principal chief of Simpson's River |
| 64 | Pen nen san | 20 | Nah tell cuss | Can hunt when he choses |
| 65 | Piss can nah tah | 20 | Nass chick | Kills a good number of Martens but very few Beaver |
| 66 | Piss u uck | 10 | Nass chick | A good hunter, but great Gambler which generally kept in a state of nakedness |

| Number of Indians | Names | Amouunt of debt [skins] | General place of residence | Character and remarks |
|---|---|---|---|---|
| 67 | Piss to mass | 1 | Simpson's River | A useless fellow |
| 68 | Quilt tay | 1 | Nah tell cuss | Can hunt but generally plays what he kills |
| 69 | Quilt no | 20 | Simpson's River | A good hunter |
| 70 | Saw buck | 10 | Nah tell cuss | Kills a few beaver |
| 71 | Say conde zy | 1 | Nah tell cuss | Each of these Indians [71–3] kill a few beaver but generally play them as soon as they are in their possession. |
| 72 | Seh hough | 2 | Nah tell cuss | |
| 73 | Set an ilth yai | 8 | Nah tell cuss | |
| 74 | Seet tah | 8 | Nah tell cuss | |
| 75 | Sin tock | 1 | Simpson's River | Wants the nose [?] generally trades what he kills with the people of the coast |
| 76 | Sink kaa hon uaze | 3 | Nass chick | No great hunter |

| Number of Indians | Names | Amouunt of debt [skins] | General place of residence | Character and remarks |
|---|---|---|---|---|
| 77 | Smug gle tuem | 15 | Simpson's River | A chief and better promiser han performer |
| 78 | Soutass | 4 | Nah tell cuss | Hunts tolerably at times |
| 79 | Squee | 3 | Nah tell cuss | Has in the course of the last four years killed one cat |
| 80 | Stup click | 1 | Nass chick | No great hunter |
| 81 | Sue wee et | 5 | Simpson's River | Hunts a few furs but cannot be depended upon to come to the fort. Trades with the first he meets. |
| 82 | Sun nu ah | 9 | Tatchy | Can hunt but is very often prevented by his passion to play |
| 83 | Tan nul yai | 3 | Nass chick | Hunts a little at times |
| 84 | Tah han | 10 | Nah tell cuss | A lazy useless rascal but can hunt if he pleases |

| Number of Indians | Names | Amouunt of debt [skins] | General place of residence | Character and remarks |
|---|---|---|---|---|
| 85 | Tall tick | 1 | Nass chick | A boy but generally kills more furs than his elders |
| 86 | Tass coo | 3 | Simpson's River | These two Indians generally kill a few furs in the spring but trade them with the people of the coast |
| 87 | Taugh | 1 | Simpson's River | These two Indians generally kill a few furs in the spring but trade them with the people of the coast |
| 88 | Telghee | 1 | Nass chick | Hunts very little |
| 89 | Teel zon | 23 | Nass chick | A useless fellow who would much rather steal than hunt |
| 90 | Teel gae chew | 7 | Simpson's River | A tolerable hunter & trades constantly at the fort |

| Number of Indians | Names | Amouunt of debt [skins] | General place of residence | Character and remarks |
|---|---|---|---|---|
| 91 | Teel leets | 10 | Nah tell cuss | A lad but generally kills a few beaver |
| 92 | Teel zie | 10 | Nass chick | Between hunting & gambling this fellow generally procures more furs than any in the village |
| 93 | Teez zonie | 2 | Nah tell cuss | A quiet man and tolerable hunter |
| 94 | Tin nu wull | 8 | Nass chick | Hunts a few furs |
| 95 | Tit za | 8 | Nah tell cuss | Kills carp but never ventures on any animals which has teeth |
| 96 | Thli kiss | 12 | Nah tell cuss | Kills a few beaver but it is extremely difficult to trade them from him |
| 97 | Too bah |  | Nah tell cuss | A useless boy |
| 98 | Tool lah | 1 | Simpson's River | A lazy useless fellow |

| Number of Indians | Names | Amouunt of debt [skins] | General place of residence | Character and remarks |
|---|---|---|---|---|
| 99 | Too peen at nah | 1 | Nass chick | Kills a few beaver |
| 100 | T'suck | 4 | Nass chick | A stout man but a poor hunter |
| 101 | Ull tass ee iene | 1 | Simpson's River | Kills a few furs |
| 102 | U tad at nu | 10 | Simpson's River | A steady quiet young man who kills a few furs |
| 103 | Ul ta qua | 10 | Simpson's River | A boy, son to Oss |
| 104 | Wah chaidth | 1 | Simpson's River | No great hunter |
| 105 | Willy wah | 1 | Simpson's River | Can hunt but generally plays what he kills |
| 106 | Yai ben elk tak | 4 | Nass chick | A steady honest man and a good lynx hunter |
| 107 | Yilth quote | 1 | Simpson's River | A boy of little note |

These Debts have been very much increased by the want of leather, for it would frequently happen that a Indian would come to the fort with furs to pay for a dressed skin which we had not to give him. It therefore became necessary to prevail on him to part with them for something else, which rarely could done without giving him an article which was considerably above their value consequently a Balance remained unpaid.

The Babines of the Lake, though not by any means rigidly honest in regard of property that happens to come in their way, are generally speaking pretty upright in their payment of their Debts, which whey seldom dispute when they are made ... to comprehend them. Those of Simpson's River when they come to the Fort, readily pay any debts they are due for Dressed Leather, but other property they consider of little value, and any that has been advanced to them on Credit they pay with great reluctance. It ought therefore to be made a point never to give them any goods unless they have wherewith to pay for the whole of them, for any balance that remains will be got in with difficulty.

## APPENDIX 2

### Transcript of My PowerPoint Presentation in *Samson*,
### 3 October 2000

Transcripts are provided in a format where each line is numbered, as shown in the twelve lines below. For ease in reading, we have provided this excerpt in text form.

2691[1]
01 FEDERAL COURT OF CANADA
01 TRIAL DIVISION
02 BETWEEN: T-2022-89
02 CHIEF VICTOR BUFFALO acting on his own behalf
03 and on behalf of all the other members
03 of the Samson Indian Nation and Band
04 – and –
04 THE SAMSON INDIAN BAND AND NATION
05 Plaintiffs
05 AND:
06 HER MAJESTY THE QUEEN IN RIGHT OF CANADA

FEDERAL COURT OF CANADA, TRIAL DIVISION, BETWEEN:
  T-022-89
CHIEF VICTOR BUFFALO acting on his own behalf and on behalf of
  all the other members of the Samson Indian Nation and Band
– and –
THE SAMSON INDIAN BAND AND NATION, Plaintiffs
AND: HER MAJESTY THE QUEEN IN RIGHT OF CANADA
Parliament Buildings, Ottawa, Ontario

1 I have added slide numbers.

– and –

THE MINISTER OF INDIAN AFFAIRS AND NORTHERN
    DEVELOPMENT
Parliament Buildings, Ottawa, Ontario
– and –
THE MINISTER OF FINANCE
Parliament Buildings, Ottawa, Ontario
Defendants
BETWEEN: T-1254-92 CHIEF JOHN ERMINESKIN, LAWRENCE
    WILDCAT,
GORDON LEE, ART LITTLECHILD, MAURICE WOLFE, CURTIS
    ERMINESKIN, GERRY ERMINESKIN, EARL ERMINESKIN,
    RICK WOLFE, KEN CUTARM, BRIAN LEE, LESTER FRAYNN,
    the elected Chief and councilors of the Ermineskin Indian Band
    and Nation suing on their own behalf and on behalf of the mem-
    bers of the Ermineskin Indian Band and Nation
Plaintiffs
AND:
HER MAJESTY THE QUEEN IN RIGHT OF CANADA
– and –
THE MINISTER OF INDIAN AFFAIRS AND NORTHERN
    DEVELOPMENT
Parliament Buildings, Ottawa, Ontario
– and –
THE MINISTER OF FINANCE
Parliament Buildings, Ottawa, Ontario
Defendants

---

TRIAL
October 3, 2000
Calgary, Alberta
Volume 22

---

TAKEN BEFORE: The Honourable Justice Teitelbaum /2692/
APPEARANCES
J.A. O'Reilly, Esq. For Samson Indian Nation
E.H. Molstad, Q.C.
Priscilla E.S. Kennedy, Esq.

P.W. Hutchins, Esq.
O.D. Young, Esq.
Cristina A. Scattolin, Esq.
M.R.V. Storrow, Q.C. For Ermineskin Indian Band
Maria A. Morellato, Esq.
A.D. Macleod, Q.C. For Her Majesty the Queen
W.C. Hunter, Esq.
T.E. Valentine, Esq.
Brenda A. Armitage, Esq.
J. Bazant, Esq.
Patrick Chippior Registrar
Becky Lyon, CSR(A) Realtime Reporter
Shawna Sonsteby, CSR(A) Production Reporter /2761/

MR. HUTCHINS: Now, I understand, My Lord – I don't know if the Registrar has indicated this to you – but Professor Ray would like to give us a small demonstration on his Power Point via Power Point, and I certainly don't understand technology, but there would just simply be some images which would be flashed on everybody's monitor from Professor Ray's machine. Perhaps he can explain the technology better than I. /2762/

THE WITNESS: I just use the technology. I don't understand it.

THE COURT: Just tell me what you are attempting to do, sir.

THE WITNESS: I just want to, in very few slides, give you a quick overview of what the general trend of the discussion will be with a few images, so you can – who is Morris, who is Christie, what are these ceremonies we are talking about look like.

THE COURT: Those are, I think, those pictures that –

THE WITNESS: Yes. That's correct. That's it.

THE COURT: Go ahead.

Q   MR. HUTCHINS: I understand now that it will take a few minutes for the machine to – what is the expression, boot up? And in the meantime, while that is happening, and so as not to waste the time of the Court, I would ask Professor Ray to turn to the abstract of his report, his principal report, which is found at page ii of the principal report, My Lord. I would ask you, Professor Ray, to read that abstract as an introduction to your testimony on your report, please.

A   Okay. /2771/

Q   Now, I assume the technology is capable of giving us the Power Point demonstration?

A   Power Point. I shouldn't promote Microsoft but ...

Q   I turn it over to you, Professor Ray, for that.

A   Okay. I just wanted, through a few images, to reinforce, and maybe expand on some of the points I have made here, and also put up a few images so we /2770/ can sort of visualize a little bit of the history we are talking about which can be rather abstract. And so, I am calling this <u>towards an understanding of Treaty 6</u>, and I use the word advisedly, because as I have emphasized, my training is in documentary history, and since that is my expertise, that has been my primary focus. But there are other sides to this history, the oral histories, and so don't presume that my presentation gives the full account that is needed. The oral histories, I think, will also, however, reinforce some of the points I made, and these records that I will present, I think, lead into some of the oral history accounts.

So, this is the chartering of the Hudson's Bay Company in 1670 (fig. 45). The painting is made from a calendar of the Hudson's Bay Company based on an artist's rendering of descriptions of events, probably a little bit fanciful, but gives me the opportunity just to make a couple of points about the nature of the Hudson's Bay Company in 1670 and implications that that has for understanding the history that is being presented to the Court. In 1670, Charles II gave the Hudson's Bay Company a charter which included title /2771/ to Rupert's Land which was an interesting idea since they had no idea at the time who lived out here. Charles granted it as though it was a vacant territory, whose extent was yet to be known.

He also granted to the company the right to enter into treaties with any non-Christian Princes and heads of state. And I don't have it before me, Your Honour, the charter of the company, so I am paraphrasing, from memory, key elements of that charter, but they can be verified if it is in issue. That is an important point we will come back to. In other words, the company has the right on behalf of the Crown to enter into treaties with non-Christians, heads of states, and so on. The other important point was the company was given monopoly trading rights. Now, those three things say something about the nature of mercantile companies in the mercantile age. What mercantile companies were expected to do was carry the flag of the Crown. They were to promote the Imperialism overseas, and in a sense, to use modern jargon, I think you can sort of envision the process of a privatized approach to colonization. /2772/ Rather than have the Crown bear the expense of building an empire directly out of its own coffers, they farmed it out to companies, and one of the reasons for the monopoly was for the company to undertake the spreading of the flag and establishing colonies overseas, it was granted a monopoly to guarantee itself a profit. That was the idea. Now, so when the ships begin to sail out, the Hudson's Bay Company's ships sail out to the west, as I have already pointed out to you, one of the key posts, then, for the Western Cree, the most important post in this late 17th century and early 18th century until 1774 was York Factory.

Now, take a look at the next slide (fig. 46). There is a popular misconception that the fur trade was a very simple thing where a few Indians came in to a post, exchanged a few furs, and went home. And it is an image that still persists, and it is totally wrongheaded, and it has nothing to do with the reality of the fur trade as it operated in the early years, especially in the early years of the Hudson's Bay Company, in fact throughout the Hudson's Bay Company's operation. What we are seeing here is an /2773/ artist's sketch – again, this is from a Hudson's Bay Company calendar – this sketch is a fairly good rendering of part of the description of the trading ceremony that Andrew Graham and his predecessor, James Isham, wrote about trading relations at Hudson's Bay Company. And the Andrew Graham material is material we are going to go into in some detail, so I thought it would be useful for the Court to see, to sort of try to visualize a little bit what this ceremony was all about.

Now, it should be understood that when the Hudson's Bay Company was chartered in 1670 and given under English, the eyes of the English Crown anyway, title to Rupert's Land, when the Hudson's Bay Company came over here, it faced the reality about the people living here. They don't know anything about Charles II, and Charles II is not going to send an army over here to defend their Charter rights. So the company, from the beginning, had to take a very pragmatic approach to things. And especially they had to do so during the period of the late 17th and late 18th century because from the time of the founding of the Hudson's Bay Company, really until the conquest and Treaty of /2774/ Paris in 1763, the French and English were periodically at odds with each other – in fact, in outright war – and so one of the things that the English had to do, was to try and win native people over to their side, and the French were doing the same thing. And one of the ways of doing this is through diplomatic negotiations with the First Nations.

I raise this, because this is a recurring theme, and it is a part of what is behind Treaty 6. And it is a repeat of a process that had been going on for a long time. So, the Hudson's Bay Company faced the reality of, Okay, the drafters in London send out instructions, which we will look at in detail, to the men in the bay, and they said, We want you to enter into treaties and so on with the native heads of the rivers and so on whereby they will understand that you are granting them the right to occupy your forts for purposes of trade and rites of passage and so on. And they tell them to do this in whatever custom of the country seems most appropriate.

So out of this emerges a very /2775/ complicated trading ceremony which incorporates into it the native customs of the country. And key elements of that tradition, some of which are being shown here, was as the traders point out, no serious negotiations began until the smoking of the calumet. So, there was the pipe ceremony preceded trade, and each trading party that came in, the trading captains brought in their calumets (fig. 47). If they were satisfied with the way they were treated at the post, they left their calumet as a sign of [intention to] return, and the trading captain or chief factor at the posts had to remember which pipe belonged to which chief so that the ceremony would be conducted properly.

Another important element of the ceremony was the exchange of gifts. Gifts were of both economic value and symbolic value. We cannot underestimate the importance of symbolic value of what is going on. So the gift exchange ceremony was the way in which both the Europeans, and in this case, the Hudson's Bay Company and the native leaders exchanged gifts as basically physical expressions of goodwill and cementing of their alliances. And so gift-giving was another crucial part. What we are seeing here is part of the gift-giving. When the men would arrive at the /2776/ post, the chief, the trading captains, this would be the paramount native leaders and their elders, would go in, have a brief visit with the chief factor of the post, and then they would all troop out to the native camp outside where the Hudson's Bay Company would bring out and present to the natives the gifts that the company was giving to them, and that is what is being shown here.

Now, the other very crucial part of the gift-giving ceremony was the recognition by the Hudson's Bay Company of the leaders of the First Nations that came down. So, trading captains – that is, what the Europeans referred to as the native traders who came down – were given suits of clothing which included, among other things, a coat – which we will see later on expressed as a "treaty coat" – they are given a coat, and they were given pants, hat, and beginning in the late 18th century, also medals were part of the presentations. Paramount chiefs were also given flags, company flags, and English flags as part of the exchange ceremony. So there are a number of important elements in this exchange ceremony that we will see reappearing later on, and it is part of the /2777/ way in which the Hudson's Bay Company comes to early terms with native people.

The other thing to remember, then, is that the Hudson's Bay Company is there as the representative of the Crown, so it is through the fur trade and through the Hudson's Bay Company that relations with the Crown begin; that is, in this case, the British Crown. Now, I just put in here an example what a treaty coat – or sorry; I keep saying "treaty coat" – Captain's coat looks like, and in the lower right corner here, this is out of the Hudson's Bay Company's account book showing the material that was used to actually make the coat (fig. 48). It is also an example of some of the things you can do: cross-checking the narrative written record against the company's account book records to cross-check and verify some of the things that are being said. So, the Captain's coat is both, then, a symbol of respect of native leadership, and it was also an expression of friendship. I should mention in the case of negotiating treaties, the colour of the coats was also an issue of negotiations and treaties. Red coats and blue coats were the common coats. Some /2778/ groups preferring one versus the other for very symbolic and cultural reasons.

Treaty 6: this is the etching of Fort Carleton, 1876 (fig. 49). I must say that when I read – the first time I read Morris's description of the pre-treaty ceremonies at Fort Carleton, I was struck by how many elements in that ceremony sounded like elements that were described by Graham at York Factory in the 1770s. The principal difference being the Cree were on horseback, and part of the ceremonies were done on horseback, because by this time they had acquired horses. The other important thing to say about the relationship between the Hudson's Bay Company and the Cree between the period of the late – well, the 1670s onward to the 1876 period, it was an enduring partnership in which the Hudson's Bay Company, through a variety of means, reassured the native people of their livelihood. Native people, in return, returned their loyalty and friendship to the company. And it was a partnership that was a flexible one that was able to deal with continually changing circumstances. So, my point would be, that there is a strong connection between the early relations that were established between the First /2779/ Nations of Western Canada through the Hudson's Bay Company and through that relationship with Canada. If you read the Morris book, you will find that in many places in this book, he refers to the importance of the Hudson's Bay tradition as influencing the relations between First Nations and what would become Canada and make those relations fundamentally different from that of the country of the Long Knives, which is the way [they] referred to the Americans, which was a much more bloody affair.

Now, this image here of a blank treaty medal (fig. 50) as again, as I said, the giving of treaty medals also is rooted in the fur trade, late18th and early 19th century, it became practice to give medals to leaders, and all these – I think we can all appreciate we are in a courtroom with a lot of symbols, and these symbols are very important, and we may look back and think that they are quaint, cute, and so on, but I think it is to do injustice to the history there and to the meaning these things had for the First Nations and for the English, themselves. I think that it is important to understand the symbolic and the economic importance /2780/ of what we look at. This treaty medal, I find interesting. If you will look at the medal on the left, Canada produced medals, and then as treaties were negotiated, they would add in the dates. You will notice at the bottom of the medal, this is the flip side of the same medal. It says "18 blank." So depending on the year of the treaty, then they would punch in the numbers. But I think, also, in talking about the symbolic significance, notice the medal. It is designed to show Canada extending a hand to the First Nations which is a recurrent theme in Morris's book. We are giving you; we are taking nothing away; we are adding to what you have; we are here to help you. That is his basic message, and that is the message that made the treaties possible, and it shows right – Canada has symbolized it right here on its own medal, so I think it is a point worth bearing in mind.

So, just a quick – just to reinforce my point here, visually, I think these two ceremonies here, put side by side, speak to a long and very important history that the relationships with the Crown do not begin with Treaty 6 (fig. 51). They begin with the Hudson's Bay Company and the British /2278/ Crown in the late 17th century, and they continue on through Treaty 6 to the present.

Now, these two individuals, on the left, you have Alexander Morris, and on the right, we have Christie (fig. 52). Now, these are two crucial people at the table in 1876. Each of these men represent these two traditions we have been talking about. Alexander Morris says over and over in his book that the treaty-making traditions of Canada guided him in making his treaties. He makes specific reference to the Robinson Treaty, to treaties and Treaty 3. Treaty 3, he brings up in negotiations both at the Fort Qu'Appelle Treaty and in Treaty 6 specifically, and so, if we are going to try to understand what Treaty 6 was supposed to mean, then we have to understand what it meant to Morris; he is Canada's chief negotiator.

Now, Morris, in negotiations for Treaty 4, Morris introduces to the Cree Christie. The interesting thing about Christie – and we will go into him; we have a biography of him – Christie had been a Hudson's Bay Company trader in the Prairies for most of his adult life. He had been chief factor of the Saskatchewan /2782/ districts – we will get into the details – for several years, about 15 years at least, which means that for the Cree arriving at Treaty 6 talks, Christie is sitting there – Christie is sitting there as one of the treaty commissioners for Canada. He retires just on the eve – he retires as a company officer just on the eve of Treaty 4, and you can't underestimate the importance of Christie here because he was a chief factor in the Hudson's Bay Company. He held the highest office in the company other than that of the Governor. He is a very influential and prominent man, and so for the Cree for most of their life, they understood Christie from the position of a Hudson Bay man, and he is representing the Crown through the Hudson's Bay Company.

Q  Professor Ray, you did mention that we had a biography of Christie?
A  Yes.

Q  MR. HUTCHINS: My Lord, it might be convenient now, it is found
   at page 24 of Professor Ray's rebuttal report, where you have a
   chronology of Mr. Christie's career. I don't know if you want to
   take us to that. /2783/

A  I am not sure if I have got that one here in my piles of stuff.

Q  MR. HUTCHINS: You do have it somewhere?

A  Somewhere. Okay. Right. Pages 24. I just kept going and looking
   at the – it is William J. Christie who we are looking at here on the
   right, and you see he begins in 1843 at Rocky Mountain House
   and spends most of his time in the Prairie areas with the exception
   of 11 short stints at York Factory and Churchill, and he becomes
   chief factor. He's chief trader at Fort Edmonton – let's see. He becomes a chief trader at Fort Pelly, which is in the Prairie areas.
   1854, he becomes chief trader or chief trader at Edmonton, which
   is in the Saskatchewan district, and then chief factor in 1860. And
   I should mention that the Saskatchewan district of the Hudson's
   Bay Company covered – included most of the Treaty 6 area and beyond Treaty 4 as well.

   So, my point is, that for the Cree coming to the treaty table,
   treaty talks, they too, had a blueprint in terms of their relations
   with Europeans, and it was a blueprint that had been /2784/ shaped
   up over long years through their relationships the Hudson's Bay
   Company and through men like Christie. And Morris, in introducing Christie in Treaty 4, says to the Cree that you know this man
   well, he has spent most of his life here. So, he is there as a moder-
   ating influence and as a representative of the continuity of these
   three traditions that we have been talking about.

   Just one last image: We have an etching of Fort Carleton, and
   this is a 19th century photograph of Fort Pitt, the other chief treaty
   negotiating points. And it is also, you will notice, that the chief
   points of negotiations also were Hudson's Bay Company posts.

   So, I think the connections are strong, both in symbolic and real
   terms of linking that history behind Treaty 6, and it is why I think
   it is important to understand and to try to understand what the
   treaty meant, so …

Q  Thank you very much, Professor Ray.Certainly, I am sure that we
   all enjoyed that demonstration, and it does bring things to life. A
   picture is worth a thousand words.

   In your abstract, the reading /2785/ of your abstract and the
   material you have just covered through the Power Point demon-

stration, I understand that you are discussing the context in which
treaty-making was made. Is it your opinion that historical context
is important for an understanding of Treaty Number 6, which is at
issue in this case?

A  I think it is absolutely essential.

Q  Why is that?

A  Well, as I said, because if you look a lot of the clauses in the treaty,
they echo the fur trade. The native people are in the situation of
the old mercantile order is passing away, and they are trying to negotiate their way into the new economic order which a number of
the elders were clearly aware that was happening, and their points
of reference would have been, as I said, would have been this long
tradition that they have already established. And I made the point
that on that basis, I don't believe that what they are asking for in
the treaty was asking for anything different in a fundamental way
than what they had received from the Hudson's Bay Company in
previous years. Now, the specifics were different. The Hudson's
Bay Company wasn't educating 278/6/ them, but the Hudson's Bay
Company, as they were asking for Canada, was concerned about
their welfare and livelihood. Now, in the case of the Hudson's
Bay Company, obviously, they would have a self-interest in it, but
it was more than a self-interest.

Q  Before we move into the detail of the report, is there anything more
by way of overview that you would like to discuss with the Court?

A  I think basically my point is, and I think – I don't want to overly
restate it, is I think there are two blueprints behind that treaty;
there is the blueprint that Morris brings to the treaty based on his
experience of treaty negotiations and Canada's previous experience, since in the conclusion of his book, he spells it all out about
what his motto was. And as I said, on the native side of the question, their negotiating experiences based on their own traditions
which were there before the Hudson's Bay Company comes, in
which they modify over the years, obviously they are in contact
with the company, and they had worked out a stable relationship
over the years, and that was very much on their mind, and the
Hudson's Bay Company through credit, through sick and destitute
accounts, various sorts of relief and so on, provided welfare –
/2787/ I don't like to use the welfare – it was not the way they put
it. Made sure that their trading partners and kin – remember a lot
of these Hudson's Bay men are married into native communities –

were looked after in times of need, so that it was more than just a simple trading operation. It had these various other components to it. And the gift-giving traditions continue, and the important point about that is these trading alliances, this trading ceremony, in the native way of things, the agreements had to be renewed, and every year there was a renewal ceremony. Now, in the ceremony that we are looking at York Factory in the 1770s is quite elaborate. Over the years, the Hudson's Bay Company pares it back, but they never can eliminate it. It remains a part of trade.

So, things like annuities and so on, in part, that appear in treaties later on, are carrying over in an understandable way, the natives – it's part of this continual renewing thing. So sometimes when natives were disgruntled, treaties were not being lived up to, natives would say, We won't take treaty, because it is, again, an annual present that initially had some considerable /2788/ economic value in the 70s and 80s but also had tremendous symbolic value as well.

So, we have these two traditions that lie behind Treaty 6 and carry on through Treaty 6.

Fig. 45: Slide 1 of PowerPoint presentation in *Samson* trial: Chartering the Hudson's Bay Company, 1670.

Fig. 46: Slide 2 of PowerPoint presentation in *Samson* trial: Trading Ceremony, York Factory, c. 1770.

Fig. 47: Slide 3 of PowerPoint presentation in *Samson* trial: A Hudson's Bay Company pipe ceremony as imagined by an artist.

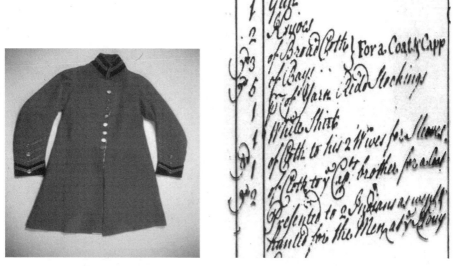

Fig. 48: Slide 4 of PowerPoint presentation in *Samson* trial: A Treaty Coat and List of Materials for a Captain's coat and other presents given at York Factory in the eighteenth century.

Fig. 49: Slide 5 of PowerPoint presentation in *Samson* trial: Treaty 6 negotiations at Fort Carleton, 1876.

Fig. 50: Slide 6 of PowerPoint presentation in *Samson* trial: Government of Canada Blank Treaty Medal. The appropriate number and date were added after negotiations had been concluded.

Fig. 51: Slide 7 of PowerPoint presentation in *Samson* trial: York Factory Trading and Fort Carleton Treaty ceremonies compared.

Fig. 52: Slide 8 of PowerPoint presentation in *Samson* trial: Treaty 6 negotiators, Lieutenant-Governor A. Morris (left) and W. Christie.

# NOTES

CHAPTER ONE

1 Provincial Court of Alberta (1986) 1 C.N.L.R., 79.

2 His father had served as a medical doctor on an Indian reserve in this province. Also, he was a lifelong friend of historian W.L. Morton, who wrote a landmark history of the province. W.L. Morton, *Manitoba: A History.*

3 A.J. Ray, *Indians in the Fur Trade: Their Roles as Hunters, Trappers and Middlemen in the Lands Southwest of Hudson Bay.*

4 Wildlife Act, R.S.A. 1980, c. W 9, ss. 18, 42.

5 The complete text of the treaty is available at Canada, Department of Indian Affairs, http://www.ainc-inac.gc.ca/al/hts/tgu/tr8-eng.asp. Accessed 22 April 2011.

6 The earliest references to the region are contained in the York Factory journals for the period 1715–20. First Nations visitors made reference to their country's including tar-like substances. Undoubtedly they were referring to the tar sands area.

7 In 1970, the company moved the originals to the Archives of Manitoba, where microfilmed copies also are available for use on site or through interlibrary loan services.

8 Originally, the archives were housed at the company's headquarters in London. By the late 1960s, when I first used them, microfilmed copies were available at the National Archives of Canada in Ottawa (now Library and Archives Canada). In 1970, the original records were moved to Winnipeg. Prior to that time, only a few scholars had consulted them. A.S. Morton was one of the most notable. He used them for his 1939 classic, *A History of the Canadian West to 1870–71: Being a History of Rupert's Land (The Hudson's Bay Company's Territory) and of the North-west Territory (including the Pacific Slope).* Another was English historian E.E. Rich, the company's official historian. Canada's most famous economic historian, Harold Innis, also used data from the company

archive for his little-known 1927 monograph, *The Fur Trade of Canada*, which was the precursor to his landmark *The Fur Trade in Canada*. Innis did not do research himself. Rather, HBC archivists provided him with the data he requested. See A.J. Ray, 1999, "Introduction," to H.A. Innis, *The Fur Trade in Canada*, 3rd edition, v–xix and A.J. Ray, 1985, "Buying and Selling Hudson's Bay Company Furs in the Eighteenth Century."

9  The Nisga'a actually began their struggle in 1890 when they created a Land Committee. The modern title case began in the courts in the 1960s.

10  In fact, since 1982, litigants have been expected to notify the court if they intend to raise Section 35 challenges.

11  At a conference in Calgary celebrating the centenary of Treaty 7 in 1977, I discussed the importance of fur trade history as an aspect of Native history. A.J. Ray, 1978, "Fur Trade History as an Aspect of Native History."

12  A principal exception was the Arctic. Most of the company's expansion into this region took place in the early twentieth century when arctic fox became a popular fur. A.J. Ray, *The Canadian Fur Trade in the Industrial Age*.

13  Archives of Manitoba, HBC archives (PAMHBCA), Fort Dunvegan Account books, 1871–91, B 56/d/14-16 and Fort Vermilion, 1871–86, B 224/d/1-8.

14  I provided analyses of this type of company document in A.J. Ray, "The Early Hudson's Bay Company Account Books as Sources for Historical Research: An Analysis and Assessment" and in A.J. Ray and D.B. Freeman, *Give Us Good Measure: An Economic Analysis of Relations between Indians and the Hudson's Bay Company*.

15  The most important and widely available are the *Sessional Papers*, which were published by the federal government. They included reports from the NWMP and the Department of Indian Affairs.

16  The force was created in 1873. In 1904, the name was changed to the Royal North West Mounted Police. This in turn was changed in 1920 to the Royal Canadian Mounted Police when the force was merged with the Dominion Police.

17  One of the most useful of these early reports was that of A.M. Jarvis, Inspector, in Charge of Northern Patrol, "Northern Patrol Report, 24 April 1897," *Canada, Sessional Papers*, 1898 (No. 15) 157–69.

18  In *Horseman* I specifically cited "Annual Report of Commissioner L.W. Herchmer, North-West Mounted Police, 1897," *Canada, Sessional Papers* 1898 (No. 15).

19  Arthur J. Ray, "Commentary on the Economic History of the Treaty 8 Area," 13 June 1985 (unpublished).

20  In 1900 and afterward, additional groups joined the treaty. It is the practice in Canada to refer to these later signings as "adhesions."

21  It should be noted also that beaver pelts traditionally provided one of the main articles of winter clothing, the beaver coat (worn with the fur turned inward) throughout the Subarctic. In the early days of the fur trade, Na-

tive people were able to sell these used garments as "coat beaver." Thus, in the first century and a half of the fur trade, they obtained use value (food and clothing) and exchange value (as coat and parchment beaver pelts) from their trapping activities.

22· During the first half of the twentieth century North American anthropologists developed the "culture area" concept. Their premise was that Native people had adapted to their environment over thousands of years. Thus, although cultures were highly varied in terms of details, these scholars supposed that common basic cultural patterns could be discerned which reflected the adaptations that groups had to make to regional environments. The Subarctic was one of the largest cultural/environmental regions that these scholars identified. The classic culture area studies are A.L. Kroeber, *Cultural and Natural Areas of Native North America* and Harold E. Driver, *Indians of North America*.

23 Actually, the animals were hunted mostly in the winter using axes and ice chisels until the late eighteenth century, when Europeans introduced steel-spring leg-hold traps.

24 I discussed this aspect of western Canadian fur trade history in: A.J. Ray, "Some Conservation Schemes of the Hudson's Bay Company, 1821–50: An Examination of the Problems of Resource Management in the Fur Trade" and A.J. Ray, "Competition and Conservation in the Early Subarctic Fur Trade." In the 1890s, Native people living in the region that is now encompassed by Treaty 8 once again faced severe food shortages. These difficulties led them to make their initial approaches the government for a treaty. See A.J. Ray, "Treaty 8: An Anomaly of the First Nations History of British Columbia."

25 This is the term used in Canada to describe the phase at trial when a lawyer asks questions of the expert he or she has retained.

26 When claims arise from civil proceedings, opposing counsel file their experts' briefs with the court before trial.

27 *Regina v. Horseman* [1986] 1 C.N.L.R. 79.

28 Before the Supreme Court Mr Staroszik argued that the government did not have the right to do this without Indian consent. The Court rejected his argument.

29 In contrast to the case with other provinces, when Manitoba joined confederation in 1870 and Alberta and Saskatchewan were created from the Northwest Territory in 1905, the federal government retained ownership of Crown lands. The NRTA resulted from a series of federal-provincial negotiations that aimed to address this issue, which had become a political grievance in the Prairie west. Three separate but similarly worded acts were passed in 1930.

30 Quoted in *R. v. Horseman* [1990] S.C.R. 901: 29.

31 Alberta is blanketed by three treaties, Treaty 6, Treaty 7, and Treaty 8.

32 *R. v. Smith,* 1935 Dominion Law Review (DLR).

33 These ideas were expressed in: *R. v. Strongquill* 1953, *Cardinal v. Attorney general of Alberta* 1974, and *Moosehunter v. The Queen* 1981.

34 Wilson cited: *R. v. Smith* 1935, *R. v. Strongquill* 1953, and *Frank v. The Queen*.

35 She paid particular attention to Richard Daniel and R. Price, eds., *The Spirit of the Alberta Indian Treaties*, and René Fumoleau, *As Long as the Land Shall Last: A History of Treaty 8 and Treaty 11, 1870–1939*.

36 The government had been sensitive about this issue since the negotiation of the Prairie treaties in the 1870s. The collapse of the bison economy before Plains First Nations were able to develop alternative sources of livelihood meant that the federal government had to mount a massive and expensive relief effort. Ray, *The Canadian Fur Trade in the Industrial Age*, 30–49.

CHAPTER TWO

1 From an early date, their actions in the political arena involved taking petitions to the provincial, federal, and Imperial governments.

2 Subsequently, they changed the spelling to Gitxsan, which is the current usage and the one I follow hereinafter.

3 After 1984 they operated as the Gitxsan-Wet'suet'en Tribal Council until they divided into two groups. Hereinafter I refer to them as the Gitxsan-Wet'suet'en, as they were identified in the *Delgamuukw v. Regina* litigation.

4 It was a subsidiary of Aluminum Company of America. Today it operates as part of Rio Tinto-Alcan.

5 In 1979 Alcan had announced its intention to develop the hydroelectric potential of the Bulkley River. In 1984 it applied to the British Columbia Utilities Commission for a certificate to use 88 percent of the river's potential.

6 The project would have augmented the power that Alcan already generated near Kemano, British Columbia, to supply its smelter at Kitimat, British Columbia.

7 I attended several meetings in January 1984 with Gitksan-Carrier Tribal Council research director Richard Overstall and other researchers to determine the historical research that would be needed for the Kemano hearings. These meetings were summarized in memos by Richard Overstall dated 4 and 23 January. A memo dated 28 June 1984 from Peter Grant, one of the legal attorneys for the tribal council, outlined the proposed schedule of evidence for the hearings. The hearings did not take place, but the project did not go forward.

8 This was published as *The Canadian Fur Trade in the Industrial Age*.

9 In 1806 Simon Fraser established a post on McLeod Lake.

10 Fraser also built a post on Stuart Lake in 1806. This post, named Fort St James, was the company's most important post in the northern interior.

11  The company's original charter, which was granted by Charles II in 1670, encompassed only the drainage area of "Hudsons Streightes." In 1821 the British Parliament extended its trading licence to the western Arctic (Mackenzie drainage basin) and the Pacific. This meant that the company came to have different legal statuses in present-day Canada. In Rupert's Land, it held title (in the eyes of the Crown) and monopoly trading privileges. Beyond this area, in the western Arctic and the Pacific drainage, it did not hold title.

12  It was originally named Fort Kilmaurs.

13  Today descendants of the latter people comprise the Lake Babine First Nation.

14  The Gitksan-Wet'suet'en prefer to describe them as "feasts."

15  Reflecting their close association, the latter people speak a common dialect – Babine-Witsuwit'en. This is spoken in the Bulkley Valley and around Francois Lake, Babine Lake, and Takla Lake in Northwestern British Columbia. It consists of two closely related dialects, Babine and Witsuwit'en. See Yinka Déné Language Institute http://www.ydli.org/langs/bw.htm (accessed 20 November 2007).

16  Babine Post Journals, 1822–23, PAMHBCA B 11/a/1-2, Microfilm Reel, 1M15.

17  Diamond Jenness, *The Carrier Indians of the Bulkley River: Their Social and Religious Life*. I was unaware of Jenness's monograph when I read Brown's accounts.

18  I summarized my research for the tribal council in two preliminary reports. I submitted the first report, which was entitled "Hudson's Bay Company Expansion into the Upper Skeena River Region in the 1820s," on 17 February 1984 and the second, lengthier one, which was entitled "The Early Economic History of the Gitxsan-Wet'suet'en-Babine Tribal Territories, 1822–1915," on 16 January 1985.

19  Also referred to as "Autcette" in the HBC records.

20  Fur trader Peter Skene Ogden visited the settlement in the late 1820s and mentioned that there were twenty-eight "chiefs" and "nobles," rather than twenty, suggesting that Brown's list may not have been complete. Peter Skene Ogden, "Notes on Western Caledonia, 1794–1854."

21  See Appendix 1.

22  This team included: Murray Adams, Michael Jackson, Louise Mandel, and Peter Grant.

23  This practice poses challenges for historians because a succession of people who appear in the historical record can have the same name. The hereditary coastal Tshimsian chiefly name of Legaic is one example. A succession of hereditary chiefs bearing this name traded on the Skeena River.

24  The final version of my second report was much lengthier (126 pages). I changed the title to "The Economic History of the Gitksan-Wet'suet'en-

Babine Tribal Territories, 1822–1915" to reflect the expanded focus. The report included a background section on the "prehistoric/protohistoric regional economy."

25 Opening Statement of the Gitksan and Wet'suwet'en Hereditary Chiefs to Chief Justice McEachern of the Supreme Court of British Columbia, 11 May 1987, 23.

26 Ibid.

27 The reason for this was that the Gitxsan-Wet'suet'en legal team had retained another expert, historical geographer Robert Galois, to focus on the later period. Several years after the conclusion of the trial, he published his report in the *Native Studies Review.* See R. Galois, "The 'Indian Land Question' in British Columbia, 1903–1916."

28 Much later, I learned that anthropologist Nancy Lurie had made this point many years earlier when noting that cross-examination was not like a doctoral oral. See Nancy O. Lurie, "A Reply to Land Claims Cases: Anthropologists in Conflict." Lurie observed that lawyers were "occupationally suspicious." In cross-examination, they often subject witnesses to "obfuscating tactics or repetitious and therefore witness-wearying questions that are the lawyer's stock in trade."

29 Proceedings at Trial in the Supreme Court of British Columbia, No. 0843, Smithers Registry, [Proceedings SCBC], 20 March 1989, vol. 202, 13330.

30 A key difference was that English/Scottish nobles held individual titles to land. Lineage heads were custodians of lands possessed collectively by the kinship group.

31 Proceedings SCBC, 20 March 1989, 13330.

32 He did so on 25 October 1989. Proceedings SCBC, vol, 288, 21562. The two specialties are very closely linked. For example, Dr Robinson's dissertation was an historical study entitled "Men and Resources on the Northern Northwest coast of North America, 1785–1840," which she completed at the University of London in 1983. When Mr Willms was leading Dr Robinson through her *curriculum vitae*, she defined cultural geography as a "branch of geography and it's concerned with the relationships between people and environments and it specifically looks at changes in those relationships through time." Proceedings SCBC, 25 October 1989, 21562.

33 Most of my pre-doctoral courses were in these fields, and two of my three doctoral supervisors were archaeologists.

34 Proceedings SCBC, 20 March 1989, 13369–13372.

35 She also noted that lawyers and judges in the United States often preferred to deal with anthropologists because they answered questions directly and in terms that members of the legal profession understood. Native witnesses often replied in their story-telling traditions, which meant that their answers were often lengthy and seemingly indirect.

36 Canada was a co-defendant in this civil action.

37 Proceedings SCBC, 13331.

38 Ibid., 13332.

39 Ibid.

40 Sheila P. Robinson explicitly states in her report: "Prior to the intensifica-tion of pressure on interior fur resources sparked by European demands for furs, there would appear to have been no need for a sophisticated and elaborate body of rules governing access to resources or for extensive and defined area of land for their exploitation. In the absence of competition over scarce resources, there is no reason for the rules to exist." "Protohis-toric Developments in Gitksan and Wet'suwet'en Territories," 6.

41 Members of the Gitxsan-Wet'suet'en team of experts referred to this idea as the "lines and nodes" thesis of Aboriginal property. In effect, she was advancing a theory of property that was similar to the one English philosopher John Locke had proposed centuries earlier. Locke proposed the labour theory of property. His ideas, and those of Thomas Hobbes, helped settlers justify dispossessing Aboriginal people by arguing that "undeveloped" lands were "waste lands."

42 In fact, she mostly ignored Brown. She lists the Fort Babine records in her bibliography but did not discuss their relevance to her argument in her re-port. Rather, they are cited as evidence for the trade of European goods from the coast by Tshimsian. Robinson, "Protohistoric Developments," 23.

43 Anthropologists labelled this notion as the "pizza Indian argument," the idea being that "Indians" who eat pizza cease to be Aboriginal. The court handed down its judgment in May 1990. *Regina v. Sparrow*, [1990] 1 S.C.R. 1075[1990] 1 S.C.R. The *Delgamuukw* trial ended 30 June 1990.

44 In this decision, the court held that traditional practices could survive in modern forms.

45 In *Sparrow*, the court stated that traditional practices could be "affirmed in a contemporary form rather than in their primeval simplicity and vigour."

46 I published my first two articles in 1972.

47 See Julian Steward, "Carrier Acculturation: The Direct Historical Ap-proach"; Charles A. Bishop, "Limiting Access to Limited Goods: The Ori-gin of Stratification in Interior British Columbia"; and Vernon Kobrinsky, "The Tsimshianization of the Carrier Indians." Robinson relied very heavily on this short speculative piece.

48 She testified 26 October to 8 November. Proceedings SCBC, vols. 289–94.

49 The commission was created by an Act of Congress in 1946 and operated for thirty years.

50 After the trial I published an article about this strategy. Arthur J. Ray, "Creating the Image of the Savage in Defense of the Crown: The Ethno-historian in Court."

51 Proceedings SCBC, vol. 205, 13678.

52 These included accounts by William Beynon (court exhibit 860A-14), who was a hereditary elder of the Nisga'a. He assisted anthropologist Marius Barbeau and became an ethnographer in his own right. His papers span the years 1933 to 1969. Macaulay also cited the 1920 reminiscences of C.F. Morrison, who worked for the Collins Overland Telegraph Company (court exhibit 969-18).

53 Proceedings SCBC, vol. 205, 13686.

54 Ibid.

55 Ibid.

56 Proceedings SCBC, vol. 205, 13699.

57 Ibid.

58 He added: "I have no doubt life in the territory was extremely difficult, and many of the badges of civilization, as we of European culture understand that term, were indeed absent." Chief Justice Allan McEachern, *Delgamuukw v. Regina, Reasons for Judgment*, Vancouver: SCBC, Vancouver, 1991: 31.

59 He did give weight to archaeological, linguistic, and genealogical evidence. Ibid., 59–61 and 68–73.

60 A.J. Ray, "Creating the Image of the Savage in Defense of the Crown: The Ethnohistorian in Court," 13–28.

61 Ibid., 13686.

62 Don Monet and Skanu'u, *Colonialism on Trial: Indigenous Land Rights and the Gitksan and Wet'suet'en Sovereignty Case*.

63 Arthur J. Ray, *I Have Lived Here Since the World Began* (3rd edition).

CHAPTER THREE

1 Treaty 3, which encompassed northwestern Ontario and bordered Treaty 9, also had a livelihood clause. There was a slight difference in wording between treaties 3 and 9. In the former, the livelihood rights clause states: "Her Majesty further agrees with Her said Indians that they, the said Indians, shall have right to pursue their avocations of hunting and fishing throughout the tract surrendered as hereinbefore described, subject to such regulations as may from time to time be made by Her Government of Her Dominion of Canada, and saving and excepting such tracts as may, from time to time, be required or taken up for settlement, mining, lumbering or other purposes by Her said Government of the Dominion of Canada, or by any of the subjects thereof duly authorized therefor by the said Government." Government of Canada, Department of Indian and Northern Affairs, http://www.ainc-inac.gc.ca/al/hts/tgu/pubs/t3/trty3-eng.asp (accessed 22 April 2011). The word "vocations" is substituted for "avocations" in Treaty 9. This was the same wording that was used in Treaty 8.

2 Ontario Court, Provincial Division.

3 Peter C. Newman, *Company of Adventurers.*

4 Bird & Thatcher, Barristers and Solicitors, 215 Camelot Street, Thunder Bay, Ontario.

5 This community and the Hudson's Bay Company trading post that was located here is variously spelled in the records as: Marten's Falls, Marten Fall, Martin Fall, and Martin Falls. Here we treat the HBC post as "Martin Fall" and the First Nation community as "Martin Falls."

6 The licence stipulated that drift nets were to be limited to 25 fathoms in length. Mr Sparrow was caught with a net that was 45 fathoms in length. Supreme Court of Canada, http://scc.lexum.umontreal.ca/en/1990/ 1990rcs1-1075/1990rcs1-1075.html (accessed 13 June 2008).

7 Ibid.

8 This treaty was completed in two stages. The 1905 agreement encompassed the lands from the Albany River southward to the Hudson Bay–St Lawrence drainage divide. Twenty-five years later the treaty was extended northward to include the rest of Northern Ontario.

9 The company built the first post in 1670. The French captured it in 1686 and renamed it Fort St Anne. The company regained the post in 1693 and controlled it thereafter.

10 The records include post journals from Fort Albany (1890–95), Henley House (1873–75), Martin Fall (1869–99), Fort Hope (1891–1903), and Osnaburgh House (1871–77), and account books from Fort Albany (1693–1799).

11 The company administered it from Moose Factory after 1821.

12 James Isham, *Observations on Hudson Bay, 1743,* 168–9.

13 Arthur J. Ray, "'Auld Betsy and Her Daughter,' Fur Trade Fisheries in Northern Ontario," 90–1. I based this chapter on the research I had undertaken for Mr Thatcher.

14 In fact, when Native people first offered to sell this product in the late seventeenth century, the Hudson's Bay Company was not interested. It was not until the London market became glutted with beaver in the early 1690s that the company encouraged their Aboriginal trading partners to bring isinglass to trade. Ibid., 90–1.

15 Tim Holzkamm, Victor Lytwyn, and Leo Waisberg, "Rainy River Sturgeon: An Ojibway Resource in the Fur Trade Economy," and Tim Holzkamm and M. McCarthy, "Potential Fishery of Lake Sturgeon (*Asipenser fulvescens*) as Indicated by the Returns of the HBC Lac La Pluie District."

16 They were Susan Roy (now Dr Roy), Terri Thompson, Kim White, and Chris Elsner.

17 This required recording the date, name of the Native person involved (if given), and the details of the transaction.

18 About eight observations per page or over 1,400 in total.

19  Jennifer Brown, *Strangers in Blood: Fur Trade Families in Indian Country.*

20  Sylvia Van Kirk, *Many Tender Ties: Women in Fur Trade Society in Western Canada.*

21  Sometimes if a male head of the family died, his account would be relisted under his widow's name.

22  J.W. Anderson, *Fur Trader's Story*, 63. To further emphasize his point, Anderson mentioned: "More than once my own life depended on the fish nets, and I am therefore in a position to appreciate the value of this food supply in the five or so half-centuries of fur trade history before my time."

23  Frank Tough, *Fisheries Economics and the Tragedy of the Commons: The Case of Manitoba's Inland Fisheries*, and *As Their Resources Fail: Native People and the Economic History of Northern Manitoba*; also, Victor Lytwyn, *The Hudson Bay Lowland Cree in the Fur Trade to 1821: A Study in Historical Geography.*

24  Often their wives and children were involved too.

25  Martin Fall Journals 1869-99, HBCA B 123/a/85–93.

26  Ibid., B 123/a/86:28.

27  For example, the journal entry for 18 October 1872 noted: "Wich ee capay got his pay for his assistance. 6 MB [made beaver] & his plug Tobacco & fall potatoes each time he came in with the full kegs ... I promised him 1 MB per trip, but was to be 4 kegs each trip." B 123/a/88: 20.

28  The journal entry for 15 October 1871, which is listed in Table 3, indicates that Auld Betsy and her daughter were building a smoke tent that was likely similar to the tent being covered in this photograph.

29  It should be noted that in the 1890s the journals make few specific references to the kinds of fish the Aboriginal people bartered. Typically the entries simply say, "Indians arrived with some fish" or "a little fish."

30  Fort Hope (Ontario) post journals, PAMHBCA AA B 291/a/1–5.

31  The Native men who operated them included Ayumeawumie, Drake, Kachang, "Lame man," Shabayorkishick, Shatagamy, and Chief Yesno. (Appendix 6, lines: 12, 55, 173–5, and 183); (Appendix 6, line 42).

32  (Appendix 6, lines: 98–113 and 142) (Appendix 6, lines: 4248).

33  Osnaburgh House Journals, 1871–77, PAMHBCA B 155/a/80–82.

34  These are found in HBCA B 135/h/1–3.

35  Tim Holzkamm and Michael McCarthy, "Potential Fishery of Lake Sturgeon (*Asipenser fulvescens*) as Indicated by the Returns of the Hudson's Bay Company Lac la Pluie District," and Holzkamm, Lytwyn, and Waisberg, "Rainy River Sturgeon."

36  Moose Factory Abstracts of Servants' Accounts, PAMHBCA B 123/a/85: 26.

37  Facsimile from Francis Thatcher to Arthur J. Ray, 2 June 1994.

38  In contrast to Treaty 3 and those that followed, Treaty 1 and Treaty 2 did not include a livelihood rights clause.

39  Tough, *Fishery Economics and the Tragedy of the Commons*, and *As Their Resources Fail.*

40 These included the 1818–19 Manitoba District Report that William Brown wrote two years before he arrived in Gitxsan-Wet'suet'en territory. PAMHBCA B 122/e/1.

41 "Journal at Water Hen River, September 6, 1849–June 5, 1850."

42 See D. Sprague and R. Frye, *The Genealogy of the Frist Métis Nation*, Table 1.

43 "Journal at Water Hen River."

44 Ibid. Entries for 14 November; 12 December; 13, 21, 25, and 31 January; 1 and 3 February; and 3 and 26 March.

45 Ibid. Entries for 12 and 17 January; 23 February; 12 and 19 March; and 13 April.

46 Arthur J. Ray, "Historical Geography of the Native Economy of the Treaty 2 Area: A Brief Overview from Pre-contact to ca. 1890." Unpublished, 1998, 34 pages.

CHAPTER FOUR

1 'Sampson Cree Lawsuit Wraps Up' http://www.cbcca/story/canada/national/2004/12/21/samsoncree0041221.html, 25 March 2005

2 That case took 365 days; it generated 9,200 documents and yielded a transcript in excess of 75,000 pages.

3 The term is used hereinafter in the legal sense to refer to people so defined according to the Indian Act.

4 O'Reilly and Hutchins also negotiated the James Bay Agreement, which was the first modern land claim settlement.

5 British historian E.E. Rich initiated the debate with his article "Trade Habits and Economic Motivation among the Indians of North America," *Canadian Journal of Economics and Political Science* 27 (1960): 35–53.

6 Arthur J. Ray and Donald B. Freeman, *"Give Us Good Measure": An Economic Analysis of Relations Between the Indians and the Hudson's Bay Company Before 1763.*

7 Subsequently I published most of my brief in chapter 1 of Arthur J. Ray, Jim Miller, and Frank Tough, *Bounty and Benevolence: A History of Saskatchewan Treaties.*

8 Thomas Flanagan, "Analysis of the Plaintiffs' Expert Reports in the Case of *Chief Victor Buffalo v. Her Majesty et al.*," 21 July 1998, Federal Court of Canada Trial Division, Trial Division, T-2022-89 and T-1254-92.

9 Von Gernet, "Assessment of Certain Evidence Relating to Plains Cree Practices," 26 May 2000 and von Gernet, "Aboriginal Oral Documents and Treaty 6," 21 March 2000, Federal Court of Canada Trial Division, Trial Division, T-2022-89 and T-1254-92.

10 Thomas Flanagan, "Surrebuttal to the Rebuttal Reports of Bob Beal, Carl Beal, Stan Cuthand, Arthur Ray, and John Tobias," 2 June 2000.

11 Von Gernet, "Assessment of Certain Evidence Relating to Plains Cree Practices," 26 May 2000 and von Gernet, "Aboriginal Oral Documents

and Treaty 6," 21 March 2000, Federal Court of Canada Trial Division, Trial Division, T-2022-89 and T-1254-92.

12 It is generally accepted that the older, pre-treaty Cree was very different from the Cree of the present day. Today very few Cree speak the older language. H.C. Wolfart, "Linguistic Aspects of Treaty 6," 24 February 2000, Federal Court of Canada Trial Division, Trial Division, T-2022-89 and T-1254-92.

13 Thomas Flanagan, "Analysis of the Plaintiffs' Experts' Reports in the case of *Chief Victor Buffalo v. Her Majesty et al.*," 21 July 1998, Federal Court of Canada Trial Division, Trial Division, T-2022-89 and T-1254-92; and "Surrebuttal to the Rebuttal Reports," 2 June 2000.

14 For a biography of Peter Erasmus and an account of his life, see Irene B. Spry, ed., *Buffalo Days and Nights: Peter Erasmus as Told to Henry Thompson.*

15 Subsequently I published my research about Kroeber. See A.J. Ray, "Kroeber and the California Claims: Historical Particularism and Cultural Ecology in Court."

16 Flanagan, 1998, 33. In his brief, Flanagan raised the issue of the linear view of time common to Western historical and judicial approaches and the Aboriginal concept of "circular time."

17 Justice Teitelbaum had been involved in the following cases: *Morin v. Canada*, [2000] F.C.J. No. 1686. (Alberta), *Cimon v. Canada*, [1999] F.C.J. No. 1736. (Ontario), *McLeod Lake Indian Band v. Chingee*, [1998] F.C.J. No. 899. (B.C.), *Yellowquill v. Canada*, [1998] F.C.J. No. 1245. (Manitoba), *Tsawwassen Indian Band v. Canada (Minister of Indian Affairs and Northern Development)* (1997), 129 F.T.R. 8. (B.C.), *Canadian Pacific Ltd. v. Matsqui Indian Band et al.* (1996), 111 F.T.R. 161. (B.C.), *Wewayakum Indian Band v. Canada and Wewayakai Indian Band* (1995), 99 F.T.R. 1. (B.C.), *Hunt v. Canada (Corrections Service)*, [1993] F.C.J. No. 552. (Ontario, Aboriginal applicant), *Derrickson v. Canada* (1991), 49 F.T.R. 295. (Ontario), *Obichon v. Heart Lake First Nation No. 176* (1988), 21 F.T.R. 1. (Alberta), *Blackfoot Band of Indians No. 146 v. Canada* (1986), 7 F.T.R. 133. (Alberta).

18 Federal Court of Canada Trial Division, Calgary, Alberta, Transcripts, 3 October 2000, 2694

19 Ibid.

20 The whole monograph was entered as an exhibit.

21 *Victor Buffalo* Transcripts, 3 October 2000, 2761.

22 Christie began his HBC career in 1843–44 as an apprentice clerk at Rocky Mountain House. Subsequently, he moved through the ranks with appointments at York Factory and Fort Churchill on Hudson Bay and at Fort Pelly in the Swan River district. In 1858 he was appointed to Fort Edmonton as chief trader. Two years later, he was appointed chief factor. He served at Fort Edmonton until he was appointed inspecting chief factor in 1872. He retired at the end of May 1873.

23  *Victor Buffalo* Transcripts, 3 October 2000, 2762.

24  Ibid., 2812.

25  This was a copy of Figure 8 from my book, *Indians in the Fur Trade*.

26  *Victor Buffalo* Transcripts, 3 October 2000, 2814.

27  *Victor Buffalo* Transcripts, 4 October 2000, 3338–40.

28  Ray, in Ray, Miller, and Tough, *Bounty and Benevolence*, 71.

29  *Victor Buffalo* Transcripts, 3 October 2000, 3040.

30  Ibid.

31  *Victor Buffalo* Transcripts, 4 October 2000, 3110–11.

32  Morris, 1880, 180.

33  *Victor Buffalo* Transcripts, 5 October 2000, 3164–5.

34  Ibid., 3165–6.

35  Ibid., 3205.

36  Ibid., 3206–7.

37  Ibid., 3208.

38  Ibid.

39  Ibid.

40  Ibid., 3319–21.

41  *Victor Buffalo* Transcripts, 5 October 2000, 3245–8.

42  These were for the government: Peter Ballenden and the Reverend John McKay.

43  This was a key reason for many of Mr O'Reilly's objections to Mr Macleod's cross-examination. It frequently was unclear if he was asking a question.

44  *Victor Buffalo* Transcripts, 5 October 2000, 3392–3. Mr Macleod had objected to Mr O'Reilly's revisiting this topic.

45  The parties mentioned in the opening paragraph are referred to as follows: "between Her Most Gracious Majesty the Queen of Great Britain and Ireland, by her Commissioners, the Honorable Alexander Morris, Lieutenant-governor of the Province of Manitoba and the North-West Territories, and the Honorable James McKay and the Honorable William Joseph Christie of the one part, and the Plain and the Wood Cree Tribes," Morris, 351.

46  *Victor Buffalo* Transcripts, 6 October 2000, 3415–17.

47  J. Teitelbaum, *Reasons for Judgment*, FC 1622, 3.

48  Ibid., 2–196.

49  Ibid., 196.

50  Justice Teitelbaum quoted Dr von Gernet's summary of his approach: "In my opinion, the most useful approach recognizes the legitimacy of self-representation and acknowledges that what people believe about their own past must be respected and receive serious historical consideration. At the same time, it assumes that there was a real past independent of what people presently believe it to be, and that valuable information about that past may be derived from various sources including oral histories and oral traditions. It accepts that both non-Aboriginal and Aborigi-

nal scholars can be biased, that various pasts can be invented or used for political reasons, and that a completely value-free history is an impossible ideal. Nevertheless, it postulates that the past constrains the way in which modern interpreters can manipulate it for various purposes. While the actual past is beyond retrieval, this must remain the aim. The reconstruction that results may not have a privileged claim on universal 'truth,' but it will have the advantage of being rigorous. The approach rejects the fashionable notion that, because Aboriginal oral documents are not Western, they cannot be assessed using Western methods and should be allowed to escape the type of scrutiny given to other forms of evidence. Ultimately, the perspective is in accord with the belief of the highly-regarded anthropologist Bruce Trigger: public wrongs cannot be atoned by abandoning scientific standards in the historical study of relations between Aboriginal and non-Aboriginal peoples. *Victor Buffalo* Transcripts, 198.

51 Ibid., 197. A key reason that she did not offer such commentary was that she was retained as an expert after the trial had resumed in October 2000. Unlike Dr von Gernet, she did not attend the oral history presentations on the reserve.

52 He did concede that Erasmus's memories probably had been contaminated by reading, or having been presented with, the accounts of other observers.

CHAPTER FIVE

1 This act has been replaced with the Fish and Wildlife Conservation Act (RSO 1997).

2 J. Peterson made passing reference to the community. See Jacqueline Peterson, "Many Roads to Red River."

3 *Regina v. Van der Peet,* 1996, 2 S.C.R. 507, 57–8.

4 Ibid., 11.

5 Ray, Arthur J. "An Economic History of the Robinson Treaties Area Before 1860," March 17, 1998.

6 I had been retained by Joyce L. Pelletier to undertake research for this First Nation, whose traditional territory overlapped the boundaries of the Robinson Huron Treaty and Treaty 9. My report was titled: "Flying Post: An Economic History." Unpublished, 1996. Questions had arisen about whether these people had treaty rights in both areas. The parties reached a settlement without going to court.

7 Alexander Henry, *Travels and Adventures in Canada and the Indian Territories Between 1760 and 1776,* 61–2. During his visit to the fort, Henry noted that the only family (apart from the French officers and men) that was resident was that of Jean Baptiste Cadotte, whose wife was Native. The Cadottes were one of the foundational Métis families. For a brief history of this family see Theresa M. Schenck, "The Cadottes: Five Generations of Fur Traders on Lake Superior," 189–98. Among the visitors to follow Henry were: G. Franchere, John Long, Alexander Mackenzie, and

Henry R. Schoolcraft. See Gabriel Franchere, *A Voyage to the Northwest Coast of America*; Alexander Mackenzie, *The Journals and Letters of Sir Alexander Mackenzie*; Johann Georg Kohl, *Kitchi-gami: Life Among the Lake Superior Ojibway*; Henry R. Schoolcraft, *Narrative Journal of Travels Through the Northwestern Regions of the United States Extending from Detroit through the Great Chain of American Lakes to the Sources of the Mississippi River in the Year 1820.*

8  I noted this in the early 1970s, as did anthropologist C.A. Bishop. See Ray (1974) and Charles A. Bishop, *The Northern Ojibwa and the Fur Trade.*

9  The report was entitled: "An Economic History of the Robinson Treaty Area before 1860."

10  Bishop, *The Northern Ojibwa and the Fur Trade.*

11  For a brief biography of Mactavish see http://www.gov.mb.ca/chc/archives/hbca/biographical/mc/mctavish_willia m.pdf.

12  The Simpson Correspondence (Outward PAMHBCA D 4/1–81and Inward PAMHBCA D 4/116–27 and D5/1–52) is an important source of information about most HBC districts. His outward letters span the years from 1821 to 1854 and the letters inward the years 1821 to 1860. Letters from district heads are included in the latter and often provide detailed information about the territories these men managed.

13  Both names have numerous spellings in the records.

14  Mactavish to Simpson, 20 November 1849. Simpson Inward, PAMHBCA D 5/26: 444.

15  Ibid., 14 December 1849, 692.

16  Alexander Vidal, "A Journal of Proceedings on My Mission to the Indians [of] Lake Superior and Huron, 1849," transcribed by George Smith with historical notes by M.E. Arthur (Bright's Grove: George Smith, 1974) and T.G. Anderson, "Diary of [Captn.] Thomas Gummersell Anderson, a visiting Supt. of Indian Affairs at this time 1849 at Cobourg."

17  The trial began on Monday 27 April 1998.

18  This course, History 302, was the basis of the first edition of my book *I Have Lived Here Since the World Began: A History of Canada's Aboriginal People.*

19  This was Thursday, 30 April 1998.

20  Registry No. 999 93 3220, Ontario Court (Provincial Division) Her Majesty the Queen against Steve Powley and Roddy C. Powley, Volume 2, Excerpts from Trial Before the Honourable Judge C. Vaillancourt at the City of Sault Ste Marie on April 30, and May 1 and 4, 1998: 258–9.

21  Ibid., 314–16.

22  Justice C. Vaillancourt, Reasons for Judgment, *Regina v. Steve Powley and Rod Powley* (No. 2) Ontario Court (Provincial Division, 26 February 1999: 26.

23  Ibid.

24 These were to the Ontario Superior Court of Justice, the Court of Appeal for Ontario, and the Supreme Court of Canada. See: *R. v. Powley*, 2000 CanLII 22327 (ON S.C.), http://www.canlii.org/eliisa/highlight.do?text= powley&language=en&searchTitle=Ontario+-+Superior+Court+of+ Justice&path=/en/on/onsc/doc/2000/2000canlii22327/2000canlii22327. html, accessed 1 October 2009, paragraph 20a; http://www.ontario courts.on.ca/decisions/search/en/OntarioCourtsSearch_VOpenFile.cfm? serverFilePath=D%3A%5CUsers%5COntario%20Courts%5Cwww%5 Cdecisions%5C2001%5Cfebruary%5Cpowley%2Ehtm.; and http://scc.lexum.umontreal.ca/en/2003/2003scc43/2003scc43.html.

25 *Regina v. Powley*, Court of Appeal for Ontario, Docket 34065, 23 February 2001, http://www.ontariocourts.on.ca/decisions/search/en/Ontario CourtsSearch_VOpenFile.cfm?serverFilePath=D%3A%5CUsers%5CO ntario%20Courts%5Cwww%5Cdecisions%5C2001%5Cfebruary%5Cp owley%2Ehtm, paragraph 136.

CHAPTER SIX

1 In *Van der Peet,* the Court wrote: "Although s. 35 [of the Constitution Act 1982] includes the Métis within its definition of 'aboriginal peoples of Canada,' and thus seems to link their claims to those of other aboriginal peoples under the general heading of 'aboriginal rights,' the history of the Métis, and the reasons underlying their inclusion in the protection given by s. 35, are quite distinct from those of other aboriginal peoples in Canada. As such, the manner in which the aboriginal rights of other aboriginal peoples are defined is not necessarily determinative of the manner in which the aboriginal rights of the Métis are defined. At the time when this Court is presented with a Métis claim under s. 35 it will then, with the benefit of the arguments of counsel, a factual context and a specific Métis claim, be able to explore the question of the purposes underlying s. 35's protection of the aboriginal rights of Métis people, and answer the question of the kinds of claims which fall within s. 35(1)'s scope when the claimants are Métis. The fact that, for other aboriginal peoples, the protection granted by s. 35 goes to the practices, customs and traditions of aboriginal peoples prior to contact, is not necessarily relevant to the answer which will be given to that question. It may, or it may not, be the case that the claims of the Métis are determined on the basis of the pre-contact practices, customs and traditions of their aboriginal ancestors; whether that is so must await determination in a case in which the issue arises. *R. v. Van der Peet*, [1996] 2 S.C.R. 507, paragraph 67.

2 *R. v. Pawley,* [2003] 2 S.C.R. 207, 2003, SCC 43, 2–3.

3 See Bibliography.

4 According to the Merriam-Webster dictionary, the word "community" has a number of common meanings: "a unified body of individuals: as a: STATE, COMMONWEALTH b: the people with common interests living in a

particular area; broadly: the area itself 'the problems of a large community' c: an interacting population of various kinds of individuals (as species) in a common location d: a group of people with a common characteristic or interest living together within a larger society 'a community of retired persons' e: a group linked by a common policy f: a body of persons or nations having a common history or common social, economic, and political interests 'the international community' g: a body of persons of common and especially professional interests scattered through a larger society 'the academic community.'" Settlement, on the other hand, refers to: "a: occupation by settlers b: a place or region newly settled c: a small village."

5 George F.G. Stanley, *The Birth of Western Canada: A History of the Riel Rebellions.* Stanley undertook this project while he was as a graduate student at Oxford University. Although he focused on these two armed conflicts, Stanley provided extensive background histories of these events.

6 Marcel Giraud, *The Métis in the Canadian West.*

7 Ibid.

8 Ibid., 271.

9 According to the court judgment, Mr Belhumeur was born in Moosomin, Saskatchewan, and moved to Regina at the age of nine. His parents had met near Fort Qu'Appelle and had married across the river at Lebret. Fish, rabbits, and game birds had been an important part of his family's diet. Judgment, Provincial Court of Saskatchewan (PCFSQ) at Fort Qu'Appelle, *Regina v. Donald Joseph Belhumeur,* 18 October 2007, 4–7.

10 PCFSQ, Exhibit D-19.

11 "Métis Economic Communities and Settlements in the 19th Century," Expert Report for *R. v. Belhumeur,* August 2005. Unpublished.

12 Cowie eventually published them as *The Company of Adventurers: A Narrative of Seven Years in the Service of the Hudson's Bay Company During 1867–1874.* Cowie had served as an apprentice clerk at the post. For his biography, see http://www.gov.mb.ca/chc/archives/hbca/biographical/c/cowie_isaac.pdf (accessed 29 June 2010).

13 Gerhard Ens, *Homeland to Hinterland: The Changing Worlds of the Red River Métis in the Nineteenth Century.* Provincial Court of Saskatchewan at Fort Qu'Appelle, Transcript of Continuation of Trial of Donald Joseph Belhumeur. Held: September 19, 20, October 3, 4, 5, 6, 2006, vol. 4: 687–775.

14 Ibid., 700.

15 Ibid., 703–4.

16 Ibid., 706–7.

17 Ibid., 207–8.

18 This was a Métis fishing rights case concerning Green Lake, Saskatchewan. In this ruling Justice J. Kalenith stated: "I find that the evidence led at this trial contains sufficient demographic information, proof of shared customs,

traditions and collective identity to support the existence of a regional historic rights-bearing Métis community, which regional community is generally defined as the triangle of the fixed communities of Green Lake, Ile à la Crosse and Lac la Biche and includes all of the settlements within and around the triangle including Meadow Lake." *R. v. Laviolette*, 15 July 2005, SKPC 70, para. 30.

CHAPTER SEVEN

1 Cuthbert Grant (1793–1854) was of Scottish-Métis ancestry. After the merger of the HBC and NWC in 1821, Governor Simpson asked Grant, a former NWC man, to establish a Métis settlement on the Assiniboine River about 16 miles (26 km) west of the Red River settlement. Initially known as Grantown, it was later renamed St Francois Xavier in honour of the town's patron saint. Later in life, Grant became known as the "warden of the plains" after his appointment in the 1830s as a sheriff and magistrate in the District of Assiniboia. See the *Dictionary of Canadian Biography* online: http://www.biographi.ca/009004-119.01-e.php?&id_nbr= 3942&interval=20&&PHPSESSID=c9u8u6ohcd6imego3jj966tro5 (accessed 24 June 2010).

2 Wildlife Act, S.M. c. W 130.

3 Transcripts, Provincial Court of Manitoba, Brandon, 16 October 2006, Exhibit 24.

4 Dr Clint Evans, "Report on the Métis in the Turtle Mountain Area of Southwestern Manitoba, 1820–1870," prepared for Manitoba Justice, Constitutional Law Branch, Winnipeg, Manitoba, 14 March 2006.

5 Ibid., 1. Despite his claim, it is clear from footnote references in his report that he did consult some of the secondary literature.

6 *Regina v. William Neal Goodon*, Provincial Court of Manitoba (PCM) Proceedings, 16 October 2006, 39.

7 Some scholars, myself among them, have described this emphasis as "Red River myopia," because it has meant that Métis from other places have received little attention. See A. J. Ray, "Reflections on Fur Trade Social History and Métis History in Canada."

8 *Regina v. William Neal Goodon* (Transcripts, 16 October 2006). Indeed, *Belhumeur* and *Goodon* are part of the ongoing effort to address this particular problem.

9 I submitted my report before Dr Evans tendered his.

10 Transcripts, 16 October 2006, 100–5.

11 Edward H. Carr, *What is History?: The George Macaulay Trevelyan Lectures Delivered in the University of Cambridge January–March, 1961.*

12 Gerhard Ens, *Homeland to Hinterland: The Changing Worlds of the Red River Métis in the Nineteenth Century.*

13 Transcripts, 19 October 2006, 4.

14 Ibid., 30–3.

15 Ibid., 33.

16 Ibid., 34.

17 Ibid., 35.

18 Justice Combs also acknowledged that this community extended beyond Manitoba. *Regina v. Goodon*, Manitoba Provincial Court, Brandon, 19 January 2009, 14–15. Available at: http://www.canlii.org/en/mb/mbpc/ doc/2009/2009canlii630/2009canlii630.html.

19 There were two plaintiffs in this case: Gary I. Hirsekorn and Ronald S. Jones.

20 The Wildlife Act, R.S.A. 2000.

21 A decision is pending.

22 PCA, Exhibit 39, CV and "Métis Economic Communities in the 19th Century," Report Prepared for the MNA, 20 May 2009, 206 pp. Hereinafter, Ray "Report," 2009.

23 The company operated two short-lived posts named Chesterfield House near the confluence of the Red Deer and South Saskatchewan rivers. The first operated from 1800 to 1802 and the second during the trading year of 1822–23.

24 Transcripts, PCA, Judicial District of Medicine Hat, E-File No.: RCPO9HIRSEKORNG, 27 October 2009, 1679.

25 Cowie, *Company of Adventurers*.

26 Relations had not always been peaceful in this area. Earlier, the Cree had expanded into the area north of the Battle River when the fur trade expanded into this region and the woodlands to the north.

27 Transcripts, 27 October 2009, 1680. Trial, volume VI, pages 1573 to 2085. Medicine Hat, Alberta, 26–30 October 2009. Transcript Management Services, Regional 4909, 48 Avenue, Red Deer, Alberta T4N 3T5.

28 Ibid., 1950.

29 For instance, the post journals indicated that hunters focused on the Stoney Plains west of Fort Edmonton and the area near the Vermilion River to the east.

30 Ray, "Report," 2009, 97–100.

31 Given that Fort Edmonton is the point of view, I argued that "outside" meant away from the fort, or the south side of the Hand Hills.

32 Entry for 11 November 1872 cited in Ray "Report," 2009, 120–1.

33 Ray, "Report," 2009, 88.

34 Transcripts, 29 October 2009.

35 One of the oldest Métis communities in the province had operated in the vicinity of this post, which the company operated, in part, to trade with them.

36 Transcripts, 29 October 2009, 1883–84.

37 I had noted in my report that there had been a large Métis community centred on Lesser Slave Lake and Utikuma Lake (referred to as Whitefish Lake in the HBC records) since the early nineteenth century.

38 This is a reference to the Stoney Nakoda First Nation of Alberta. They are Siouan speakers and were related to the Assiniboine.

39 Transcripts, 29 October 2009, 1876.

40 Ibid.

41 Ibid., 1878. I did not have the opportunity to point out that in 1800–02 the Blackfoot were not the only ones to be hostile. The Gros Ventre attacked the fort.

42 Transcripts, 29 October 2009, 1967.

43 Ibid., 1931.

44 Ibid.

45 Ibid., 1934–35.

46 Ibid., 1997–98.

47 Without explaining why, he determined that the latter event happened in 1874 with the arrival of the first contingent of North West Mounted Police.

48 Judge F.C. Fisher, *Her Majesty the Queen and Garry Hirsekorn and Ron Jones: Reasons for Judgment*, Provincial Court of Alberta, 12 December 2010, page 10, paragraph 63.

49 I have added underlining for emphasis. The company men stationed in the area would have included those from Fort Edmonton, most of whom were Métis, as were the people from Red River. The full quotation is from London Inward Correspondence from Governors of HBC Territories: Sir George Simpson, 1856–67 PAMHBCA A 12/8: 13–13d.

50 Transcripts, 29 October 2009, 1926.

51 In 1795 Aaron Arrowsmith (1750–1823) initially mapped only the Rocky Mountains and the headwaters of the South Saskatchewan River. The portion from the confluence of the South Saskathewan and Red Deer rivers is shown tentatively with a dashed line. Following the establishment and abandonment of Chesterfield House in 1822–23, subsequent maps, most notably perhaps John Arrowsmith's Map of British North America (1854), portrayed the whole river system. R.C. Harris, ed., *Historical Atlas of Canada: From the Beginning to 1800*, Plate 67 and *Atlas of Canada: Historical Map: 1854 British North America (John Arrowsmith)*, Ottawa, Government of Canada: http://atlas.nrcan.gc.ca/auth/english/maps/historical/preconfederation/britishnorthamerica1823/95.gif/image_view. The area in question was part of the Saskatchewan District of the Hudson's Bay Company and is described in the Fort Edmonton district reports.

CHAPTER EIGHT

1 Ms Teillet, personal communication, 9 August 2010.

2 The Powley case originally was supposed to have been heard by a justice of the peace (not a judge), because it involved a provincial offence. Ms

Teillet wrote to the Regional Chief Justice and requested that a judge of the provincial court hear it. The Regional Chief Justice agreed and asked for volunteers from his provincial court judges. Vaillancourt volunteered.

3   A trial day amounts to about six hours a day after allowance is made for coffee and lunch breaks. Invariably some of that time, usually in the morning opening session, is devoted to administrative issues such as scheduling and legal issues arising from motions brought before the court. Also, the court in this case did not sit continuously.

4   This problem arose during the opening testimony of ethnoarchaeologist Sylvia L. Albright. She explained that hearths were places where archaeological evidence indicated that people had maintained fires for cooking, heating, and social purposes. She also had to define the discipline of ethnoarchaeology. Monet and Skanu'u, *Colonialism on Trial*, 114.

5   This geographical term was coined by Canadian geographer John Warkentin to refer to the area between western Hudson Bay and the Rocky Mountains.

6   Chief Justice Allan McEachern, *Reasons for Judgment*, Supreme Court of British Columbia, No. 0843 Smithers Registry, 8 March 1991: viii.

7   Justice Teitelbaum, 234.

8   It is likely that Justice Teitelbaum's error was based in part on a mistaken paraphrasing of my report. In my report, I had made the ambiguous statement that "shortly after the founding of the HBC in 1670, some groups began direct involvement by venturing to York Factory." Ray, "Economic Background to Treaty 6," 3. Clearly, I should have specified that they ventured to the post almost two decades after the company's establishment in 1670. The testimony of Dr von Gernet, who was not an expert on fur trade history, probably contributed to Justice Teitelbaum's error as well. Dr von Gernet equated contact throughout the Prairies with the establishment of the HBC. Arguably the founding date of 1694 for York Factory is not as significant for First Nations of the Manitoba prairies to the east of the Treaty 6 territory, who would have had indirect and some direct access to HBC posts on western James Bay beginning in the early 1670s.

9   This area is approximately 1,300 kilometres from York Factory "as the crow flies."

10  It was only in *Spade and Wasseykessic* and *Victor Buffalo* that I was given the opportunity to help formulate these questions.

11  Alexander Reilly, "The Ghost of Truganini: Use of Historical Evidence as Proof of Native Title."

12  He made specific references to critiques by Robin Fisher, "Judging History: Reflections on the Reasons for Judgment in *Delgamuukw v. B.C.*," and Arthur J. Ray, "Creating the Image of the Savage in Defense of the Crown: The Ethnohistorian in Court." SCC *R. v. Marshall* (5 November 1999).

13 Supreme Court of Canada, Judgment, *Regina v. Marshall*, 1998: 35.

14 In *Victor Buffalo*, lawyers for the plaintiffs did emphasize the methodologies of their experts, which is not commonly the practice.

15 This was the labour theory of property. It justified colonial regimes' treating Aboriginal lands as vacant if they lacked visible signs of human alteration as exhibited at village sites, burial places, etc. See Barbara Arneil, *John Locke and America: The Defence of English Colonialism.*

16 These models emphasized subsistence and ceremonial use of the land, whereas most of the treaty-rights cases I have been involved in address commercial hunting and fishing. Evolutionary perspectives concerning Canadian native culture history held sway until relatively recently. The best example would be Diamond Jenness, *Indians of Canada*. It was first published in 1933 by the National Museum of Canada, republished in 1977, and reprinted thereafter by the University of Toronto Press. Until the 1990s it was the only widely read general synthesis.

17 Usually these narratives portrayed Canada as a more humane colonizer than the United States. See Arthur Ray, J.R. Miller, and Frank Tough, *Bounty and Benevolence: A History of Saskatchewan Treaties* and Jill St Germain, *Indian Treaty-Making Policy in the United States and Canada, 1867–1877*. Also, they tended to celebrate Canadian expansion and dismiss native resistance by casting the colonization process as a clash of civilization against barbarism. An example would be G.F.G. Stanley, *The Birth of Western Canada: A History of the Riel Rebellions* (Toronto: University of Toronto Press, 1992 [1936 and 1962]).

18 They were Wilson Duff, Associate Professor, Anthropology Department, University of British Columbia, and Willard Ernest Ireland, Official Archivist for the Province of British Columbia.

19 In these respects, the Canadian circumstance is different from that of the early USICC cases in which government experts often advanced the new framework of cultural ecology, whereas experts for Indian tribes frequently championed the older perspective of the cultural area. Arthur Ray, "Kroeber and the California Claims: Myth and Reality" and Arthur J. Ray, "From the United States Indian Claims Commission Cases to Delgamuukw."

20 A.J. Ray, 1996, "Commentary on the Economic History of the Treaty 8 Area."

21 Research-based or problem-based teaching is a common teaching model at research-oriented universities where professors are expected to have active research careers.

22 The teaching parallel here would be with those who teach in smaller liberal arts colleges and universities that emphasize teaching and do not expect professors to have active research and publishing agendas.

23 In his briefs for *Victor Buffalo*, for example, Dr von Gernet cited positive citations of his testimony and briefs by courts in prior cases as proof of

his authority and reliability in the absence of scholarly publications on the topics at issue. See von Gernet, "An Assessment," 2 and footnotes 1 and 3.

24 In Delgamuukw, provincial Crown counsel advanced the latter proposition when I was being qualified as an expert. They argued that it was not necessary for me to explain the significance and meaning of Hudson's Bay Company documents because "in most cases the documents – the documents are plain on their face." "Proceedings at Trial": 13330. Tough also discusses this issue. See Tough, 62.

25 In Delgamuukw, as mentioned, before I was qualified as an expert, the lawyers discussed at length whether they needed an historical geographer. In the end, the judge decided it would be helpful to the court to have me direct them to the relevant Hudson's Bay Company records, given the vast size of that archive.

APPENDIX ONE

1 PAMHBC B 11/e/1. This document and the one following were included in Exhibit 964, which were the Hudson's Bay Company documents submitted in support of my report. Here I have added editorial notes in square brackets and endnotes below.

2 The Tache Band is one of several groups who amalgamated into the Tl'azt'en First Nation in 1988. The present-day Tache reserve is located approximately 50 kilometres northwest of Fort St James on the shores of Stuart Lake. For a map of their territory see: http://www.cstc.bc.ca/downloads/Tlazten1.pdf. They are members of the Carrier-Sekani Tribal Council.

3 Brown spelled this name "Caupine" in his 1826 report.

4 Brown's reports and journals make it clear that Native men did not bluntly say they were unwilling to go hunting and trapping when he asked them to. Rather, they usually offered excuses for not doing so.

5 This was the large Wet'suet'en settlement near their present-day community of Moricetown, British Columbia.

6 Here and after Brown is using the term Babine inclusively to include the western groups of Athabascan speakers known as the Dakelh [Carrier]. In his 1826 report, he divides them into the "Babines of the Lake" and the "Babines of the River." Much later, amateur ethnologist Father Morice, who probably was unfamiliar with Brown's observations, identified several Dakelh "sub-tribes" on the basis of dialects: these were Babines, whom he subdivided into those of Babine Lake and the Bulkley Valley, the Upper Dakelh of Stuart Lake and Trembleur Lake, and the Lower Dakelh, who included the remaining groups living farther south. Late twentieth-century linguistic research largely confirmed Morice's classifications. See Margaret Tobey, "Carrier."

7 This would be a reference to the Dakelh ancestors of the Stellat'en First Nation, who live in the vicinity of southwestern Fraser Lake. The Stellat'en

Reserve is located on the banks of the Fraser Lake (Nadleh Bun) west of present-day Fort Fraser. For a map of their traditional territory see: http://www.cstc.bc.ca/downloads/Stellaten1.pdf.

8  Gitxsan.

9  Confluence of Bulkley and Skeena rivers. There are two major forks on the Skeena River. This is one of them. The other is the confluence with the Babine River. The former was a major trading place where the Coast Tsimshian came to meet the Gitxsan, Wet'suet'en, and their neighbours. In his report of 1824, Brown specifically states that the Simpson's and McDougall's rivers joined at the forks.

10  The Hudson's Bay Company operated Fort St James on the southeastern shore of this lake. Simon Fraser of the North West Company established the post in 1806. The same year he also built a post on the east end of Fraser Lake. The two companies merged in 1821.

11  Brown was very likely referring the practice of competitors, First Nations and Europeans alike, of encouraging trappers and traders to part with their furs even though they may have been owed owed in debt to others.

12  Commissioned officers.

13  This reference points to one of the means by which inter-group disputes were settled and peaceful relationships established or restored. In this instance, the Babine, Gitxsan, Wet'suet'en, and Coast Tsimshian planned to attend.

14  He often refers to this location as "The Forks."

15  Bulkley River.

16  Groundhog.

17  Tsek'ene. Historically the terms Siccanie, Sikani, and Sekani were used by English speakers.

18  The name suggests the Meadow Sekani identified by Simon Fraser in 1806. However, these people lived on the western flanks of the Rocky Mountains. Brown's geographic reference suggests a different group, the Sasuchan, Sekani. Glenda Denniston, "Sekani."

19  Bear Lake is a large lake located at 54°29′41″N and 122°41′2″W. There is no other large lake in the vicinity draining into the headwater tributaries of the Skeena River, or of the Nass River. So, it is unclear what lake Brown's informants were referring to.

20  These were woollens named after Stroud, Gloucestershire, England.

21  This is the northern tributary of the Peace River.

22  This group would be the Sasuchan, Sekani.

23  There are two copies of this report. B 11/e/2 appears to be the original signed by Brown and B11/e/3 is a copy. The formatting of the two is slightly different because they were written in booklets of different size.

24  Rainbow trout (*Oncorhy nchusmykiss*) and lake trout (*Salvelinus namay-cush*) are both present in the lake.

25  Burbot (*Lota lota*).

26 Named Tachy in his 1822–23 report. Brown's comment suggests that these people may have relocated elsewhere, perhaps to Fraser Lake.

27 Gitxsan.

28 Brown's discussion of Ack koo shaw, Cabbah, and Caupin [Caspin] suggest the following socio-political structure. There was a nominal leader for all of the villages on the lake, which in effect comprised a regional group, perhaps a phratry, and two or more "tribes," which in turn included various lineage heads, who managed territories on behalf of their relatives. Brown's use of the term "tribe" here is unclear. He does indicate that they included more than one village. So, perhaps he is referring to different clans. Ack koo shaw belonged to one extra-village group and Cabbah and Caupin to another.

29 Hagwilget.

30 Based on Brown's statement, Simon McGillivray attempted to travel to the forks by canoe in June 1833, but he found the current too dangerous and had to make the trip overland. McGillivray remarked about this in his journal: "We got to the end of Babine Lake about 6 PM and began to descend the river, which for its small size and breadth astonished me very much, the moment we entered the river, it became a succession of rapids without intermission and although the water was high, there was not a sufficiency to float our Canoe, with all hands into it, and to avoid breaking, 5 of us walked about 4 miles the rapidity at which the Canoe went down this part of the river baffles all description, and I became alarmed for the safety of those, who were in it ... finding the river to be of such a dangerous nature, the following morning I abandoned it altogether ... In abandoning the navigation of the river which I had never calculated upon (for I had taken it for granted it was navigable, as the late Mr. Chief Trader Brown had pronounced it so March 1826) it struck me the object of the voyage was entirely defeated by this unforeseen event." "From Simon McGillivray to the Govr. & Chief Factors & Ch. Trader, dated Stuarts Lake 20 Feby. 1834," PAMHBC D 4/125: 35–46.

31 Brown is referring to the Gispakloats, who were one of the Coast Tsimshian groups living along the lower Skeena River.

32 A coarse Indian muslin.

# BIBLIOGRAPHY

PUBLISHED SOURCES

Arneil, Barbara, *John Locke and America: The Defence of English Colonialism.* Oxford: Clarendon Press, 1996.

*Atlas of Canada: Historical Map: 1854 British North America* (John Arrowsmith). Ottawa, Government of Canada: http://atlas.nrcan.gc.ca/auth/english/maps/historical/preconfederation/britishnorthamerica1823/95.gif/image_view.

Anderson, J.W. *Fur Trader's Story.* Toronto: Ryerson Press, 1961.

Bishop, Charles A. "Limiting Access to Limited Goods: The Origin of Stratification in Interior British Columbia." In E. Tooker, ed., *The Development of Political Organization in Native North America.* New York: Proceedings of the American Ethnological Society, 1979: 148–61.

Brown, Jennifer. *Strangers in Blood: Fur Trade Families in Indian Country.* Vancouver: University of British Columbia Press, 1980.

Carr, Edward H. *What is History?: The George Macaulay Trevelyan Lectures Delivered in the University of Cambridge January–March, 1961.* London: Macmillan, 1986.

Cowie, Isaac. *The Company of Adventurers: A Narrative of Seven Years in the Service of the Hudson's Bay Company During 1867–1874.* Toronto, 1913.

Denniston Glenda. "Sekani." In June Helm, ed. *Handbook of North American Indians: Subarctic.* Washington: Smithsonian Institution, 1981: 433–4.

Driver, Harold E. *Indians of North America.* Chicago: University of Chicago Press, 1961.

Ens, Gerhard. *Homeland to Hinterland: The Changing Worlds of the Red River Métis in the Nineteenth Century.* Toronto: University of Toronto Press, 1996.

Fisher, Robin. "Judging History: Reflections on the Reasons for Judgment in *Delgamuukw v. B.C.*" *BC Studies,* 95 (autumn 1992): 43–54.

Franchere, Gabriel. *A Voyage to the Northwest Coast of America*. Edited by Milo Milton Quaife. New York: Citadel Press, 1968.

Fumoleau, René. *As Long as the Land Shall Last: A History of Treaty 8 and Treaty 11, 1870–1939*. Toronto: McClelland & Stewart, 1973.

Galois, R. "The 'Indian Land Question' in British Columbia, 1903–1916," *Native Studies Review* 8 (2) (1993): 1–34.

Giraud, Marcel. *The Métis in the Canadian West*. Translated by G. Woodcock. Edmonton: University of Alberta, 1986 [1945]).

Harris, R.C., ed. *Historical Atlas of Canada: From the Beginning to 1800*. Toronto: University of Toronto Press, 1987.

Henry, Alexander. *Travels and Adventures in Canada and the Indian Territories Between 1760 and 1776*. Edmonton: Hurtig [reprint], 1969.

Herchmer, L.W., Commissioner, North-West Mounted Police. *Sessional Papers*, 1898 (No. 15). Ottawa: Queen's Printer, 1898.

Holzkamm, Tim, Victor Lytwyn, and Leo Waisberg. "Rainy River Sturgeon: An Ojibway Resource in the Fur Trade Economy." *Canadian Geographer* 33 (3) (1988): 194–205.

– and M. McCarthy. "Potential Fishery of Lake Sturgeon (*Asipenser fulvescens*) as Indicated by the Returns of the HBC Lac la Pluie District." *Canadian Journal of Fisheries and Aquatic Sciences* 45 (1988): 921–3.

Hutchins, Peter W. "Cede, Release and Surrender: Treaty-Making, the Aboriginal Perspective and the Great Juridical Oxymoron Or Let's Face It – It Didn't Happen." In Maria Morellato, ed., *Aboriginal Law and Delgamuukw*. Aurora: Canada Law Book, 2009: 431–64.

– "Power and Principle: State-Indigenous Relations across Time and Space." In Lou Knafla & Haijo Westra, eds., *Aboriginal Title and Indigenous Peoples: Comparative Essays on Canada, Australia, and New Zealand*. Vancouver: UBC Press, 2010: 214–28.

– and Anjali Choksi. "From *Calder* to *Mitchell*: Should the Court Patrol Cultural Borders?" *Supreme Court Law Review* 16 (2nd Series) (2002): 241–83.

Innis, Harold A. *The Fur-Trade of Canada*. Toronto: University of Toronto Library, 1927.

– *The Fur Trade in Canada*. Toronto: University of Toronto Press, 1930 and 1985 with a new introduction by A.J. Ray.

Isham, James. *Observations on Hudson Bay, 1743*. E.E. Rich, ed., Hudson's Bay Record Society, 1949.

Jarvis, A.M. Inspector, "Northern Patrol Report, 24 April." Canada, *Sessional Papers* (No. 15), 1898: 157–69.

Jenness, Diamond. *The Carrier Indians of the Bulkley River: Their Social and Religious Life*. Anthropological papers, Smithsonian Institution, Bureau of American Ethnology, 25, 1943.

Kobrinsky, Vernon. "The Tsimshianization of the Carrier Indians." In *Proceedings of the Ninth Annual Conference, Problems in Prehistory of the*

North American Subarctic: The Athabaskan Question. Calgary: University of Calgary Department of Archaeology (1977): 201–10.

Kohl, Johann Georg. *Kitchi-gami: Life Among the Lake Superior Ojibway*. Translated by L. Wraxall; R. Neufang and U. Bocker, eds. St Paul: Minnesota Historical Society, 1985.

Kroeber, A.L. *Cultural and Natural Areas of Native North America*. Berkeley and Los Angeles: University of California Press, 1963.

Lurie, Nancy O. "A Reply to Land Claims Cases: Anthropologists in Conflict," *Ethnohistory* 3 (3) (1956): 256–79.

Lytwyn, Victor. *The Hudson Bay Lowland Cree in the Fur Trade to 1821: A Study in Historical Geography*. Winnipeg: University of Manitoba Press, 1993.

Mackenzie, Alexander. *The Journals and Letters of Sir Alexander Mackenzie*. W.K. Lamb ed. Toronto: Macmillan of Canada, 1970.

Monet, Don and Skanu'u (A. Wilson). *Colonialism on Trial: Indigenous Land Rights and the Gitksan and Wet'suet'en Sovereignty Case*. Philadelphia and Gabriola Island: New Society Publishers, 1992.

Morton, Arthur S. *A History of the Canadian West to 1870–71: Being a History of Rupert's Land (The Hudson's Bay Company's Territory) and of the North-West Territory (including the Pacific Slope)*. Toronto: University of Toronto Press [1939] 1973.

Morton, W.L. *Manitoba: A History*. Toronto: University of Toronto Press, 1967.

Newman, Peter C. *Company of Adventurers*. Markham: Viking Press, 1985.

Ogden, Peter Skene. "Notes on Western Caledonia, 1794–1854." *British Columbia Historical Quarterly*, 1 (1) (1937): 45–56.

Peterson, Jacqueline. "Many Roads to Red River." In J. Peterson and J. Brown, eds., *The New Peoples: Being and Becoming Métis in North America*. Winnipeg: University of Manitoba Press, 1985: 41–5.

Price, R., ed., *The Spirit of the Alberta Indian Treaties*. Montreal: Institute for Research on Public Policy, 1979.

Ray, Arthur J. "'Auld Betsy and Her Daughter,' Fur Trade Fisheries in Northern Ontario." In Dianne C. Newell and Rosemary Omer, eds., *Fishing Places, Fishing People: Traditions and Issues in Canadian Small-Scale Fisheries*. Toronto: University of Toronto Press, 1999: 90–1.

– "Buying and Selling Hudson's Bay Company Furs in the Eighteenth Century." In D. Cameron, ed., *Explorations in Canadian Economic History: Essays in Honour of Irene M. Spry*. Ottawa: University of Ottawa Press, 1985: 95–115.

– *The Canadian Fur Trade in the Industrial Age*. Toronto: University of Toronto Press, 1990.

– "Commentary on the Economic History of the Treaty 8 Area." *Native Studies Review* 10 (2): 169–95.

– "Competition and Conservation in the Early Subarctic Fur Trade." *Ethnohistory* 25 (1987) (4): 347–58.

- "Creating the Image of the Savage in Defense of the Crown: The Ethno-historian in Court." Special Issue, *Native Studies Review* 1993 6 (2): 13–28.
- "The Early Hudson's Bay Company Account Books as Sources for Histori-cal Research: An Analysis and Assessment." *Archivaria*, (1976) 1 (1): 3–38.
- "From the United States Indian Claims Commission Cases to Delga-muukw." In Louis Knafla, *Aboriginal Title and Indigenous Peoples: Com-parative Essays on Australia, New Zealand, and Western Canada.* Calgary: University of Calgary Press, 2010: 37–52.
- "Fur Trade History as an Aspect of Native History." In D. Smith and I. Getty, eds., *One Century Later.* Vancouver: University of British Columbia Press (1978): 7–19.
- *I Have Lived Here Since the World Began* (3rd edition). Toronto: Key Porter, 2009 [1996].
- "History Wars and Treaty Rights in Canada: A Canadian Case Study." In Alexandra Harmon, ed., *The Power of Promises: Rethinking Indian Treaties in the Pacific Northwest.* Seattle: University of Washington Press, 2008: 279–96.
- *Indians in the Fur Trade: Their Roles as Hunters, Trappers and Middlemen in the Lands Southwest of Hudson Bay.* Toronto: University of Toronto Press, 1998 [1974].
- "Kroeber and the California Claims: Historical Particularism and Cultural Ecology in Court." In Richard Handler, ed., *Central Sites, Peripheral Vi-sions: Cultural and Institutional Crossings in the History of Anthropology.* History of Anthropology Volume 11. Madison: University of Wisconsin Press, 2006: 248–74.
- "Reflections on Fur Trade Social History and Métis History in Canada." *American Indian Culture and Research Journal,* 1982 6 (2): 91–207.
- "Shading a Promise: Interpreting the Livelihood Rights Clauses in Nine-teenth-Century Canadian Treaties with First Nations." In Jerry P. White, Erik Anderson, Jean-Pierre Morin, and Dan Beavon, eds., *Aboriginal Policy Research: A History of Treaties and Policies*, vol. 7. Toronto: Thompson Educational Publishing, 2010: 59–72.
- "Some Conservation Schemes of the Hudson's Bay Company, 1821–50: An Examination of the Problems of Resource Management in the Fur Trade." *Journal of Historical Geography,* 1 (1975) (1): 49–68.
- "Treaty 8: An Anomaly of the First Nations History of British Columbia." *BC Studies,* 123 (autumn) (1999): 5–58.
- and D.B. Freeman, *Give Us Good Measure: An Economic Analysis of Rela-tions Between Indians and the Hudson's Bay Company.* Toronto: University of Toronto Press, 1978.
- Jim Miller, and Frank Tough. *Bounty and Benevolence: A History of Saskatchewan Treaties.* Montreal: McGill-Queen's University Press, 2000.
Reilly, Alexander. "The Ghost of Truganini: Use of Historical Evidence as Proof of Native Title." *Federal Law Review,* 28 (2000): 3–5.

Rich, E.E., "Trade Habits and Economic Motivation among the Indians of North America," *Canadian Journal of Economics and Political Science* 27 (1960): 35–53.

St. Germain, Jill, *Indian Treaty-Making Policy in the United States and Canada, 1867–1877*. Toronto: University of Toronto Press, 2001.

"Sampson Cree Lawsuit Wraps Up." http://www.cbcca/story/canada/ national/2004/12/21/samsoncree0041221.html, 25 March 2005.

Schenck, Theresa M. "The Cadottes: Five Generations of Fur Traders on Lake Superior." In J. Brown et al., *The Fur Trade Revisited: Selected Papers of the Sixth North American Fur Trade Conference, Mackinac Island, Michigan, 1991*. East Lansing: Michigan State University Press, 1994.

Schoolcraft, Henry R. *Narrative Journal of Travels Through the Northwestern Regions of the United States Extending from Detroit through the Great Chain of American Lakes to the Sources of The Mississippi River in the Year 1820*. Mentor Williams, ed. East Lansing: Michigan State University Press, 1953.

Sprague, Douglas and Ronald Frye. *The Genealogy of the First Métis Nation*. Winnipeg: Pemmican Publications, 1983.

Spry, Irene B., ed. *Buffalo Days and Nights: Peter Erasmus as told to Henry Thompson*. Calgary: Glenbow-Alberta Institute, 1976.

Stanley, George F.G. *The Birth of Western Canada: A History of the Riel Rebellions*. London: Longmans, Green and Company, 1936.

Steward, Julian. "Carrier Acculturation: The Direct Historical Approach." In Stanley Diamond, ed. *Culture in History*. New York: Columbia University Press, 1960: 732–44.

Teillet, Jean. *Métis Law in Canada*. Vancouver: Pape Salter Teillet, 2010.

Tobey, Margaret. "Carrier." In June Helm, ed., *Handbook of North American Indians: Subarctic*, vol. 6. Washington: Smithsonian Institution, 1981: 418–20.

Tough, Frank. *As Their Resources Fail: Native People and the Economic History of Northern Manitoba*. Vancouver: University of British Columbia Press, 1996.

– *Fisheries Economics and the Tragedy of the Commons: The Case of Manitoba's Inland Fisheries*. Downsview: York University Geography Department, 1987.

Van Kirk, Sylvia. *Many Tender Ties: Women in Fur Trade Society in Western Canada*. Winnipeg: Watson and Dwyer, 1980.

UNPUBLISHED
*Archival sources*

"Journal at Water Hen River, September 6, 1849 – June 5, 1850," University of Washington–Pullman, Manuscripts, Archives and Special Collections, (Shelfmark) Cage 200.

Provincial Archives of Manitoba, Hudson's Bay Company Records

Babine Post Journals, 1822–23, B 11/a/1–2.
Babine Post District Reports, 1823 and 1826, B 11/e/1–2.
Fort Dunvegan Account books, 1871–91, B 56/d/14–16.
Fort Hope (Ontario) post journals, 291/a/1–5.
Fort Vermilion, 1871–86, B 224/d/1–8.
Manitoba Lake House District Report, 1818–19, B 122/e/1.
Martin Fall Journals 1869–99, B 123/a/85–93.
Moose Factory, 135/h/-

*Court Transcripts*
Federal Court of Canada Trial Division, Calgary, Alberta, Docket T–2022–89,
    Transcripts 3–5 October 2000.
Supreme Court of British Columbia, No. 0843, Smithers Registry, *Delga-
    muukw v. Regina*: 20–23 March 1989, volumes 202–05; and 25–28 October
    and 7–8 November, Volumes 288–94.
Provincial Court of Alberta, Medicine Hat Registry, *Regina v. Hirsekorn*,
    Trial Transcripts, vol. 6., 27–29 October 2009.
Provincial Court of Manitoba, Brandon, *Regina v. Goodon*, Transcripts,
    16–19 October 2006.
Provincial Court of Saskatchewan at Fort Qu'Appelle, Transcript of Continu-
    ation of Trial of Donald Joseph Belhumeur, September 19, 20, October 3, 4,
    5, 6, 2006.

*Judgments*
Combs, Provincial Justice J., *Regina v. Goodon: Reasons for Decision Deliv-
    ered on the 31st Day of December, 2008 at the City of Brandon*.
    http://www.canlii.org/eliisa/highlight.do?text=r.+v.+goodon&language=en&
    searchTitle=Manitoba&path=/en/mb/mbpc/doc/2009/2009canlii630/2009c
    anlii630.html.
Fisher, Provincial Court Justice F. C. "*Regina v. Hirsekorn: Reasons for Judg-
    ment*," 1 December 2010. http://www.canlii.org/eliisa/highlight.do?text
    =r.+v.+Hirsekorn&language=en&searchTitle=Alberta&path=/en/ab/abpc/
    doc/2010/2010abpc385/2010abpc385.html.
McEachern, Chief Justice Allan, *Delgamuukw v. Regina: Reasons for Judg-
    ment*. Vancouver: Supreme Court of British Columbia, 1991.
Morris, Provincial Court Justice, D.I. "*Regina v. Donald Joseph Belhumeur*,"
    18 October 2007. http://www.canlii.org/eliisa/highlight.do?text=r.+v.+bel
    humeur&language=en&searchTitle=Saskatchewan&path=/en/sk/skpc/doc/
    2007/2007skpc114/2007skpc114.html.
Teitelbaum, M. *Reasons for Judgment*. Federal Court of Canada, 30 Novem-
    ber 2005, http://decisions.fct-cf.gc.ca/en/2005/2005fc1622/2005fc1622.html.
Vaillancourt, Provincial Justice. "*Regina. v. Powley: Reasons for Judgment,
    Ontario Court of Justice (Provincial Division)*." Sault Ste Marie, 21 Decem-
    ber 1998.

*Reports*

Evans, Clint. "Report on the Métis in the Turtle Mountain Area of Southwestern Manitoba, 1820–1870," 14 March 2006.

Flanagan, Thomas. "Analysis of the Plaintiffs' Expert Reports in the Case of *Chief Victor Buffalo v. Her Majesty et al.*" Federal Court of Canada Trial Division, Trial Division, Docket T-2022-89 and T-1254-92 21, July 1998.

– "Surrebuttal to the Rebuttal Reports of Bob Beal, Carl Beal, Stan Cuthand, Arthur Ray, and John Tobias," Federal Court of Canada Docket T-2022-89 and T-1254-92, 2 June 2000.

Ray, Arthur J. "Aboriginal Fishing for Commercial Purposes in Northern Ontario Before Treaty 9: A Report for the Marten Falls First Nation," 1993.

– "An Economic History of the Robinson Treaties Area Before, 1860," March 17, 1998.

– "Commentary on the Economic History of the Treaty 8 Area," 13 June 1985 (for *Regina v. Horseman*).

– "Determining Effective European Control in Alberta." Report for the Office of the federal Interlocutor for Métis and Non-Status Indians, 17 March 2009.

– "The Early Economic History of the Gitxsan-Wet'suet'en-Babine Tribal Territories, 1822–1915." Exhibit 961, Supreme Court of British Columbia, *Delgamuukw v. Regina*, 16 January 1985.

– "The Economic Background to Treaty 6, Expert Report for the Samson Plaintiffs." 3 vols., 3 appendices, 26 June 1997.

– with assistance from Wayne Campbell and Megan Schlase. "Flying Post: An Economic History." Prepared for Joyce L. Pelletier, 2 April 1996.

– "Historical Geography of the Native Economy of the Treaty 2 Area: A Brief Overview from Pre-contact to ca. 1890," 1998.

– "Hudson's Bay Company Expansion into the Upper Skeena River Region in the 1820s," 17 February 1984 (Exhibit 962, *Delgamuukw v. Regina*).

– "Métis Economic Communities and Settlements in the 19th Century." Expert Report for *R. v. Belhumeur*, August 2005; Report for *R. v. Goodon*, 2005; Report for *R. v. Bates; R. v. Hirsekorn; R. v. Jones*, 16 June 2009.

Robinson, Sheila. "Protohistoric Developments in Gitksan and Wet'suwet'en Territories," 12 May 1987 (Exhibit number 1191-6, *Delgamuukw v. Regina*).

Von Gernet. "Aboriginal Oral Documents and Treaty 6." 21 March 2000. Federal Court of Canada Trial Division, Trial Division, T-1254-92.

– "Assessment of Certain Evidence Relating to Plains Cree Practices," 26 May 2000. Federal Court of Canada Trial Division, T-2022-89.

Wolfart, H.C., "Linguistic Aspects of Treaty 6," 24 February 2000, Federal Court of Canada Trial Division, Trial Division, T-2022-89 and T-1254-92.

# INDEX